200 Marlboro Red

A Russian Odyssey

A True Story of One Man's Journey Through The Land They Called "The Wild East"

Geraint Bowen

MAPLE
PUBLISHERS

200 Marlboro Red – A Russian Odyssey

Author: Geraint Bowen

Copyright © Geraint Bowen (2023)

The right of Geraint Bowen to be identified as author of this work has been asserted by the author in accordance with section 77 and 78 of the Copyright, Designs and Patents Act 1988.

First Edition 2023

ISBN 978-1-915996-56-5 (Paperback)

978-1-915996-57-2 (eBook)

Book Layout by:

White Magic Studios

www.whitemagicstudios.co.uk

Published by:

Maple Publishers

Fairbourne Drive, Atterbury,

Milton Keynes,

MK10 9RG, UK

www.maplepublishers.com

A CIP catalogue record for this title is available from the British Library.

While the story in this book is true, in order to protect the innocent, some names have been changed.

Although every precaution has been taken in the preparation of this book, the publisher and author assume no responsibility for errors or omissions. Neither is any liability assumed for damages, misinterpretation or misguidance by others resulting from the use of this information contained herein.

For Luisa, 'yellow blue bus'

Acknowledgements

Cover Design – Tanya Wragg – Get Fresh Brands

Editor – Paula Kench – Brontë Proofreading and Editing Services

About the Author

Currently running a successful Airbnb out of his family home in the city of Leeds, for the first time, Geraint found the time and, more importantly, the motivation, to finally put on record, some of the stories he had been recounting to friends and family, for over twenty-five years.

To his surprise, he found the writing process came naturally to him and the book only took four months to complete, aided by the fact there were few distractions during the first period of the COVID-19 pandemic. With no sequel planned, he hopes the book will stand alone, as an entertaining and hopefully, thought-provoking account of a seminal moment in twentieth century history.

Contents

1

Boats for Cigarettes

Smoking Kills! I think these days everyone accepts this fact, however, when I was growing up there seemed to be some debate. My father gave me a puff on one of his Rio 6 cigars, when I was barely seven and luckily, it put me off smoking for life. Nevertheless, back in Kyiv, in the early autumn of 1991, 200 *Marlboro Red* nearly cost me my life. My name is Geraint Lloyd Bowen, AKA Geri, AKA Geriochka and this is the story of my Russian Odyssey.

At the time, I was two years into a stint of leading tours around what was, up till then, the Soviet Union. During this period, you were only allowed to visit the country in an organised group and due to the fact I spoke Russian, I had secured a freelance tour director position, with an upmarket UK-based tour operator. I had already worked in places as diverse as Tallinn, Irkutsk and Tbilisi, but no matter where you were, the system run by the state tour operator, Intourist, was the same. You had to be accompanied throughout your visit by an Intourist guide known as a *perevodchik*[1]. These were invariably women, who had attended the Moscow Institute of Foreign Languages (Maurice Thorez) and had vastly superior knowledge of the history and culture of the country, than I could ever hope to obtain. They also spoke perfect English, despite never having been outside the Soviet Union. One thing they didn't have however, was my entrepreneurial instinct.

The format for any day in a new city was always the same. Breakfast, followed by a guided city tour by coach, usually carried

---

1   *Perevodchik* – Interpreter.

out by a local guide, with me and the national guide taking the morning off. Lunch would follow the city tour and then an optional tour would be available in the afternoon, paid for in dollars or sterling. It was the optional tours which interested me because this was where I was able to make some much needed, additional income.

On this cool September morning, a rather fraught looking local guide, came to my breakfast table, to tell me that, unfortunately, the planned optional tour to the war museum, under the 62m statue of Mother Ukraine, was not going to take place, as the museum was closed for renovation. During the past two years, I had become accustomed to attractions being unexpectedly unavailable but this was a blow, as my normal routine was to get my own tickets for the afternoon excursion at local prices, while my clients were on the morning guided tour and then sell them at lunch for hard currency. By exchanging money on the black market, the cost to me would literally be a few pence, so I was easily able to undercut the official Intourist prices, saving my clients money but also ensuring I made a fairly honest buck. Faced with the prospect of my group of thirty having a wasted afternoon, sitting around the hotel or perusing the not overly exciting shops, I decided to organise a river excursion on the Dnieper which flows through the city.

Ironically, I had made my first decent commission, on an optional river excursion on the Volga, by pure chance, on my first ever tour of the Golden Ring[2] (the ancient Russian cities to the north and east of Moscow) back in 1989. For some reason, the local Intourist office in Yaroslavl, was unable to accept hard currency and so my group was asked to pay for the excursion in roubles, albeit at an inflated price of 14 roubles a person (NB at this time

---

2   The Golden Ring (*Zolotoe Kol'tso*) comprises a dozen medieval towns north-east of Moscow that once formed Russia's political, spiritual and cultural heartland.

the official exchange rate was £1 = 1 rouble). Groups were always discouraged from changing much money into roubles, as there was literally nothing to buy and all the hotels only accepted hard currency. I however, had had the foresight to do my first "black market" transaction with a waiter, in the laundry of the 25-storey Hotel Cosmos, in Moscow, built to provide accommodation for the 1980 Summer Olympics. Without much haggling, I had managed to get 7 roubles to the pound and so I was easily able to pay for my whole group's river trip, with them paying me in hard cash at the official rate. Therefore for an outlay of £2 per person, I was able to recoup £14 – a 700 per cent profit! And so became the model, for all future optional excursions on my tours.

Having seen my group off on the morning Kyiv city tour, from the Hotel Lybid and with assurances that they wouldn't have a free afternoon, I flagged down a passing car, negotiated a "fare" down to the port and as usual, hoped that the driver hadn't been drinking! I very rarely used official taxis, as the drivers were harder to haggle with and their interpretation of *"The Highway Code"*, left a lot to be desired. Inevitably, the car I found myself in was a Lada (old Russian joke: Why do Ladas have heated rear windows? So you don't get your hands cold when you are pushing them) and as usual, the driver was smoking. At least with it being September, I was able to open the window, but through the winter months, I must have passively smoked hundreds of the poor-quality, Russian-brand cigarettes. However, I couldn't complain about the Soviets' propensity to smoke, as the box of 200 *Marlboro Red* under my arm, was going to secure me that "river excursion"!

From my very first time in the Soviet Union, I had realised I could get most things I wanted with *Marlboro Red* cigarettes. The locals loved anything that came from outside the Soviet bloc, be it jeans, music or books. At the time, it was illegal to possess hard

10

currency and many of the older generation were too scared to accept dollars in the way of payment or a bribe. This, however, did not apply to cigarettes. Such was the "buying power" of branded western packs, that I was allowed by the tour operator I worked for, to claim up to two boxes of 200 *Marlboro Red* (20 packs) for every week I worked.

We arrived at the river port around 11 a.m. and I paid the driver the pre-agreed sum of roubles. He must have been in his sixties and seemed happy with what I'd given him, probably the equivalent of a week's salary. In fact most drivers I hitched lifts with, were from the older generation, given the inordinately long waits one had to endure to secure a new Lada. Ten years was not unusual and the vast majority of the population never got to own a private vehicle.

For this reason public transport was the most common way of getting about, be it train, bus, trolley bus, tram or *Metro*. There also were river taxis in many of the major cities and in the case of the Dnieper, the river on which Kyiv stands, they had hydrofoils which linked the city with other population centres to the south as far as the Black Sea. For obvious reasons, it was a hydrofoil I was after, as it would be big enough to accommodate my group of thirty and would also go fast enough to see a decent amount of the region south of the city in the time available, around two hours. I already knew I had to have my group back at the Hotel Lybid, for their evening meal at 5.30 p.m. because I had procured tickets for a Ukrainian dance show which started at 7 p.m.. This was how I operated; trying to cram as many money-making opportunities into the limited time available. For example, on this tour, which also included Moscow and St Petersburg[3], we only had two nights in Kyiv and our flight to Vnukovo airport, Moscow, was scheduled for 9 a.m. the following morning.

---

3   Prior to 6th September, 1991, St Petersburg was known as Leningrad.

Following the bad luck of the War Museum being closed, I thought I might just be having one of those days, but my spirits lifted when I spotted a relatively new hydrofoil docked at the terminal building and more importantly, empty of passengers. Things got better when I saw the guy who was clearly the captain, sitting on the bridge leisurely smoking a cigarette. I called out to him in Russian and waved the pack of 200 cigarettes in the air. He gestured for me to come on board and I explained to him briefly, the predicament I was in and asked if he would be able to help me out. He gave me a knowing look and explained that it would be difficult, as he was scheduled to leave for Cherkasy a city 100 miles to the south, at 4 p.m.. The fact that he hadn't simply said, 'Nyet,' ('No') gave me hope and after a couple of minutes negotiation (i.e., the acceptance of 200 Marlboro Red as a "gift") he agreed to a two-hour trip, starting at 2 p.m., which would just give me enough time for the group to have a quick lunch and get them down to the port. I'd already arranged with the coach driver on the morning's city tour, to be available for a bit of extra work in the afternoon. Coach drivers were a bit more savvy than the average citizen but basically, I could guarantee a coach for $10 an afternoon, rising to $15 for an evening event, such as a ballet performance.

With the deal done, I made my way back to the hotel, just in time to meet my group returning from the city tour. The beauty of the Intourist system was that breakfast, lunch and dinner were always included in the price of the holiday. This was traditionally to keep a close eye on foreign visitors but also a practical necessity, as trying to find anything remotely edible to eat outside of the hotels, was virtually impossible. It also helped me hugely, as at any given time, I always knew where my group was going to be. Everyone seemed to be in good spirits, having enjoyed the morning tour with the highlight of St Sophia's and St Andrew's churches and the weather was improving. It was quickly agreed that a river excursion for $10 dollars a head was a great idea and I settled back to try to enjoy the rather meagre fare the Hotel Lybid provided for lunch, as always with my eye on the clock. One thing I learnt very early on in my career as a tour director, was to allow more time than you think you need when moving large groups of people around.

The coach, as previously agreed, met us outside the hotel at 1.45 p.m. and we made the short transfer down to the river port in less than ten minutes. To be honest, working in Kyiv was a doddle when compared to leading tours in St Petersburg and particularly Moscow, where the traffic at times could be absolutely horrendous. To my relief, the hydrofoil was still docked where I had left it that morning, with the captain smiling and beckoning us to come on board. No matter how many times I arranged "optionals" of my own, I always had a nagging doubt that someone would welch on the deal. I was once seriously let down by a coach driver in Moscow, who got cold feet and refused to take part in a "Geri optional", leaving me to deal with fifty annoyed clients, who were looking forward to their morning trip to the Trinity Monastery of St Sergius, located in the town of Zagorsk[4] an hour's drive north of the capital. But that story's for a later time.

---

4   Zagorsk changed its name to Sergiyev Posad, after collapse of Soviet Union, on 25th December, 1991

13

2

A Cruise with a Difference

We set "sail" just after 2 p.m. and I was immediately struck by the power at the captain's disposal. It reminded me of the catamaran crossings I used to take between Folkestone and Boulogne, when I had been living in France. By now the sun had come out and the majority of the group had decided to stand on the outside deck, soaking up the rays, subconsciously knowing perhaps, that we were heading north, to the colder climes of Moscow the following day. For once, I gave up on the chance of a bit of extra sunbathing, preferring to chat to the captain on the bridge, partly with a view to arranging a similar trip for the next time I was in Kyiv. We had been heading south down the Dnieper for about thirty minutes, when suddenly in the distance, I saw what looked to me, like the biggest lock in the world, barring our onward journey. I had grown up in Leeds and so was used to the locks on the Leeds Liverpool Canal, but this was something on an altogether different scale, what you might call a "Soviet scale". For a moment my heart sank, thinking that the trip would have to be curtailed, with possible refund implications. However, the captain assured me that everything would be ok and it would only take twenty minutes to get through the lock. I quickly did the time calculations and realised that this was really an unexpected bonus, as the scenery so far on the trip, had been rather underwhelming and this might provide a bit of excitement, little did I know how much excitement!

As we approached the massive lock gates, the captain cut the engine and as if by magic the gates started to open slowly. By this time, all my group had gathered on the outside deck and I started to relay some of the information about passing through locks, that the captain was supplying to me. The hydrofoil edged into the lock and gradually, the huge iron doors closed behind us. Once fully closed, slowly, the boat began to descend, to what I estimated to be about a 20-metre difference in level. It was at this point that suddenly, seemingly from nowhere, an old man appeared, looking slightly the worse for wear but nevertheless pointing a rifle directly at me. My being on the bridge meant I was closest to his eyeline, he must have been about 10 metres away and he was screaming something at me in Ukrainian, which I was struggling to understand. All I could shout back in Russian was, '*Ne strelyay!*' ('Don't shoot!'). The captain standing next to me said it was the lock keeper and he was saying that the hydrofoil wasn't due to pass through the lock for another two hours. At this point, I really didn't care about hydrofoil timetables, I was only concerned that 200 *Marlboro Red* were going to cost me my life, as the lock keeper's finger hovered over the trigger. Then suddenly I realised that cigarettes might be my salvation. I always kept two packs of *Marlboro Red* in the deep pockets of my mustard-coloured raincoat for "emergencies" and this certainly seemed to qualify as an "emergency". Still yelling, 'Don't shoot!' I reached into my pocket, grabbed the first pack of *Marlboro Red* and threw it in the general direction of the old man, at the same time shouting the word, *podarok* (gift). Luckily, my aim was pretty good and the pack landed only a couple of feet away, causing a vaguely bewildered look to appear on the lock keeper's face. He was in a bit of a dilemma. Being from the older generation, he was very much conditioned to follow orders and clearly, allowing a group of unauthorised westerners to pass through his lock, didn't sit comfortably. On the other hand, from his sallow complexion, I could tell he was a heavy smoker and I thought the second pack of *Marlboro Red* might clinch the deal, with the promise of more to come. Sure enough, he slowly lowered the rifle to the ground and picked up the second pack I had thrown. Gradually, a smile appeared on his face and I shouted one of my favourite Russian words *druzba* (friendship).

While all this had been occurring, my group had been staring on incredulously, some of the more cynical, maybe thinking I had staged the whole thing as a form of entertainment, to compensate for what might otherwise have been considered a rather "over-priced" optional. In truth, the most logical explanation was that the lock keeper had been drinking vodka, fallen asleep and only woken up in a confused state, when he heard the sound of the water starting to empty out of the lock as we slowly descended to the lower level. In any case, this was the explanation I gave to the group, as I didn't want to get into the intricacies of explaining how what we were doing, was effectively breaking the law.

Happily for me, the rest of the "voyage" passed off without incident. The lock keeper even waved to us on our return journey, as he sat on a chair outside his small "gatehouse", puffing on undoubtably, the first western cigarette he had ever tasted. As we pulled into the river port at exactly 4 p.m., I could see a line of local people queueing up with slightly bemused faces, clearly concerned that the scheduled hydrofoil was only making an appearance at the last possible minute. These looks became even more confused as my well-dressed group of westerners returned to shore, chatting in English about the rather unusual river trip they had just been on. It's not every day that a state-controlled hydrofoil gets commandeered by a slightly crazy guy called Geri, wearing a mustard coloured raincoat! But these were extraordinary times. As the Soviet Union collapsed all around me, "The Escapade on the Dnieper" was just one of the many surreal events that occurred during my time, in the land that came to be known as "The Wild East".

3

The Early Years

I was born in the midst of the "Cold War", on the 25th March, 1964, less than eighteen months after, the "Cuban missile crisis" and only four months after, the assassination of John F Kennedy in Dallas[5]. The ongoing joke in the family was, that like most people, I knew exactly where I was when JFK was shot! My father was an architect and my mother a French teacher, they having met at the "freshers ball", Liverpool University, in 1954. At the time of my birth, they had recently re-located to Leeds for work reasons, so I was destined to spend the whole of my childhood explaining to bemused Yorkshire folk, how to pronounce the rather unusual name that my Welsh father had insisted on giving me. Things didn't get much better for my sister, born two years later and given the name Angharad. Perhaps the feeling of being different from the rest, led to my pursuing a career path at odds with that of my peers, in any case, my mother's motto was, "'Just because everyone else is doing it, doesn't mean that you have to.'" I remember not being allowed to go to bonfire parties because they were, according to my mother, "anti-Catholic" and from the age of four, I used to walk home on my own from school for lunch, barely having time to scoff down the meal our housekeeper had prepared, before running the half mile back, to try and get a game of football with my friends. I know things were a bit different in the sixties, with children having much more freedom than they do today, but I do think our family pushed at the limits of what was deemed acceptable. For example, I remember being told that it was ok to leave your children home alone, as long as there was an

---

5   22nd November, 1963.

eight-year-old child present! I had my own house key from the age of nine, although I struggled with the mortice lock and sometimes had to wait in the outhouse, for one of my parents to come back from work to let me in. This rather relaxed view of health and safety also manifested itself in the vehicle my mother chose to drive, an old green Austin Mini van. Evidently, there were no seats in the rear and my sister and I used to rattle around in the back, clinging on to the luggage cords, my father had kindly thought to install. However, with hindsight, all this was great preparation for dealing with the total lack of health and safety I was to encounter in the Soviet Union.

By the time I was nine, Leeds City Council had decided to introduce a middle school system and my cohort was the first to complete the four requisite years, up to the age of thirteen, thereby avoiding the horrors of the "Eleven Plus". One of the beauties of the system, was that you got to learn French two years earlier, than if you had gone straight from primary school to secondary school. Not surprisingly, given my mother's profession, I had a natural aptitude for French and was also helped by the radical, "*En Avant*" method of teaching the language, which required that you saw no written text for the first two years, with all lessons being carried out orally. As it turned out, this couldn't have been more different from the way I was subsequently taught Russian, where text books dating from the 1950s were the order of the day and grammar ruled.

With the liberal teaching methods of Holt Park Middle School, which I came to adore, I flourished both linguistically and academically. My French was also greatly aided by spending a month in a *Colonie de Vacances* (summer camp) based in Chambery, south-east France, when I was eleven. The *Colonie* was run in a beautiful, seventeenth-century chateau, set in majestic grounds. I shared a dorm with boys from all over the world and had my first experience of meeting someone from the "eastern bloc", a boy called Florin, from Bucharest. In truth, we didn't get on very well, especially as I beat him in the final of the table tennis competition I helped to organise. He seemed rather surly and reserved. I much preferred spending time with my new French friend Jerome, particularly as he seemed to have no problem attracting the stunning Scandinavian girls, who formed a significant contingent of the *Colonie's* female population. The chance to mix with children from countries as diverse as Brazil and Denmark, for four sun-drenched weeks, in the summer of 1975, no doubt fuelled my wanderlust from an early age. This was abetted by the fact that from the age of five, I had been going on regular family skiing holidays.

With the arrival of artificial ski slopes in the UK in the mid-seventies, I had developed my technique to become good enough to be chosen to represent England, in a junior international competition in Pamporovo, Bulgaria, in 1978. This was fortuitous, as by this time, I had already started to learn Russian at my new secondary school, Lawnswood. The fact that the school offered Russian, was a hangover from its grammar school days and I remember my mother being rather annoyed that if I wanted to do a second language, it would have to be Russian. She would have preferred me to do German, which was her second language and because it would be useful for my burgeoning skiing career, with Austria being the home of Alpine ski racing. However, the school policy, probably to protect the jobs of the small Russian department, was to alternate each year's intake, between Russian and German. In a sense, this was logical, as at the time no one would have chosen to do Russian. It was virtually impossible to visit the Soviet Union and the career prospects seemed limited to either working at GCHQ[6] in Cheltenham, or teaching the subject.

---

6   Government Communications Headquarters.

Although my mother wrote to the school to complain, asking, given my perceived linguistic ability, for me to study German with the year above, the school remained adamant and so it was, that in early September 1977, I had my first encounter with the *Cyrillic*[7] alphabet.

Lawnswood School dated back to the nineteenth century and at the time of my arrival, comprised two identical buildings: the Leeds Modern Boys (east) and Lawnswood High Girls (west) built in the early thirties, which had then merged in 1972, with the introduction of the comprehensive system. My mother had taught in the girls' school, from 1967 to 1974 but thankfully, had decided to move into higher education, thereby sparing me the indignity of having my mum teaching in the same school, always a recipe for disaster. Although many of the teachers had been colleagues of my mother's, no mention was ever made of the link and I certainly wasn't going to tell any of my new friends about "my shameful secret", I just wanted to be one of the cool kids and a "teacher mum" was definitely not cool. As it turned out, my new Russian teacher, Mr Ward, was a fairly recent arrival and so there was no "baggage" there.

Russian was offered as an extra 'O' Level to the more academic pupils and suited me fine, as it got me out of doing metalwork, with some of the more challenging students that attended Lawnswood at the time. As my family will attest, I am probably the world's worst DIYer, even now I have to rely on Halfords to fix the punctures on my bike – apparently I have the most used bike care plan in the UK!

The home for the next five years of Russian study, was to be room 32, West Building. This never changed, even when I went on to study 'A' level. The wall behind the massive chalkboard by the

---

7   Russian Alphabet.

teacher's desk, was covered by a map showing the whole of the Soviet Union, comprising the 15 Republics we now know today as independent countries. From day one the map fascinated me. As a child, I had always drawn maps of countries from around the world, being relatively skilled at copying from the atlases that littered the family home. However, I had never seen such a big map and the addition of the Cyrillic alphabet, intensified the sense of adventure. I must have stared at that map for hours on end, particularly during Russian Literature lessons. One aim, was to try to memorise the names of the cities on the Trans-Siberian Railway, running from Moscow to Vladivostok, not knowing that one day I would get together with my future wife, in one of its compartments, following a night of drinking Azerbaijani cognac.

The seating plan for the majority of classes at Lawnswood was decided by the teachers, normally to ensure that the "naughty kids" were kept to the front. However, as there were no "naughty kids" in our "academically gifted" troupe, we were allowed to sit where we wanted. This meant, in my case, a window seat at the very back, so I could survey the whole scene. There were about thirty of us in the class and I remember the first question Mr Ward asked, was if any of us had been to the Soviet Union. This to me, appeared a stupid question and so I was amazed when a girl new to me, called Anna Douglas, raised her hand to say that she and her mother had been to Moscow and Leningrad[8] and even more amazingly, she knew how to say, 'hello' in Russian. I was deeply impressed and resolved to get to know Anna better. Unfortunately, she turned out to be from the cool, left-wing, hippy set and being an "international" ski racer was far too bourgeois for her!

Mr Ward's teaching methods could best be described as "old school". We were mainly taught by rote, hardly understanding

---

8 On 26th January 1924, shortly after the death of Vladimir Lenin, St Petersburg was renamed Leningrad, reverting to St Petersburg on 6th September, 1991.

the sentences we were copying down. The only bit of "oral" work in the early days, seemed to be getting asked our name and age. Strangely, everyone in our class answered that they were thirteen, although many were fourteen, the reason being, "four" in Russian, is: *chyTYry* (chetyre) and is particularly difficult to pronounce! The one advantage of concentrating on the grammatical aspect of the language, was that I did learn to write Russian correctly. This would surprise many of the friends I came to make, who thought I could only speak the language. To this day, I am still able to write comprehensible sentences in free hand, containing the thirty-three letters that make up the Russian alphabet, so thank you, Mr Ward. In fact, some of the grammatical lessons were so engrained, that even after nearly forty years not studying Russian, my best friend Mike, can still translate the really useful sentence: "The dog ran under the bus" (*sobaka pobezhala pod avtobus*)! In truth, I didn't really take to Russian at the beginning. The teaching methods were light years away from the *"En Avant"* programme I had followed, learning French at middle school and there seemed very little chance I would ever get to use it in a social setting. I therefore, concentrated on my French and skiing and continued to stare at that map. However, things were about to change, as for the next seven years, I got to experience the joys of one of the Soviet Union's poorest satellite states, "The Land of the Evergreen Orange", Bulgaria.

4

First Time in the East

With hindsight, the many times I visited Bulgaria in the late seventies, early eighties, were ideal preparation for my later Russian adventures. Every February there was a training camp, followed by a slalom and giant slalom competition, for the national team in Pamporovo, situated in the southern Rhodope Mountains, close to the border with Greece. The only way to get there was by charter flight with Balkan Airlines, from Stansted to Plovdiv. I remember my father driving me down to Stansted for the first time and being surprised by how rural the area was, my being used to the busier airports of Heathrow, Gatwick and Manchester. We were getting close to the airport, driving down what was no more than a country lane, when suddenly out of nowhere appeared some traffic lights, showing red. My father was a bit confused, only to realise we were about to inadvertently cross the runway, when a large cargo plane taxied across about 50 metres in front of us. At this time, Stansted Airport bore no resemblance to the current Norman Foster designed, award-winning building, being little more than a large shack. In the days before low-cost flights, Balkan Airlines was one of the few carriers with regular flights out of Stansted and they certainly did things a bit differently from the airlines I was used to flying with. One particular quirk was to give you a boiled sweet just before take-off, along with a small wet wipe, to clean your hands. This was aimed at helping your ears deal with the change in air pressure but also introduced me to the fact that my learning of the *Cyrillic* alphabet might be useful after all. I managed to decipher the word *voda* (water) on the packaging containing the wet wipe. As things

23

turned out, wet wipes proved to be just about the most luxurious thing I ever encountered on my trips to Bulgaria. Despite the fact it had the perfect climate for growing fruit and vegetables, see more recently the great wines it has been producing, it was virtually impossible to get anything decent to eat, the whole economy being riddled with corruption and incompetence. The other problem was that being under Soviet control, as with the other members of the Warsaw Pact, Bulgaria was forced to send most of the good stuff it produced to Moscow.

The Hotel Panorama in Pamporovo was symptomatic of the problems at the time. I particularly remember the evening meals, almost invariably a soup starter (best described as brown sludge) which nobody ate, only to see it reappear poured over a bit of gristly meat, for our main course. This would usually be followed by some green fruit, unfortunately, not an apple but an orange! In fact, I don't think any fruit I ever saw was the correct colour. In theory, there was the possibility of buying something reasonable to eat, for hard currency, in the tourist shop, located in the centre of the resort. However, when me and a few mates walked the 20 minutes into town, to satisfy our raging hunger, the only thing we could get to buy, was some out-of-date Swiss Toblerone. I don't even like Toblerone, especially at the then exorbitant price of £1 a bar.

However, the trip to the tourist shop did open my eyes to what would later become a way of life for me, namely changing money on the "black market". As we were about to enter the shop, we were approached by a group of locals, probably in their late teens to early twenties. They were very friendly and spoke good English. At first, I rather naively thought they just wanted to practice their English but it soon became clear that their main aim, was to change their Bulgarian lev and stotinki into British pounds. When we refused, having been warned by the team management that it was illegal to change money on the streets and who wanted to end up in a Bulgarian prison cell, they changed tack and asked us if we would buy them some electrical goods, with the sterling they had already accrued. I thought this seemed even more dodgy but one of the more impressionable boys in our group agreed, saying he felt sorry for them. I saw little point in taking any risk for no appreciable gain and so left Mark to discuss with his new friends, what was on their shopping list and proceeded into the shop, to discover the delights of out-of-date confectionery. I found out later, that Mark had gone really "native", agreeing to sell his best pair of jeans for some ridiculous amount of *lev*. To this day, I don't know what he did with the money, as there really was nothing worth buying, unless of course you liked a glass of wine.

Like most teenagers, the thought of having an illicit drink preoccupied my thoughts. From the age of six, in keeping with my parents view of the world, I had been allowed to have a glass of watered-down wine with my evening meal, when on holiday, or on special occasions. When most of my contemporaries were collecting stamps, I had started to collate an album full of wine labels. However, being on the small side (I'm 5ft. 4in.) and not having an older sibling, I'd always struggled to get hold of the "real stuff". This, however, I soon discovered, was not a problem in Bulgaria. When I was fifteen, for the price of an out-of-date Toblerone (£1) I was able, via one of the "friendly" waiters in our hotel, to get a bottle of local red wine. Unfortunately, I couldn't get anyone else to drink it with me, some of the older squad members, having got hold of a couple of bottles of vodka. Needless to say, I ended up downing the whole bottle on my own, with the inevitable "sickly" outcome about two hours later. Unsurprisingly, I didn't perform at my best in the team slalom the next day and in fact, it put me off drinking red wine for the next three years. If only that had continued!

Despite my poor, alcohol induced performance in Bulgaria, I continued to get selected for the national team and my late teens were dominated by the notion that I might be able to make my name as an Olympic ski racer. This led to me spending far more time attending ski training camps and competitions, than concentrating on my academic studies. Christmas holidays were always spent training in the Alps, in preparation for the British Championships, in early January and this was followed straight away by the Scottish circuit, a series of weekend races in the "resorts" of Aviemore, Glenshee and Glencoe. With the arrival of global warming, it is difficult now to imagine that you could have a guaranteed race every weekend throughout January, February and March. In fact, the only time races were cancelled, was due to there being too much snow. My father would pick me up from school at 4 p.m. on a Friday afternoon and we would then have the joy of a seven hour car journey from Leeds, to one of the Scottish ski resorts. Accommodation for Friday and Saturday night would be in some freezing bed and breakfast, where the orange juice in the morning, would always be of the watered-down variety. The races themselves consisted of a two-run slalom competition on the Saturday, followed by a one-run giant slalom on the Sunday, enabling competitors from south of the border, the theoretical chance of getting back home on the same day. You need to be aware, that at this time, the roads north to the Highlands, particularly the A1 and the A9, were much more challenging than they are today, especially as we were often driving in atrocious conditions. Luckily, my father, being from north Wales, was used to driving in the snow and we never failed to reach our destination. He did however get tired, particularly on the return journey. Like most ski racers, I was obsessed with speed and had started learning to drive on my seventeenth birthday. This meant that from March 1981, I had a provisional licence and could drive under adult supervision. True to my family's traditional view of "adult supervision", this meant me careering down the A1, in the middle of the night, in a high powered VW, with my father fast asleep beside me. I didn't actually pass my test until the October of that year, managing to fail twice for something called, "undue care and attention". At least I didn't fail for being the first person to have points on their provisional licence.

I would like to claim that all the skiing I did, affected my academic performance; I found it impossible to do any work while I was away, saving everything up for possibly a late Sunday evening session or more usually, a rushed attempt to get something produced during Monday morning registration. For my French 'A' Level, this was not really a problem but Russian was a different matter. Luckily, my great friend Lyn, was kind enough to let me "check" the translations she had done over the weekend and with one free period on a Monday morning, I was usually able to meet Mr Ward's deadline. Unfortunately, on one occasion Lyn had inadvertently missed out a whole paragraph, which was a surprise to Mr Ward, as she was an A-star student and an even bigger surprise, when he noticed that I had missed out exactly the same paragraph! In the long run of course, "cheating never pays", as I struggled to scrape a pass (i.e., grade E) while Lyn went on to get a Russian degree from Birmingham University and subsequently, to work for Intourist in their London bureau.

5

Olympic Dreams

For a few years after leaving the sixth form, Russia completely dropped off my radar. By some miracle, I had managed to get an A grade in French, which had secured me a place to study the language at Warwick University. Even better, was that I had managed to get sponsorship from an English ski-tour operator, who were happy to put me up in one of their hotels in the French Alps, while Warwick agreed to defer my place until I had finished my "skiing career". With hindsight, the main aim of my "skiing career", was to make me more attractive to the opposite sex. I spent far too much time in the night club located under the Hotel du Mont Charvin, Notre Dame de Bellecombe, where I partied the nights away with the English guests staying in the hotel and with the local girls I had got to know. Probably the best example of my rather amateur approach to ski racing, came during my second winter season in the Alps. A fellow racer, called Richard, who was also sponsored by an English tour operator, was living in the ski resort of Chatel on the Franco-Swiss border. By chance, the Welsh National Championships were taking place in his home resort and so he asked me if I'd like to come over for three days of racing. At first I was a bit reticent, as although Chatel was only 60 miles away as the crow flies, it would take me nearly six hours to get there by bus and train. In addition, there would be no chance of improving my ranking points, as the level of competition would be lower than I was used to, on the European FIS circuit[9] and so I would literally be doing the Welsh a favour by competing. However, Richard was a good friend, offering free accommodation and of

---

9   The level below World Cup.

course my father was from Colwyn Bay, so slightly reluctantly, I agreed to go.

As soon as I got there I knew I'd made a big mistake. The accommodation turned out to be a slightly damp mattress, on the floor of what could best be described as a covered balcony. Richard's sponsor, although a much bigger company than mine, was notoriously badly organised, so instead of having his own hotel room, like me, he had been forced to share an apartment with four seasonal workers, with him getting the worst "sleeping quarters". Anyone who knows anything about winter season workers, will tell you that they're not renowned for going to bed early and I could see from Richard's rather drawn expression, that he probably hadn't been getting much sleep recently. Checking out the bathroom confirmed that personal hygiene wasn't high on the agenda either. The problem was, it was already mid-March and my funds were starting to run low, so paying for a hotel room for three nights was totally out of the question. It looked like I was just going to have to "lump it". Things improved a bit when Richard said that, although he was stuck with rubbish accommodation, at least all his meals were provided for him, at one of the company's hotels, just around the corner. It was already early evening and he said there would be no problem eating with him in the hotel kitchen, as one of his four flatmates was in actual fact, the head chef. As usual, the food was a bit basic, given that it was aimed at catering for the school groups, that formed the basis of his sponsor's clientele. However, at least it was filling and accompanied by a couple of glasses of red wine, my mood started to improve. Things got even better when I discovered that the school group staying at the hotel that week, was from Roedean[10] sixth form. From my time at The Mont Charvin, I knew that the vast majority of teachers, usually from the PE (physical

---

10 One of the top girls' boarding schools in the UK.

29

education) department, regarded the annual school ski trip as a perk of the job and treated it pretty much as a free holiday. Supervision of the students seemed to be regarded as "optional" and I had already benefited from this on a number of occasions. It wasn't until a few years later, with the deaths of four British boys on a school trip to Salzburg, ironically not on a skiing holiday, that things changed dramatically[11].

Assuming that the Roedean teachers would be propping up the hotel bar after dinner, benefiting from the discounted drinks the tour operator was happy to provide, I asked Richard which bar the sixth-form girls would be most likely to sneak out to. He said, The Avalanche was the most popular bar in town but why was I bothered, as we had three days of racing coming up? By this point, any interest I had once had in becoming the Welsh open champion had completely disappeared. The prospect of a bit of "posh totty" was all consuming. Reluctantly, Richard agreed to accompany me, with the proviso that he would only stay for one drink. Sure enough, six Roedean girls had already made it to the bar and when they spotted our National Team jackets, I knew we were onto a good thing. After only a couple of minutes, I was deep in conversation with a girl called Lucinda, who was obsessed with show jumping. Of course, she asked me if I liked to ride, only to be a bit shocked when I replied with a knowing look, 'Yes... but not horses!' Unfortunately, Richard was showing much less interest in getting to know the other sixth formers and pretty soon he was gesturing that it was time to go. I however, have always had a thing about "posh girls" (I used to say to my wife that the only woman I would ever leave her for is Kristin Scott Thomas) and so I was definitely up for staying. Shrugging his shoulders, he grabbed his jacket and headed for the door, calling out that course inspection was at 9 a.m. the following morning, if I could

---

11 April 1988.

be bothered. With Lucinda wedged up beside me and giving me encouraging looks, I certainly wasn't bothered. It turned out, that as she and her five friends were in the upper-sixth, they were allowed out of the hotel on their own, with a theoretical curfew of 11 p.m., which in effect, meant midnight. Unused to male company, they were all boarders, it was easy to impress them with my tales of "life as an international ski racer" and in addition, I was two years older, which in my experience always helps. It was already past midnight, when a little bit "the worse for wear" the seven of us crept back into the hotel lobby, me tightly holding Lucinda's hand and looking forward to getting to know her better. I was about to be severely disappointed. Suddenly a light came on and there standing in front of us was the senior games mistress, who had obviously decided that this time the girls had pushed the curfew too far. Sending them straight to their rooms and giving me a disapproving look, she went back to the table in the corner, where she had been sitting in the dark and picked up the tumbler of whisky, that had been serving as a nightcap, while she waited for the girls to return. With no other option, I returned to Richard's apartment, crawled into the sleeping bag I always travelled with and tried to get to sleep, while bemoaning the missed opportunity with Lucinda.

The next morning, complete with hangover, I decided there was no way I was going to spend another night on a balcony and so started to get my stuff together for my return to Notre Dame de Bellecombe. Suddenly, Richard appeared in all his ski racing gear and told me to get a move on, as it was already 8.15 a.m. and the slalom course inspection was starting in less than an hour. I'll always remember the look of incredulity that appeared on his face, when I told him I was going home. He simply couldn't understand why I would choose not to race, having already made a six hour journey to get there. But then again, I've always liked to be different. That day a big DNS (Did Not Start) appeared against my name on the race results for the Welsh Open Slalom, while Richard's name occupied first place!

It is possible my preference for partying, was linked to the fact that I very quickly realised that the chasm between UK national based racing and international racing, was one I was never going to bridge. While I would have to hitch rides and travel on trains and buses, to get to races across Europe, lugging at least two pairs of skis and assorted equipment, my competitors would turn up in national team minibuses, driven by members of their support team. Maybe due to the mediocre results I recorded on the European circuit, I came to realise that what I really liked was the journey rather than the arrival. Towards the end of my time on the tour, I was picking races due to the distance I would have to travel to get there. I once travelled over 500 miles to a multi-race event, in Piancavallo (Italian Dolomites) with four pairs of skis, a bag of training poles, boot bag and suitcase. Arriving in Pordenone, 50 miles to the north of Venice, I was disheartened to find that the bus station, where I had to get the transfer up to Piancavallo, was a mile away from the train station where I had just arrived. As usual, I had no money for a taxi and in any case, there was no way all my kit would fit in one. I thus simply dumped my bags on the station forecourt and worked out that it would take me three trips to carry all my stuff across town. The thought nowadays of unattended luggage being left in bus and train stations for a considerable length of time, is unimaginable but these were more innocent times and an hour and a half later, I was sitting on the coach transfer up to Piancavallo, totally knackered but happy. Luckily, on the return journey, me and a fellow team member, Finlay, I had met up with for the four days of competition, were able to hitch a ride in the French team minibus, to the station at Venice Mestre, so avoiding the need for, what could be best described as, something akin to being a Himalayan Sherpa. As it turned out Finlay was going to Milan, so we loaded all our stuff on to the train (destination Turin) which is where I was heading. By this time, it was early evening and after all the exertions of the previous days I was soon nodding off. Finlay, however, remained awake. After a while, I sensed we were pulling into a station and so I sleepily asked Finlay, 'Where are we?' He mumbled something back which I didn't quite catch, other than it ended in "A". I dropped off again, only to be woken by Finlay, about 30 minutes later, exclaiming that the train was going round in circles and we were back in *Uscita*. To be fair, Finlay had never claimed to be a linguist but it was with a certain smugness, that I explained to him that *Uscita*, was the Italian for "exit".

By the summer of 1984, I realised my ski racing days were over. I had been nowhere close to making the Sarajevo Olympic Team and the prospect of another four years "on the road", didn't fill me with joy. I did remain involved in the sport for a while longer as a coach, actually training future Olympic competitors but with Warwick University beckoning, this chapter of my life effectively closed.

6

This is not Warwick

On an early October day, I drove my mother's VW Polo the 130 miles, from Leeds to Warwick University, with my younger sister Angharad, sitting in the passenger seat beside me. She had just passed her driving test at the fourth attempt, continuing the family tradition of multiple failures and had very bravely offered to drive the car back. I can't quite remember why one of my parents wasn't able to accompany me and it did seem like I was the only person being "dropped off" by their little sister. The other thing that struck me, was that Warwick University is nowhere near Warwick and is in fact, situated on the outskirts of Coventry. Unlike today, when there is an endless number of open days to attend over the summer, prior to students submitting their applications (and with three academic sons I've been to a lot!) I had simply had one interview, which was now nearly three years ago. I had even applied to Leicester and Cardiff universities without going there. With the benefit of hindsight, I think the new way of doing things is better. To this day, Coventry has a slightly chequered reputation. At the time, the expression "sent to Coventry" (i.e., to be ostracised) was still in common parlance and my favourite band, *The Specials*, who were from Coventry, had only recently recorded the Number 1 song, *Ghost Town*, an earlier hit having been, *Concrete Jungle*. I remember in the first week of term, me and my new flatmate, Steve, venturing into Coventry around 6 p.m. in the evening, keen to see the just released Oscar winning film, *The Killing Fields*, which was showing at the Odeon. Not only did we struggle to find the cinema, but we struggled to find anyone to ask where it was, we truly were in a "ghost town".

Perhaps I'm being too hard on Coventry and there were other reasons for my time at Warwick not being the greatest. Having lived in France for two years I already spoke the language fluently and with only eight hours tutor contact time a week, I had plenty of opportunity to pursue the hedonistic lifestyle I had envisaged university to be. However, the bars took last orders at 10.30 p.m. and being two years older than most of my contemporaries, not for the first time in my life, set me apart. To a certain extent I played on this.

In my second year, while living off campus in Leamington Spa, I bought an old left hand-drive Polo from a skiing friend, whose dad had a chain of VW franchises in London. I deemed the car a necessity, as it was a 10-mile commute into the campus and the bus was notoriously slow and unreliable. It also allowed me to make some money, as there was a well-established hitch-hiking point on the edge of town, where you could pick up fellow students for £1 a ride. Of course, having the only left-hand drive car in the area, caused problems at pick-up time, with people invariably trying to get in through my door, while I gestured frantically for them to go round the other side. When people asked if it was difficult to drive, I used to say, 'No,' and that it made it easier to overtake on the pavement! In any case, my being right-handed, makes it a more natural way to drive. Over the years, I have driven thousands of miles in left-hand drive cars and never had an accident. I do, however, possess a number of speeding violations on the continent and possibly hold some kind of record for recently getting caught on camera, three different times, in a three-hour period! By the time I'd paid the fines and Europcar's admin fee, I had managed to double the cost of the car hire. As some form of compensation, I decided to get the rather impressive French speeding notifications framed, along with a fourth one, I had managed to get two days later!

The highlight of my time at Warwick, was ironically the year when I wasn't actually there. One of the reasons I had applied, was that they guaranteed you a year working as an English language teaching assistant in "a place of your choice". This seemed to me far better than studying in some French university, where the social life is practically non-existent, as most of the students live at home. It would also allow me to make some money, as you were paid a salary and it was a good way to pick up private tutoring work. I was also lucky in having the offer of rent-free accommodation, in a beautiful old town house in the centre of Reims, the capital of the Champagne region.

In my early teens I had become close friends with a French correspondent, Renaud, and we had spent many happy summer holidays together. I had always got on particularly well with his grandmother Yvonne, and it was she who made the offer of the attic room, provided I contributed towards the extra cost of heating, the upper part of the house having been closed off following the death of her husband. Yvonne was a real character with family connections to the Laurent Perrier Champagne house. During the war, she had worked for the resistance, carrying messages hidden in balls of wool, through German checkpoints. She told me stories of being flown down to Paris for the night by an old boyfriend, in a rickety bi-plane, also of treks across Africa with her hunting-obsessed husband. In fact, the large entrance lobby to the house was framed by two massive ivory tusks and all the walls dripped with the heads of stuffed animals, collected as trophies. Returning on my own late of an evening, I always had an eerie sense that these animals with their piercing eyes, were judging me for the wrong that had been done to them.

I had a great year in Reims. I was the only English language assistant in the city, which suited me perfectly, as I only wanted to mix with French speakers. It also meant it was easy for me to pick up private lessons. By the time I left, I was making more money from these, than I was from my assistant's salary. In theory, I should have returned to Warwick for my final year, as one of the richest students ever, however, true to form, my hedonistic lifestyle proved a barrier to my amassing any savings. Drinks in nightclubs were 50 Francs (£5) each, which led me to develop a taste for Malibu and orange, as unlike the normal spirits: whiskey, vodka, gin, etc., Malibu wasn't on an optic, so you could encourage the bartender to be a bit more generous when pouring a shot.

I remember a week's partying in Corsica proving particularly costly and it also presaged some of the *Aeroflot*[12] airline adventures, I was to have a few years later. On the return flight from Ajaccio to Paris, we had barely reached our cruising altitude, when I felt the plane starting to descend. Sure enough, a couple of minutes later, the captain came on the tannoy, to announce that we were going to have to make an emergency landing at Lyon Airport. I had already experienced a few dodgy landings, including nearly ending up in the Black Sea, at Varna in Bulgaria, but none had ever been described as an "emergency". My apprehension levels increased, when I saw out of the cabin window, a Mirage jet fighter, which was clearly accompanying us on our descent. Still, at least the plane seemed to be handling ok and sure enough, we touched down on the runway at Lyon without incident. We were, however, met by a cavalcade of fire engines and police vehicles. It turned out that Corsican separatists had telephoned to say that there was a bomb on the plane, which given the lax security at Ajaccio Airport, was easy to believe. With the airport closed to all flights, the authorities then made the rather strange decision to get all the passengers to assemble on the runway and to identify their own bags, as they were unloaded from the aircraft's hold. Nowadays, it is impossible for an unaccompanied bag to be

---

12 Russian state carrier.

carried but this was at a time before the Lockerbie bombing[13], when things were very different. I quickly realised that the "bag identification process" was going to take a while, so I thought I'd use the time to "top up" my ever so important tan. Asking a friend to alert me when my bag appeared, I took my Sony Walkman out of my jacket, put on my Pierre Cardin sunglasses and settled down in the middle of the runway, using my rolled-up jacket as a pillow. To this day, I have yet to meet anyone else who has sunbathed on an international airport runway. In fact, sunbathing in strange places is something of a hobby of mine.

I once had three days between tours to kill in Moscow. It was early July and I was staying in the Intourist hotel on Tverskaya Street (formerly Gorky Street) located in the centre of the city and a stone's throw from the Kremlin. Contrary to popular belief, Moscow given its continental climate, enjoys relatively warm weather in the summer months and for my "mini break", the temperature was in the low thirties. I decided that the best place for sunbathing would be on the large circle of benches, situated in the Alexander Gardens, at the foot of the Kremlin walls and close to the Eternal Flame of The Unknown Soldier. Due to the good weather, most of the benches were occupied, mainly by Russian grannies (*babushkas*) who, despite the heat, were all wearing the obligatory black overcoat and patterned headscarf. I did, however, manage to get a bench with the correct orientation towards the sun and having stripped down to my skimpy shorts, I settled down to listen to some *Soft Cell*, on my ever present Walkman. It must have made for a slightly strange sight, a bronzed, bleach-blond westerner, miming along to *Tainted Love*, while a crowd of Russian matriarchs looked on disapprovingly. After about an hour and a half, I realised I was starting to lose the direct sunlight I craved and so started to look around for a

---

13 21ˢᵗ December 1988.

new bench. The problem was that the one I wanted was already occupied. However, I suddenly realised how I could make myself more popular with my fellow "sunbathers". I was sure that for 20 roubles, the two *babushkas* currently occupying my desired perch, would be happy to swap places. Sure enough, the deal was quickly sealed and "normal" sunbathing resumed. Unfortunately, my great idea had unexpected consequences, as word quickly spread that some crazy foreigner was prepared to give you a week's wages, if you let him have your bench. When the time came for my next "sun re-orientation", all twenty-four benches in the huge circle were fully occupied and the price for moving had gone up to 30 roubles. It was said at the time, that the Russian people would never embrace the capitalist system, I, however, wasn't so sure!

As my time at Warwick drew to a close, thoughts turned to what future lay ahead for me. Since my Corsican adventure, I had been dating a Spanish girl called Carmen, who had been studying French at Reims University. She had subsequently come to live with my parents in Leeds, to study English, while I finished my finals. We always spoke French together, which was helpful in maintaining the fluency I had achieved during my year abroad. However, when asked how good my French was, in a desire to shock, I would simply reply, 'I'm bisexual,' instead of the more usual, 'bilingual.' Despite hardly ever attending lectures, with a bit of last-minute swatting, I was able to get a 2:1[14] (note that: unlike today, Firsts were incredibly rare, for example, no one in my year got one). Unfortunately, I was unable to celebrate with Carmen, as she had by then returned to Galicia, NW Spain, to take the national exam to become a French teacher. Vague plans to both work as EU translators in Brussels, soon disappeared and when her family made it clear that, were I to visit, there would

---

14 First-Class Honours (First or 1st) (70% and above) Upper Second-Class Honours (2:1, 2. i) (60-70%) Lower Second-Class Honours (2:2, 2. ii) (50-60%).

be no chance of my staying in the same house, they being ardent Catholics, the relationship ended. Alone and not sure what to do next, I headed back to Yvonne's house in Reims for the summer and consoled myself with champagne and the occasional "French dalliance"! It was only on my return to Leeds, in the autumn of 1988, that the "road to Russia" started to reveal itself.

7

How to Become a Tour Director

My old friend Lyn was back home after completing her Russian degree at Birmingham University and I arranged to meet up for a drink, in what had been our old sixth form drinking spot. She and another good friend Ailsa had spent their third year studying in Moscow, although from the vast quantities of vodka they were now able to consume, it was clear they hadn't just been studying. In fact, Lyn had fallen in love with a Russian student and had spent much of her final year in Birmingham trying to maintain a long-distance romance. This was incredibly difficult at the time, with all phone calls having to be approved by the Soviet authorities and with the sure knowledge that they would record the conversation. Lyn however, was very determined to continue the relationship, even when she found out that Andrei had been conscripted and was likely to be sent to fight in Afghanistan. With her fluent Russian, she had been able to get a job as a freelance tour director, taking groups of American high school students on tours of Moscow and Leningrad, during the school holidays. This had initially helped to keep some form of contact with Andrei, but as I already knew from my Carmen experience, long-distance love rarely survives and when Andrei was eventually sent to war, the relationship ended. Lyn had however, continued to work on an ad-hoc basis for the American tour operator and as the conversation turned to what I was planning to do next, she mentioned that in addition, they did tours of Europe and had a small ski programme. I had already spent three years living on the continent and with my ski racing background it seemed an ideal fit. Sure enough, I got the job and two months later I was once again packing my bags and heading off to spend Christmas in the French Alps.

For the next few months I jetted in and out of the UK, combining skiing tours with cultural ones to cities like Rome, Florence, Amsterdam and Paris. At the end of each tour I would have a de-brief in the company's London office and hand in my, as usual, over-inflated expenses claim. It was at one of these meetings that I had the encounter that was to change my life for ever. I had already met Pierre, a fellow tour director "out on the road" and knew him to be a bit of a chancer. Given he had a French name and a French mother, everyone assumed he could speak the language fluently. I, for a fact, knew that he only spoke the odd word, something he had never felt necessary to divulge to the various companies he freelanced for. Anyway, as usual, he was full of chat about all the money he was making through the various kickbacks we used to get, while plying our trade. Basically, wherever you were there was an opportunity to make money. If it was Paris, it was the perfume "factory"; Florence, it was the leather "supermarket"; Lucerne, it was watches etc.. With 50-seat coaches crammed full of American tourists, anxious to snap up the tax-free "bargains" we were taking them to, easy pickings were there to be made. As a rule, we would get 10 per cent of the overall spend, handed over in a white envelope at the end of the "visit". We had just come to the end of the Easter period and given the way the holiday seasons fell, there would be no more work with the American tour operator until June. Pierre was therefore keen to tell me about an English tour operator he had got a job with, who were looking for French speaking tour directors, for an immediate start. I'm not a great one for believing in fate, my mantra has always been: "'The harder I work, the luckier I get,'" but this time there did seem to be something pre-destined, as the company's headquarters was in Leicester and that was where I was already heading. By this time, I had exhausted all the opportunities to stay with London based friends for the odd night between tours and so, I had decided to go and stay with my sister, who had recently taken up a position as a prison psychologist in Leicester. While waiting for my train north at St Pancras, I put a call through to the contact Pierre had given me and managed to secure an interview for the following day.

Given that everything had been arranged last minute, I rolled up for the interview totally unprepared. In those pre-internet days, I had been unable to do any research on the company and I didn't even have a *curriculum vitae* (CV) with me. However, I needn't have worried. Paul, who ran the French desk, was a really laid back, former Thomson Travel rep and Rick, who was the overall operations manager, had worked a number of winter seasons in the Alps and seemed more keen to chat about skiing, than to quiz me on why they should take me on. In truth, the fact that I had managed to "survive" with the American tour operator, automatically made me suitable, as they had a terrible reputation within the travel industry and the general consensus was, that if you could work for them, you could work for anyone. The only problem was, Paul had just taken on a couple of new French speaking freelancers and he didn't have any work available for the next few months. Of course, they would keep my details on file and contact me if things changed. Resigned to spending the next couple of months back in Leeds, I thanked them for the opportunity and started to make my way to the door. Suddenly from out of the blue Rick asked, 'You don't fancy going to Russia in a couple of weeks' time do you?' Trying to hide my incredulity, I immediately replied, 'Of course.' Up to this point, I hadn't even realised they did Russian tours and had only mentioned in passing that I had done Russian 'A' level. As it turned out, the fact that my Russian might be a bit rusty wasn't going to be a problem. In fact, the married couple who ran all the Russian tours at the time and who were based in Moscow, didn't speak a word of the language, instead relying on the ever-dependable Intourist guides, to do the majority of the work. I couldn't believe my luck. I was going to get paid to go to a country I'd always wanted to visit and even better, I wasn't going to have to do much. Rick introduced me to Tina, who ran the Russian desk and she explained if I could let her have some photos, she could fast track the visa application via an agency they used in London. I later found out that "fast track" entailed a little old man, employed by the agency, getting to the Soviet Consulate in Kensington Park Gardens, at some inordinately early time, to ensure he was first in line for when the visa section opened at 9 a.m.. Further down the line, I came to rely on this agency when I started travelling to Russia independently.

Clutching a copy of the tour itinerary for Moscow and the Golden Ring and determined to purchase an up-to-date travel guide book for the Soviet Union, I was just leaving the office, when a voice called out from a different section of the open-plan office. This turned out to be Sharon, who was the dynamic head of UK operations. She said she couldn't help hearing that I was looking for work and did I want to go to Durham next weekend? Things seemed to be getting a bit surreal. Within the space of ten minutes, I had been asked to lead tours to two places I'd never been. Who knew what next? Maybe a tour to China? Keen to maintain a favourable impression, I immediately said, 'Yes,' to Sharon and sat down to go through the tour details, subconsciously thinking that I would be able to drive up from Leeds to Durham midweek, to make sure I had some idea of what I was doing. Above all, I didn't want to jeopardize my Russia trip. Thus two days later, I drove the 80 miles north from Leeds and left my mum's VW Polo in the car park of The Royal County Hotel, to familiarise myself with the walking tour of Durham, I was going to have to lead the following Sunday morning. Looking back, I think the weekend tour ran pretty smoothly, at least no complaints were made that would have precluded my working for the company again and I even got some tips as the group alighted the coach, on our return to London. In fact, my main memory of the weekend, was me and the coach driver watching the title decider between Arsenal and my team Liverpool, on the TV in our hotel room. To this day, I remember the agony I felt, as Michael Thomas scored Arsenal's second, in the dying seconds, thereby securing the title on goal difference. Many years later, I was back at The Royal County Hotel visiting my son, Vito, who had decided to study Economics at Durham University but on this occasion, it was he who acted as the tour guide.

8

The Adventure Begins

Preparations for my first tour to Russia were a little rushed, as I only had three days between returning from Durham and having to be at London Heathrow for the flight out. I had managed to find an old Harpers pocket dictionary, stuffed to the back of one of the bookcases in my mother's study and purchased the *Collins Guide to the Soviet Union*, by Martin Walker, which had only just been published. Martin Walker had been *The Guardian's* Moscow correspondent, from 1984 to 1988, living in the city with his wife and young children and like all my family, I had always trusted *The Guardian* as a reliable source. I was keen to have the most up-to-date information, as I was going to the Soviet Union at a time of immense change. Four years earlier, Mikhail Gorbachev had been elected General Secretary of the Communist Party, thereby, effectively becoming leader of the whole Soviet Union. Unlike his predecessor, Konstantin Chernenko, a member of the "old guard", who typified "the Cold War" spirit of the post-war period, Gorbachev, with his youthful energy and enthusiasm (he was only 54 when elected) looked to improve relations with the West. By introducing the twin programmes of *Glasnost* (openness) and *Perestroika* (restructuring) he had worked towards establishing a market economy that was more socially oriented. His reforms were also geared towards increasing productivity and reducing waste. For example, one of his first actions had been to triple the price of vodka and to severely limit its sale. At the time of my arrival, in late May 1989, Gorbachev's policies had started to encourage real debate about the problems facing the country. By sheer coincidence, my first week in Russia coincided with a meeting of the Supreme Soviet (the country's legislative body) which, for the first time, had been voted in through relatively free elections. I remember everywhere my group went TVs would be turned on, with people staring dumbfounded, as delegates openly criticised the existing system.

I met my group, thirty in number, at one of the British Airways check-ins, in terminal 1, Heathrow. Ours was a scheduled flight, so we would be flying out as individuals and I needed to hand them their visas, so they would be able to get through passport control in Moscow, at which point, we would meet up with our Intourist guide. I had already been at the airport since 6 a.m. to get the visas from the agency representative and was slightly bleared-eyed as I introduced myself to the mainly middle-aged couples, who were to be my clients. Early morning starts were to prove typical over the next few years, as the *British Airways* (*BA*) Moscow flight always left at 9.45 a.m., meaning I had to be at Heathrow no later than 6.30 a.m.. I much preferred the flight out to St Petersburg, which left a couple of hours later. There was, however, one slight consolation, in that *BA's Concorde* transatlantic flight to New York, had a take-off slot just three planes ahead on the taxiing rank. I still remember being struck, by how such a small plane could make so much noise.

It took just over three and a half hours for our *Boeing 757* to cover the 1,500 miles between London and Moscow. With the prevailing wind behind, flights were always quicker west to east, the return journey often took over four hours. During the flight, I continued to familiarise myself with the Martin Walker guide, hoping to be prepared for any unexpected questions. I had been told by Rick, not to mention to my group, that this was my first trip to Russia, as this might not inspire confidence and I had resolved to say, that if caught out, I would claim to having only been to Leningrad and Murmansk in the far north. At least I was able to carry out my studies without fear of being rumbled, as I had deliberately chosen a seat at the rear of the plane, just in front of the smoker's section, where no one ever sat. And yes, you could still smoke on *BA* flights in 1989!

We arrived at Moscow Sheremetyevo Airport just after 4 p.m. local time (Moscow is three hours ahead of London) and joined the rather long queue for passport control. I had been advised not to speak any Russian while entering the country, as this might arouse suspicion, however, when finally standing in front of the rather attractive blonde-haired, female border guard, I couldn't help saying, '*Prevyet, Kak delya?*' a bit like Joey in *Friends*, "'Hey, how you doin?'" I have to admit, she remained rather stern-faced, clearly impervious to my charms, however, at least she let me through and I, twelve years after my first lesson with Mr Ward, had finally met a real Russian.

The second real Russian I met was equally attractive, namely Alina, the designated Intourist national guide for our seven-day trip. She was quite petite, blonde-haired and dressed smart-casual. Unlike me however, she didn't have a name badge, clearly, somethings were more relaxed in the Soviet Union. Having got the group together, we made our way out to the coach that was waiting for us in the parking lot outside. The thing that struck me most about the arrivals hall, was how dark it was. It almost felt like somebody had forgotten to pay the electricity bill and they had been cut off. The overall dinginess of the place wasn't helped by the thousands of, what appeared to be baking tins, that had been affixed to the ceiling. At least the coach, for our 25-minute transfer to the Hotel Cosmos, situated to the north of the city centre, appeared to be one of the newer ones in the parking lot and the driver, Valodya had a friendly smile. Alina settled herself into her front row seat, microphone in hand, with me in the seat alongside and the coach slowly pulled away. Thus began the first of the thousands of miles I would spend on the pot-holed highways of the Soviet Union.

The first point of interest you come to when taking the road south towards the city centre, are the three huge sculptures of anti-tank hedgehogs, marking the fullest extent of the German advance on Moscow during World War II. It was sobering to realise just how close the Germans had come to defeating the Russians, a fact I was reminded of a year later, when I saw one of the menus that Hitler had had printed for a celebratory dinner, at the Hotel Astoria in Leningrad. These days, in many quarters, the Russians get a bad press but the huge sacrifices that were made on all our behalf, in the fight against fascism, should never be forgotten. The next sight to grab my attention was an *Agip* petrol station, something I was used to seeing on my European travels but totally unexpected here. In fact, it was a sign that the changes Gorbachev had initiated were starting to have an effect. The term "joint venture", where the Soviets went into partnership with a western company, in this case the Italian conglomerate AGIP, would come to dominate my life over the next few years, as I struggled to set up my own trading deals, between the UK and Russia. The contrast between the sparkly new petrol station and the motley collection of Ladas queuing to use its pumps, couldn't have been greater and served to demonstrate just how far the Gorbachev reforms still had to go. After another five minutes, Alina asked us, in her perfect English, to look to the left and pointed out the stadium where *Dynamo Moscow* played. Being a keen student of football history, I knew that during the 1950s and early 1960s *Dynamo Moscow* had been one of the strongest teams in Europe, with players such as the goalkeeper, Lev Yashin, nicknamed "The Black Spider", becoming world famous. However, what I didn't know at the time, was how closely linked the club was to the hated KGB[15] (the Russian secret

---

15 KGB stands for *Komitet Gosudarstvennoy Bezopasnosti*, which translates to "Committee for State Security."

police). Supporters of rival teams actually referred to the club as "garbage", a slang term for "police". I later discovered that true Muscovites usually supported *Moscow Spartak*, a bit like true Mancunians follow Manchester City and not the "Salford based" Manchester United.

Soon afterwards, Alina announced we were approaching the Hotel Cosmos and sure enough the imposing 25 floor, crescent-shaped structure, loomed into view. The hotel had been built to serve the XXII Summer Olympic Games, held in Moscow, in 1980 and already had a place in my affections, as my schoolboy hero, Steve Ovett, had famously got drunk in one of its bars, following his unexpected victory over Sebastian Coe, in the final of the 800 metres. I always liked to think this is the reason he went on to lose the final of the 1,500 metres to Coe, a few days later. At the time, with its 1,777 rooms, it was the second-largest hotel in Russia, only surpassed by the gigantic, Hotel Rossiya (3,000 rooms) situated opposite the Kremlin and registered in *The Guinness Book of Records* at the time, as the largest hotel in the world.

The check-in procedure which followed, was to become all too familiar over the next few years. While hotel porters unloaded cases from the boot of the coach, we entered the imposing lobby and formed an orderly queue at the reception desk. A few of my group had already been a bit nervous about letting their luggage out of their sight and had become even more uneasy when they were told they would have to surrender their passports for the duration of their stay. However, "rules are rules" and in fact, the system worked surprisingly efficiently. On surrender of ones passport, you were given a room card which would then be handed to the *dezhurnaya*[16] (pronounced *dejournaya* (key lady)) who were dotted along the floor landings throughout the

---

16 *dezhurnaya* translates as 'duty' but in this context refers to "floor lady", "floor guard" etc..

hotel. Meanwhile, cases were hand delivered to your rooms, Alina, having taken the room numbers down to the porters in the baggage room below. In all my time tour directing in the Soviet Union, I never experienced the loss of a single bag or passport, so at least some things worked.

With the group all settling into their rooms, Alina took me to the cavernous dining room, where dinner was to be served and introduced me to Sergei, who was going to be our waiter for the evening meal. We then arranged to meet up the following morning at 9.45 a.m., in time for the Moscow city tour starting at 10 a.m.. No matter where you are in the world, the "golden rule of tour directing" is that city tours start at 10 a.m.. With Alina having departed, I suddenly noticed that Sergei was gesturing for me to come over to him. He had clearly been waiting for her to leave so that he could broach the subject of my first illegal transaction. In a murmured whisper, he asked if I was willing to change pounds into roubles at an advantageous rate? The official rate of exchange was £1 for 1 rouble but he could do it for 5 roubles. A little wary but not wishing to miss out on a deal, I managed to negotiate a rate of 7 roubles to the pound and feeling pretty pleased with myself, asked if he wanted to come to my room to complete the transaction. Judging by the way he vigorously shook his head, I realised this wouldn't be a good idea and so a rendezvous was set for half an hour later, in, of all places, the hotel laundry, located in the basement. Surrounded by baskets of dirty bed linen, I, to use a euphemism, "lost my cherry" and entered the underground world of the *chyorny rynok* (black market). It soon transpired that I should have been better at haggling, as the going rate on the street, was actually 10 roubles to the pound! I would only make one more mistake while changing money illicitly, when a wide-boy in Tallinn, Estonia, counted out a number of 10 rouble notes into the palm of his hand only to switch them at the last moment for a bundle of 1 rouble notes, wrapped up in the sole surviving 10.

I met up with my new "friend" Sergei at dinner and not surprisingly he was very attentive to my needs, although he couldn't do much about the rather tasteless meat that was on offer. Still, as most of my group agreed, no one came to Russia for the culinary delights on offer and at least the ubiquitous ice cream, that always appeared at dessert time, didn't taste too bad. After dinner, I headed for my room and picked up my key from the *dezhurnaya,* sitting at her desk in the dimly-lit corridor, with the obligatory book in hand. These women came to play an important role in my life. In theory, they were meant to be the "eyes and ears" of the state, making sure no illicit contact was made between Soviet citizens and "decadent" westerners. However, for me, they were a great intermediary for getting my washing and ironing done, when I had been on the road for weeks on end.

I remember struggling to get to sleep on my first night in the Cosmos. Neither of the twin beds in the room was particularly comfortable (Note: double beds in hotels, simply didn't exist, there is a puritanical streak to the Russian mentality) and in any case, with the three hour time difference, it was still relatively early for me. Instead, I stared out across the Moscow night skyline, from the vantage of my 20th-floor room, taking in the twin sights of the Ostankino Telecom Tower and "The Conquerors of Space" monument and wondered what the next day would have in store.

9

A Bit of a Problem

For my first full day in Russia, the weather was unseasonably warm. I was already regretting having put on one of the two woollen suits I'd brought, when I met up with Alina in the coach parking lot, situated at the bottom of the long, sweeping drive, which forms the approach to the Hotel Cosmos. Unlike the previous day, she was looking a bit flustered, as she explained to me that because the Supreme Soviet was meeting in the Kremlin, the whole of the area, including Red Square, was cordoned off, meaning the planned city tour was going to be severely compromised. At first, although a bit annoyed, I thought that as we would be returning to Moscow at the end of our trip around the Golden Ring, before flying home, we would get the chance to visit the Kremlin and Red Square on our final morning. Alina however, quickly disabused me of this hope, by saying that the meeting of the Supreme Soviet was scheduled to last for at least a further ten days. Clearly, she had known all this the previous day but, as was to prove the case on numerous occasions in the future, Intourist preferred to keep bad news to the last possible moment. Concerned that I was going to be the first tour director in living memory, to not have a group see Red Square, I determined to go and find out for myself what was really going on. I had already arranged with Alina to be dropped off from the city coach tour near to the Intourist office, situated close to Gorky Street, in the city centre. The Leicester office had given me a parcel containing important documents to hand-deliver to a lady called Lara Karlina, who was in charge of all UK tour groups visiting the Soviet Union. For the next few years Lara was to play an integral part in my life;

in the process, becoming a good friend. As the coach pulled out of the parking lot and on to Prospect Mira (Peace Avenue) to head south towards the city centre, Alina broke the news about the amended itinerary. To my surprise, everyone seemed remarkably sanguine about not getting to see Red Square. Living through the Cold War years, people were used to the Russians continually saying, "'*N'yet*,'" to everything and so, this seemed just "par for the course". I however, was not going to be so easily dissuaded. Having left the group and located the Intourist office, while handing over the parcel, I asked Lara, a statuesque blonde in her mid- thirties, whether there really was no way to get a view of Red Square. After a minute's reflection she said the only possibility would be to go into GUM[17], the massive department store, whose façade ran along the opposite side of Red Square to the Kremlin and hope to find a window big enough to offer a decent vista. Slightly encouraged, I set off to walk the short distance from the Intourist office, to GUM, in the process, passing the imposing structure of the Hotel Moskva. In the distance, I could make out the towers of the Kremlin but sure enough, the twin entrances to Red Square were blocked off by huge screens, with large numbers of police and soldiers milling around. The entrance to GUM was rather uninspiring but once inside, it was easy to be impressed by the glass roofed design, which had been unique at the time of its construction, in the late nineteenth century. In fact, it very much reminded me of the Victorian shopping arcades, found in my home city of Leeds. However, here on the ground floor, instead of designer boutiques, were endless stalls of cheap textiles, plastic briefcases and tacky souvenirs, a salutary reminder of how much Gorbachev's reforms still had to do. Realising any decent view of Red Square would more likely be available from higher up,

---

17 GUM, in full *Glavny Universalny Magazin* (Main Department Store) formerly *Gosudarstvenny Universalny Magazin* (State Department Store) the largest department store in Russia.

I took one of the narrow staircases up to the first of the three floors and immediately came across a much bigger shop selling men's overcoats. Beyond the rails and rails of universally black coats, I spotted a large arched window which might get me the view I was looking for. The window itself was relatively high off the ground but by standing on tip-toe I was finally able to get my first sight of what, still to this day, remains the most magical place I have ever been. As it turned out, I was directly opposite Lenin's Mausoleum, the resting place of the first Soviet leader, Vladimir Lenin and by pure chance, the changing of the guard was just taking place. This involved two goose-stepping soldiers, accompanied by a commanding officer, swapping places with two of their comrades, who were standing guard, motionless, at the entrance to the tomb. This spectacle occurred on the hour, every hour, 365 days a year. Many a time, I would ensure my late night walks home coincided with this hourly spectacle. Sometimes, around 2 a.m. there would be just me and the five soldiers, alone with our thoughts, on the whole of Red Square.

Having found the best vantage point, I now had to get my group here. Lunch, following the city tour, was pre-booked at the Cosmos, which meant I was going to have to get the *Metro* back to the hotel. In central Moscow, you are never more than two minutes away from the nearest station and without too much trouble, I came across the large interchange, where the red, blue and green lines meet. Alina had told me I would need to take the red line from Marx Prospect and then change onto the orange line at Kirovskaya, which would take me north to VDNKh[18] (the Park of Economic Achievement) which was the closest *Metro* station to the Cosmos. At the automatic barrier, I realised I would have to change one of the rouble notes that Sergei had given me

---

18 VDNKh was opened on 1 May 1958. The name stands for Exhibition of Achievements of the National Economy *Vystavka Dostizheniy Narodnovo Khozyaystva* (abbreviated to VDNKh).

for some kopeks, the fare being a five-kopek coin. I spotted a small window to the left, marked *"Kassa"* and assumed correctly that this was the place to get coins. As was universally the case, it was a woman who served me and as I descended the escalator into the depths of the system, I quickly realised I was entering a very female environment, for at the bottom of every escalator there was a uniformed female worker, sitting in a glass booth staring morbidly at the thousands of passengers passing by. I often thought this must be one of the worst jobs in the world, cooped up in a tiny space, devoid of natural light, for hours on end, with basically nothing to do. In truth it was symptomatic of a country where unemployment officially "didn't exist" and so everyone had a job, no matter how trivial the role. Once on the platform, I spotted the illuminated sign that tells you how long since the last train left and with it saying 45 seconds, was very surprised when I heard the rumble of another train approaching. Even to this day, the Moscow *Metro* is one of the most efficient in the world, with waiting times during peak periods, little more than one minute. Unlike the endless delays I was used to on the London Underground, I never had any problems in either Moscow, Leningrad or Kyiv and the other difference was as the train drew up to the platform, I noticed it was a woman driving. I came to quickly realise that it was women who did the bulk of the work in the Soviet Union, while their male contemporaries lazed around drinking vodka!

Having successfully negotiated the change of lines at Kirovskaya, I was soon exiting the station at VDNKh, with the Hotel Cosmos looming in front of me. Luckily, I was just in time for lunch and despite the omission of Red Square, my group seemed to be in good spirits. Alina and I, as was the norm, sat on a separate table and she told me that instead of the intended afternoon visit to the Kremlin Armoury Museum, to see the world-famous *Faberge Eggs*, we would be going on a tour of the nearby, Park of Economic

Achievement (VDNKh). This seemed to me to be a bit of a poor substitute, so I explained my plan to get the group to see Red Square, from the vantage point of the coat shop in GUM. At first, Alina was a bit dubious but the coach was already available for the afternoon and I also made the suggestion that we could combine the trip with a tour of the *Metro*'s most beautiful stations. So it came to pass, that to the incredulity of two po-faced shop assistants, thirty expensively-attired westerners "invaded" their meagrely stocked emporium, to witness the "changing of the guard" on Red Square, at 3 p.m. precisely. The *Metro* tour proved a similar success, with the group awestruck by the Art Deco masterpiece that is Mayakovskaya Station, as well as the elegant bronze chandeliers, marble arcades and monumental mosaics, found in Komsomolskaya Station. Luckily, the tour of VDNKh would have to wait for another day, as we were leaving early the next morning, for our trip around the Golden Ring. I did, however, get to discover its limited delights, when a couple of months later, accompanied by a national Intourist guide, a Moscow city guide and a park guide (surely the highest ratio of guides to tourists ever recorded) we traipsed through a steady drizzle, listening to how the Soviet Union had consistently over-achieved in its five year economic plans, a fact rather at odds with the numerous rusting tractors on display. For me VDNKh will always be known as "The Park of Economic Under-Achievement"!

10
Out in the Country

The next morning, the sun was still shining, as our coach with two drivers, Valodya and Misha, pulled out of the Cosmos Hotel parking lot, heading for Zagorsk, 40 miles away and our first stop on the Golden Ring. Over the next few years, the tour would become one of my favourites, as while Moscow and Leningrad changed dramatically, places such as Suzdal, Vladimir and Rostov seemed to be "frozen in time" and gave me an insight into the heart and soul of Russia. After about an hour's driving, the golden domes and the great bell tower of the Trinity Monastery of St Sergius, appeared in the distance. During the Soviet period, Zagorsk had been the centre of the Russian Orthodox Church. The patriarch lived within the monastery, which also housed the main seminary, to train future priests and acted as a shrine for the faithful. However, as a sign of the changing times, the previous year, the seat of the patriarch had been allowed to return to Moscow's Danilovsky Monastery. Our tour of the monastery, led by Alina, lasted a couple of hours and I got to see the first of the many thousands of icons I would encounter. Little did I know that a couple of years later, I would be making money out of icons, selling them on, through a dealer in London's Camden Market.

After Zagorsk, we set off for Suzdal, 100 miles away and where we had two night's accommodation booked. Now, travelling through the depths of the Russian countryside, I soon realised it was going to take a few hours to reach our intended destination, as the roads were becoming increasingly pot-holed. Glancing at my watch, I saw it was already well past one o'clock in the afternoon and I started to feel a little concerned that lunch might be a bit of a problem, there being no sign of human life, let alone anywhere to eat. Just as I was about to express my concerns to Alina, the coach rounded a bend and to the side of the road I saw what could only be described as a huge wooden wigwam, with parking spaces in front. Sure enough, this turned out to be our lunch venue, one of the strangest places I've ever eaten. Not only did the place look like a wigwam but there was a large, carved totem pole at the side. I half-expected the waiters to be dressed as native Indians. However, when the food arrived it was served, as usual, by men wearing the obligatory uniform of black trousers, white shirt and tatty bow-tie. The other thing was that buffalo was definitely not on the menu! Instead it was the usual fare of watery soup, gristly meat with potatoes and very sweet ice cream. Given that the temperature had continued to rise all day, I was desperate to have something to quench my thirst and I started to stare longingly at the carafes of iced-water that had been placed on the table. Before leaving for Russia, I had been advised by Lyn not to drink the tap water and instead to rely on the omnipresent bottles of mineral water that littered hotel dining rooms. These however, tasted more like Baltic seawater, than natural spring water and surely, given that we were in the depths of the countryside, the water would be fine to drink. Noting that Alina was pouring herself a glass, I decided to take a chance. Big mistake! Although the water tasted ok, it's effects were to stay with me for the next few months, with intermittent bouts of upset tummy. Still, at least I learnt my lesson, going so far as to not even brush my teeth in tap water and to scrupulously avoid having ice in my gin and tonic (G&T).

After lunch, it was another two hours before we reached the Motel Suzdal and what a pleasant surprise. Unlike the towering Hotel Cosmos, this single-storey, purpose-built accommodation was the pride and joy of Intourist. Set in well-maintained gardens and with parquet flooring throughout, it was to become a particular favourite of mine. The reason for Intourist's investment, is that it formed part of one vast museum and tourism complex, showcasing the whole of traditional Russian life, including the churches, the private houses of townspeople and peasants plus numerous wooden carvings. Maybe it hadn't been a totem pole outside our lunch venue after all!

The next day, accompanied by a local guide, we got to visit the whole of the site, which had the slightly strange feel of a half-deserted theme park. Apart from us, there were a few small groups of schoolchildren, exercise books in hand, listening attentively, as their teachers explained what life had been like, as far back as the fourteenth century. We also came across another group of tourists, who at first glance, appeared to be fellow westerners. I was just about to greet them, when I heard that they were speaking German, definitely not one of my languages and then I noticed their footwear. Although their clothes wouldn't have looked out of place on the streets of Leeds, the shoes and trainers they had on, were universally of a poor quality. The group, it transpired, was from the DDR i.e., East Germany. Although over the next few years, the continent of Europe was to experience monumental changes, the one thing you could still rely on, was the inability of the old communist bloc countries to produce decent footwear.

By mid-afternoon, having visited the blue-domed Cathedral of the Nativity, the Monastery of the Saviour and St Euthymius and numerous other churches, I sensed that the group was starting to flag, particularly as the sun was continuing to beat down. So when I suggested a return to the motel and a couple of hours of free time, the offer was gratefully accepted. I also had an ulterior motive, as I had noticed a small river running through the motel's extensive grounds and I fancied a cooling swim, followed by a bit of impromptu sunbathing. I got changed quickly and set off to find a quiet spot, where I would be in no danger of coming across any of my group. The banks of the river were covered in waist-high reeds, perfect for nestling down in, well out of sight of the motel. Just as I was trampling down some reeds in order to spread my towel out, I heard the vague sound of pop music, emanating from a spot about 30 feet to my left. Deciding to investigate, to my great surprise I came across Alina, already stretched out on a much nicer towel than mine, wearing a fetching bikini and listening to a *Sony Walkman* that was a more up-to-date model than mine. Immersed in her music, she was a little startled when she saw there was a man in skimpy *Speedos* standing above her but quickly regained her composure, when she realised it was me. Thinking this was the perfect opportunity for me to get to know Alina better, I suggested she might like to come for a swim with me. However, this was obviously not going to be on the agenda. Very politely she declined my "gallant" offer and made it quite clear that she would like to get back to her music. Feeling a little rebuffed, I consoled myself with a leisurely dip in the slow flowing river, followed by a couple of hours listening to Marc Almond on my own *Walkman*. Luckily, not all Russian women were to prove as impervious to my charms as Alina!

The following day I was pleased I had suggested some "free time" for the group, as the weather had turned and swimming was definitely "off limits." The itinerary for the day included visiting two more cities, Ivanovo and Vladimir. First up, was Ivanovo, where a city tour led by a monotone local guide, called Olga, made the Park of Economic Achievement seem interesting. When I tell you that the "highlight" of the tour was a visit to a textile museum, I think you get the idea. Vladimir, however, with its golden gates, dating back to 1164 and twin cathedrals of the Dormition and St Demetrius, proved much more up-lifting and it was a tired but happy group, that returned to the Suzdal Motel, for our second night. Being in the depths of the Russian countryside meant there was no evening entertainment put on for the motel guests. There

61

was, nevertheless, a fairly well-stocked bar and I thought an after-dinner Geri-led pub quiz might be a good idea. Sure enough, the group who after four days together, were starting to bond well, were enthusiastic and luckily, I had had the foresight to bring a quiz book based on the popular TV gameshow, *Masterteam,* hosted by the presenter Angela Rippon. With a bottle of *Sovetskoye Shampanskoye* (Soviet Champagne) as the prize and me taking the role of Angela, we passed an enjoyable couple of hours, which got increasingly lively, as the beer and vodka started to flow. A married couple from Scarborough, called Jim and Margaret, were the first winners of the many "Geri quizzes" that were to follow and they very kindly offered to share their winning prize with me. If there is one thing in life that I've subsequently learnt, it is never to mix vodka with champagne. I once had a client who only saw Moscow from the inside of a hotel room for three days, his having accepted the friendly invitation of a railway attendant to join him for a drink, on the overnight train down from Leningrad.

Sure enough, the next day I was feeling a bit ropey, as we set off on the road to Yaroslavl, our final port of call on the Golden Ring. The good weather had returned and with the sun blazing through the front window of the coach, I abandoned my usual seat and headed for the comparative cool to be found at the rear. Here I found Valodya, the older of the two drivers and even though it was only 9.30 a.m., he had a bottle of vodka pressed to his lips. He gestured for me to join him and took a small glass out of his jacket pocket. In my delicate state I could think of nothing less appealing than trying some "hair of the dog" and I very politely refused, explaining that I was working and therefore not allowed to drink while "on duty". This seemed a bit of an alien concept to Valodya. I had already noticed that he and Misha only drove on alternate days, the result of the Soviet obsession with full-employment. Given that this was Valodya's "day off", he had clearly been drinking all night and was keen to keep going on his own 24-

hour bender. Where drink is concerned, Russians can be very persuasive, or maybe I'm just weak-willed, but for once I stood my ground, particularly as we weren't exactly hidden from view and I had no desire to mess up my chances of future tour directing. Making my excuses I returned to the cauldron of heat that was the front of the coach, resolving to avoid any future late-night drinking sessions. After a couple of hours driving, to my intense relief we reached Rostov, one of the oldest towns of northern Russia, dating back to the ninth century AD. Despite my hangover, I couldn't help but be impressed by the sheer beauty of the place, a highlight being the cube shaped and single-domed, Saviour in the Vestibule, containing its fresco of the *Last Judgement*, painted by the local priest Timothy, Dmitry of Vologda and rightly considered one of the great masterpieces of Russian art. From Rostov to Yaroslavl, our final destination on the Golden Ring, it is a little over 30 miles and with empty and relatively straight roads, we were able to make the originally named Hotel Yaroslval, in time for a late lunch. As it turned out, luckily, we only had one night's accommodation booked here. After the splendours of Rostov, Yaroslavl was an instant disappointment. Standing on the banks of the River Kotorosl, where it flows into the mighty Volga, it reminded me of some industrial landscape from Victorian Britain, with its smoking factory chimneys and synthetic tyre factories. In addition, after the relative comfort of the Hotel Cosmos and Suzdal Motel, here we were in the heart of provincial Russia, staying in the type of room that was to become all too familiar to me, over the next few years. Threadbare carpets, wafer-thin curtains that failed to keep out the sunlight, tiny baths and rudimentary plumbing. The local Intourist guide, who had been there to meet us at lunch, told me and Alina that the city coach tour was planned for the following morning but if we wanted, we could have an "optional" river excursion that afternoon, for the princely sum of 14 roubles per person. Thinking immediately that Yaroslavl might possibly look better from the river, I asked the group if they were interested. Everyone thought it was a good idea, only they didn't have any roubles left, having already spent the small amounts they had exchanged officially, over the previous five days. Jim, the pub quiz winner from the previous night, asked if they could pay in sterling but the local guide, who was very much "old school" said definitely not. Seeing the group's disappointment and sensing a money-making opportunity, I said if the group paid me in sterling I could use the imaginary "rouble float", my company had provided, to cover the cost of the trip. Alina gave me a knowing look but said nothing and the local guide just seemed relieved I was taking on the responsibility. And so, it came to pass, that in the space of just a couple of hours I made a £300 profit, appreciably more than the weekly fee I was being paid by the tour operator. Suddenly Russia didn't just seem a "place of interest", more "a land of opportunity" and no, Yaroslavl didn't look better from the water!

Returning from the excursion, I still had an hour to kill before dinner and inspired by the sight of locals bathing in the Volga, I thought it would be nice to say I had swum in one of the world's longest rivers. In addition, I thought dipping into its cooling waters might be a remedy for the nagging headache I was still experiencing. With the temperature still in the high twenties, it was lovely to breaststroke gently downriver, smiling at my fellow bathers, the majority of whom I noted, were wearing swim caps. Maybe Yaroslavl wasn't so bad after all. Then out of nowhere I heard an incredibly loud klaxon sound. Immediately people started to head to shore, not quite like an excerpt from *Jaws* but still fairly rapidly. I however, was still enjoying the thrill of open-water swimming and was in no hurry to join them. This was soon to change. A couple of minutes after the sound of the klaxon a tampon bobbed into view, closely followed by the traces of what was soon to become a sea of human excrement. Realising I was the only person still in the river, I quickly reverted to front crawl and made as fast as I could for the riverbank, straining to keep my head above water and keeping my mouth tightly closed. As it turned out, the Yaroslavl authorities treated the Volga like one big open sewer, regularly releasing the city's human waste into its flowing waters. In fact, at the time Yaroslavl had the reputation of being the most polluted city in the whole of the Soviet Union. The first factory ever closed and fined for breaking pollution laws was in Yaroslavl. As you can imagine, my pre-dinner ablutions were more assiduous than normal, wedged into the tiny bath with my feet dangling over the adjacent hand basin. Unsurprisingly, to this day, the Volga and the Kamenka at Suzdal, remain the only Russian rivers in my "open water" collection.

11

Falling for Russian Women

As expected, the coach city tour the following morning, proved decidedly under-whelming and it was with some relief, that we hit the road straight after lunch, for the five-hour return journey to Moscow and our final night's accommodation at the Hotel Cosmos. Despite the relative disappointment of Yaroslavl, the group were in good spirits and that evening at dinner, the *shampanskoye* and wine flowed freely. It must have been well after ten, when the impromptu party started to break up but I decided to have one last drink, on my own, in the bar on the mezzanine floor in the huge central lobby. I must admit, my decision had been slightly influenced by the stunning blonde I had noticed earlier in the evening, lounging on one of the comfortable leather sofas that formed the seating area for the aptly named *Heineken* bar, *Heineken* being the only beer available. Luckily, she was still there but had now been joined by an equally attractive brunette. The two women were immaculately turned out and were both, to my surprise, clutching Gucci handbags. I could hear they were speaking Russian but I supposed they must be part of the emerging wave of second or third generation Russians, who were starting to return to the land of their ancestors, lured by the Gorbachev reforms. Having ordered a beer at the bar, I chose one of the sofas in close proximity to the object of my attention and placed the lukewarm can down on the glass coffee table in front of me. It quickly became apparent that I had been noticed and to my intense pleasure the blonde gave me a winning smile. Buoyed by the not insignificant amount of alcohol I had already consumed, I called over in English to see if it would be ok to join

66

them. A slightly confused look appeared on the blonde girl's face and I realised these were actually locals and not returning emigres. Switching to Russian, I asked the same question and was pleased to get a positive response. As I was sitting down, naturally closer to the blonde than the brunette, as if by magic the barman appeared. Up to this point the barmen I had encountered had been invariably surly, usually giving the impression that they were doing you a favour by letting you have a drink. However, this one was all smiles, as he asked my new friends if they would like something from the bar. Ever the gentleman and feeling cash rich after the previous day's river trip, I immediately offered to pay, only slightly surprised when both women said, 'the usual.' Having quickly established that I was in conversation with Olga (the blonde) and Nadia (the brunette) and with two large vodka and oranges now on the table in front of us, I started my first proper attempt at flirting in Russian. In truth, I was only really flirting with Olga, as I became instantly aware that I was clearly not Nadia's type. Still, the conversation between me and Olga flowed relatively smoothly. She said she was a secretary in a government department and that she loved western music, with Elton John a particular favourite. I asked if she was staying in the hotel but she said no, it was too expensive and she and Nadia had just come for a drink to celebrate the end of the working week. Noticing how quickly the vodka and oranges were disappearing, I offered to buy another round and Olga immediately accepted. Nadia however was more reticent and declined, saying it was getting late and she didn't want to miss the last *Metro* home. With Olga inching ever closer to me on the sofa, this seemed like the perfect scenario. Downing the last of her drink in one, Nadia said her goodbyes to Olga and headed off towards the cloakroom, which was situated on the ground floor level off the hotel lobby. I, meanwhile, decided to join Olga on the vodka and oranges. By this time, I was getting quite tipsy and was starting to wax lyrical about how unfair it was that there were so many barriers between the UK and Soviet Union. Suddenly I noticed that Olga's hand was on my knee, as she softly whispered in my ear that barriers were there to be crossed! Following her lead I asked if she would like to come for a nightcap in my room and was really pleased when she agreed. There was however, a bit of a problem. As Olga explained the only way for us to be together was for me to go up alone, get my key from the *dezhurnaya* on my floor and wait in the room. She would come up ten minutes later and if I could give her five dollars, the cost of a vodka and orange, she would be able to bribe the *dezhurnaya* to turn a blind eye. This seemed a cheap price to pay for what I imagined was going to be a great ending to my first week in Russia. Putting a five dollar bill under Olga's glass I gave her my room number and headed for the lifts downstairs, to make the ascent to the twentieth floor. Just as I was approaching the set of four lifts, located to the right of the huge reception desk, I noticed Nadia, hand-in-hand with an aged Italian businessman, who I had bumped into earlier in the week, getting into the nearest lift and heading for the upper floors. Clearly, she was no longer worried about missing the last *Metro* home! Slowly, it began to dawn on me that it might be costing me a bit more than five dollars to spend the night with Olga. Although, I wouldn't claim to have the highest moral standards, I am rather puritanical about the notion of paying for sex, I never have done it and I never will. The Hotel Cosmos however, had a completely different ethos. As I came to find out, prostitution in its 1,777 rooms, was on an epic scale. At one time, in the early nineties, it was nicknamed "The Biggest Brothel in the World". Olga and Nadia were just the human face of a huge, mafia-run operation, that paid off hotel doormen, nightclub bouncers, receptionists, barmen and waiters, to ensure a constant stream of ready, non-traceable, hard currency. Needless to say, Olga never made it to my room. Clearly she had realised there were better "marks" to be made and had probably headed for the nightclub, situated in the hotel basement, where even if there were no potential clients at this late hour, at least she had five dollars to get herself a final vodka and orange.

I was a little subdued the following morning as I checked out of my room and headed for the parking lot, to ensure the coach was ready for our transfer to Sheremetyevo airport. It had been an amazing week full of new experiences and at the time, it wasn't clear if I would ever be coming back. As per the Intourist rules, Alina was obliged to accompany us up to the point of check-in, which gave me the chance to give her a thank you card from the group, containing a selection of dollar bills and pound notes, I had collected at breakfast time. I was pretty sure that unlike some of her older colleagues, she would have no qualms about accepting such a *podarok* (gift) and so it proved. Once through customs, I still had plenty of time to kill before the *BA* return flight to Heathrow. The Intourist way of doing things was, just like an army, always to be early when transport was involved. The first time I left the Hotel Moskva, in Leningrad, to catch the midnight train to Talinn, we left at 10 p.m., when the transfer to the station only took five minutes! Seeing a sign for "Duty Free", I thought I might as well stock-up on a few bottles of spirits for the coming months (Note: this was a time when prices were genuinely cheaper than in the supermarkets back home). To my surprise, the Moscow airport "Duty Free" was a large, well-supplied retail outlet, mirroring those I had come across on my European travels. In fact, it was one of the very first joint ventures, with the western capital being provided by the company running Ireland's airports. The link with Ireland had been formed due to *Aeroflot* planes, on their way to New York, refuelling at Shannon Airport, situated on the country's western coast. One infamous story has it, that an enterprising *Aeroflot* pilot on the New York run, managed, over a number of years, to accumulate enough car components, to build his own *Ford Mustang*.

With my trolley well-stashed with booze and some much-needed chocolate bars, I made my way to the check-out. By now, it was mid-afternoon and the place was pretty much deserted. There was just the one till open and no queue. As I approached, I realised it was going to be a young, extremely attractive woman serving me. Her name badge read "Juliyanna" and so naturally, I said, '*Kak delya?*'

'I'm fine,' she replied in English, with only the hint of an accent. 'Where are you flying to?'

'London,' I replied, 'Would you like to come with me?' only half joking.

'If only I could,' she said, giving me a wistful look, which melted my heart. And so began my first Russian romance, initiated by a postcard I sent on my return, simply addressed to Juliyanna, at Moscow Airport Duty Free, Russia and giving her my contact details in the UK. To this day, it amazes me that she ever received the card but as she later told me, she was the only Juliyanna on the staff and her supervisor, who took delivery of the unusual communication, had a soft spot for her. Over the next few years, every time I was in Moscow, we would meet up and with her as my expert guide, I discovered parts of the city "off limits" to the normal westerner. For a while, I was infatuated with her. She was the spitting-image of Mary Nightingale, a popular TV presenter of the time, but for obvious reasons, ours was a complicated relationship, not helped by the fact I married someone else! But that story will have to wait. As the *BA, Boeing 757* lifted off effortlessly, from the Sheremetyevo tarmac, the first part of my Russian Odyssey came to an end, little did I know at the time, that the real journey was only just beginning.

12

Collecting Air Miles

People often ask me, 'Did you have a good flight?' to which I always reply, 'It landed!' One time, flying back to Moscow from Irkutsk, in the far east of Russia, the *Ilyushin 62* (aeroplane) I was on, seemed to be preparing to land. We had descended through thick cloud cover, for about twenty minutes and I had already heard the undercarriage go down, so naturally, I assumed touchdown was imminent. It was therefore with some surprise that when we did emerge from the clouds, all I could see below was forest. Now the *Ilyushin 62* is a big plane, in fact, it was the world's largest jet liner, when it was first flown in 1963 and even I, with my very basic grasp of aeronautics, knew that it shouldn't be flying so low, with no landing strip in sight. Sure enough, I immediately heard the pilot increase the engine revs, as we were clearly in danger of stalling. The problem was, we were nowhere near Domodedovo Airport, our intended destination and unfortunately, the *Ilyushin 62* was not fitted with an automatic pilot, landing system. In other words, the pilot had to be able to see the runway from a long way off, in order to complete a successful touchdown. For the next twenty minutes, he displayed incredible skill, managing to bob in and out of the low-lying clouds, literally searching for the airport, while managing to avoid stalling the plane and sending us crashing into the canopy below. It was with immense relief, that I finally felt the plane get into a normal landing trajectory and to spot the outlying buildings of Moscow's fourth and most antiquated airport. Once landed, as was the custom with all *Aeroflot* flights at the time, the pilot, co-pilot and navigation officer, exited the plane before the passengers and as they passed my seat, I was sorely tempted to

71

jump up and give them all a big hug and of course, a few packets of *Marlboro Red*. However, not wishing to look uncool in front of my group, I resisted the temptation, instead, limiting myself to a smile and a celebratory thumbs up. I don't wish to appear over-dramatic but a couple of months later, I took the same flight, having been told by the coach driver, on the way to the airport, that the previous day's flight had taken off but there had been no report of a landing! This was typical of news management during "Soviet times" i.e., no *Aeroflot* flight had ever "crashed", it simply "hadn't landed". An infamous story dating back to 1950, was of a plane carrying the ice hockey team, VVS[19] Moscow, crashing, as they travelled to a game against Tractor Chelyabinsk, in west-central Russia. Although the whole team was wiped out, incredibly, the fixture was still completed the following day with a hastily assembled "fake team" and *pravda*[20] reporting the result, as if nothing had happened. Ironically *pravda* means "truth" in Russian.

I think it is fair to say that air safety wasn't a top priority during my flying days across the Soviet Union. Most of my flights in and out of the country were with British Airways, accompanied by the soothing voice of the captain, who always seemed to sound the same. *Aeroflot* however was an altogether different matter. For one thing, the captain never uttered a single word. They also had different grades of plane, pilot and mechanic. Grade 1 (the best) was for international flights, Grade 2 for inter-republic flights and Grade 3 for internal flights in any given republic. By definition, the majority of my *Aeroflot* flights were of the Grade 2 variety, and although, occasionally, I would fly back to Heathrow with *Aeroflot* i.e., Grade 1, I never got to experience the joys of Grade 3. This was unlike my friend Lyn, who, while on her honeymoon, discovering the five central Asian republics, was on a plane that managed to

---

19 VVS - *Voenno-Vozdushniye Sily* (Russian Air Forces).
20 Official newspaper of the Soviet Union Communist Party.

miss the runway three times in succession at Samarkand, on the short flight from Tashkent, despite there being perfect weather conditions.

Most of the planes I travelled on dated back to the 1960s. For short-haul flights of less than two hours, it was usually a *Tupolev 134*. The original version featured a glazed-nose design and it had the unique feature of allowing you to face backwards when flying. This was because the two front rows were taken up with four-person wooden tables, arranged as you might find on an *Intercity* train in the UK. Having noticed for many years, that cabin crew invariably faced backwards during take-off and landing, I decided this must be the safest option and so, wherever possible, I ensured I was assigned a seat in row A, 1–4, facing my fellow passengers in row B 5–8. Apparently, it is only the inordinate cost of re-designing the interiors of planes, which means that this safety feature will never be implemented, so in a sense, for once, the Soviets were ahead of the game, if only for four people!

Whenever I flew between St Petersburg and Moscow, it was always on a *Tupolev 134*. I remember one time, arriving late at Pulkovo Airport, 14 miles south of the city centre, to be met by a stony-faced, female check-in assistant, telling me that the flight was closed. I did have to admit, that me and my two English travelling companions, were cutting it fine but there were still twenty minutes to the scheduled departure time. As usual, when someone said, "'*nyet*'" to me, I took this as a sign to open negotiations but this "brute" of a woman was having none of it, clearly, she had already sold our seats to someone else. Now, this presented a problem, as if we didn't get this flight, we would miss our *BA* connection to Heathrow from Sheremetyevo. Realising our only chance was to "negotiate" directly with the airline crew and, armed with the usual supply of *Marlboro Red,* I headed for the departure gate, with the woman screaming, *'Ostanovis!'* ('Stop!') behind us.

Now, the first thing to understand, is that at this time, Pulkovo Airport was on a scale comparable to Stansted, back in the 1970s i.e., it wasn't very big. From check-in to the departure gate was no more than 70 metres and because we were taking an internal flight, there were no border controls or safety checks on luggage. Waving our tickets in the air and shouting that we were British and had a London connection to make, we forged ahead, with me making sure that packets of *Marlboro Red* were on hand, to enable our smooth passage. Sure enough, we sailed through the departure gate and were soon sitting on the aged bus that was to transfer us out to the plane, our luggage at our feet. It was at this point, that I started to realise that cigarettes alone, would not be enough to get us on the flight, but I didn't despair. By this time, I had been in the Soviet Union for over two years and had come to realise, that basically anything was possible, if you were armed with hard currency. I had recently heard the story of an Israeli businessman who had been flying back to Moscow from the Siberian city of Omsk, in order to catch an *El Al*[21] flight home to Tel Aviv. Now, flights from the East always landed at Domodedovo Airport, 25 miles to the south of Moscow and of course, the *El Al* flight was from Sheremetyevo International, at least a 90-minute transfer away. As was often the case, the plane from Omsk was delayed and pretty soon into the six-hour flight, the guy had realised there was no way he was going to make his connection. So, what to do? Well, why not get the plane to land at Sheremetyevo instead of Domodedovo, ensuring he would make his connection? And so it came to pass that for a "present" of $200, an unscheduled *Ilyushin 62* touched down on the second of Sheremetyevo's two runways. I was told

---

21 Established in 1948 as the National *Airline* of Israel.

74

that the pilot even agreed to taxi right up to the waiting *El Al* flight, to ensure the smooth transfer of his "special" passenger. What the rest of the passengers thought, especially those with internal connecting flights to the Caucasus, is anyone's guess but I suppose, as was the custom, they would have simply shrugged their shoulders and started to work out how they were going to make it to Domodedovo.

Thinking, *'if you could get an entire flight re-routed for $200,'* then I quickly calculated that *'$20 should be enough to get the three of us on the plane.'* In the ensuing "negotiation" with the captain, via the smiling intermediary Sasha, one of the cabin crew, the price rose to $30, which seemed to be loosely based on $10 per person. Relieved that we were no longer going to miss our connection and noting that Sasha was getting three passengers at the rear of the packed plane to vacate their seats, I started to consider where to put our luggage. My friends Dave and Brendan, each had relatively large suitcases, while I, given that I was only going back to the UK for a couple of days, luckily just had a holdall. The problem was that the *Tupolev 134,* that ran between St Petersburg and Moscow, was really more of a commuter plane, it didn't even have overhead lockers, just a narrow shelf running down each side of the cabin, definitely no room for a suitcase. The space problem only became more acute when I realised that the three young Russian men who had been asked to move, were not actually leaving the plane, obviously they had bribed the woman at check-in to get us "bumped-off" the flight and saw no reason why they shouldn't travel. It is hard to believe now, that the solution that was reached, entailed one of them sitting on the aeroplane toilet with the door open, the second occupying Sasha's jump seat, situated alongside and the third perched on Dave and Brendan's suitcases, in the middle of the aisle. Unlike Dave, this was Brendan's first time in Russia and I could see he was rather uneasy with the new "seating plan." However, Manchester United had a game that evening and there was no way he was going to get to see it if we were stuck in Moscow for the night. Slowly, the plane began to taxi towards the runway and I could see Brendan's knuckles begin to whiten, as he gripped the arm rest between us. As was my usual practice, I turned on my *Sony Walkman* full-blast, to cut out the sometime troubling noises that *Aeroflot* planes made and started to chew on the *Wrigley's* gum, which was going to prevent my ears from popping. Taking off from Pulkovo was always a bit bumpy but with the plane clearly over loaded, this was going to be a "bit special". As we accelerated down the runway, the whole plane started to vibrate madly and items started to drop from the overhead shelves. Then, the central light fitting at the rear of the plane, where we were sitting, came loose, falling onto the head of the unfortunate Russian, sitting on the suitcases, in the aisle beside us. By this time Brendan's face was ashen and I could see him resolving never to come to Russia again. Eventually, after what seemed an age, I felt us leave the ground and almost immediately, Sasha appeared from where he had been standing at the rear, to refix the light fitting. Luckily, the guy had only suffered a glancing blow and in any case, Russian men are made of strong stuff. Amazingly, the rest of the flight passed without incident and for a while, I chatted with my new friend Boris, as he shifted uncomfortably on his "suitcase seat." He had, like us, been desperate to get the flight as *Zenit*, the local football team, were playing *Dynamo Moscow* that evening and he and his two mates were ardent fans. Having landed at Sheremetyevo 1 (Internal Flights) we made the short bus transfer to Sheremetyevo 2 (International Flights) and once through customs, made straight for the Irish bar, where Brendan was able to calm his rather frayed nerves, with a soothing pint of *Guinness*. Needless to say, he never came back!

13

Riding a Carousel

As mentioned before, Pulkovo Airport, which dated back to the 1930s, was on a much smaller scale than Sheremetyevo. However, by the time my mother came out to visit me in the autumn of 1993, work had begun on a brand-new terminal, being built to cope with the increased passenger numbers, linked to the greater freedom enjoyed by the citizens of the newly formed Russian Federation[22]. As with most building work, there was an impact on the existing service and in this case, the biggest problem was the creation of a tiny baggage reclaim section, with just one carousel serving all recently-landed planes. As I arrived by car, outside the original terminal building, with my friend Tolya, I noticed that there were more coaches than usual, standing in the parking lot and sure enough, as I entered the arrivals hall, the board was displaying four, newly landed flights, including my mother's *BA* flight from Heathrow. Immediately, I realised there was going to be a problem. The previous week, I had picked up a group of fifty from the airport and although there had only been one other flight landing within 30 minutes of the *BA Boeing 737,* it had taken over an hour to get all the bags reclaimed. Now, with four flights landing within 15 minutes, I knew it was going to be absolute chaos. It was already mid-afternoon and I had only just secured two, highly-prized tickets for that evening's performance of Tchaikovsy's ballet, *Sleeping Beauty*, at the *Marinsky* (previously known as the *Kirov*) theatre, in the centre of town. If I didn't do something quick, we were

---

22 In 1991, the Russian SFSR (Soviet Federative Socialist Republic) emerged from the dissolution of the Soviet Union as the independent Russian Federation.

going to miss the spectacle and I would be $40 out of pocket. The section acting temporarily as baggage reclaim, was in fact the original departure hall, with its beautiful Soviet era frescos adorning the ceiling. However, the beauty of the frescos couldn't detract from the scene of carnage that greeted me, as I slipped a packet of *Marlboro Red* to a security guard, to allow me to go "airside". Completed in 1932, when passenger numbers were clearly much lower, it was simply too small to cope with the influx of over six hundred travellers. All I could see in front of me was a mass of people, struggling to get a position close enough to the single carousel, that was starting, very slowly, to dispense their luggage. Being small and used to queue jumping, from my skiing days, I was able, after about ten minutes, to get into a good spot to grab a bag, but the problem was, how long would it be before my mother's case appeared? There was only one thing for it, jump on the carousel, go through the hole in the wall and bribe a baggage handler on the other side, to locate the bright red suitcase, my mother always travelled with. The look of incredulity on the faces of the two baggage handlers, as I appeared through the wall, will stay with me for ever. I had already done some pretty crazy things during my time in Russia but this, even for me, was new territory. Shouting 'I need my mother's case,' and waving a $5 bill as an incentive, I jumped off the carousel and started to scan the numerous luggage cages, that had been rather shambolically lined up. Spotting one with a *BA* bag tag sticking out of the side, I started to rummage through it and to my great relief, quickly came across the required item. Stuffing the $5 bill into the palm of the older baggage handler, I jumped back on the carousel, ducked my head, as I passed through the hole in the wall and, to the utter bewilderment of the hundreds of passengers still waiting for their luggage, re-entered the baggage reclaim area, triumphantly clutching my mother's case in my arms. I will always remember, as I alighted from the carousel, being asked by an English guy, if anyone could do that but spotting my mother in a distant corner, I decided it was up to him to find out! Thanks to my "carousel escapade", we even had time to eat with Tolya's parents, in their small, two-bedroom apartment, before heading off for a delightful evening of ballet and champagne, at the *Marinsky Theatre*.

Flying around the old Soviet Union was always an experience. Early morning flights from Kyiv to Moscow, meant having to endure the risible fare offered for breakfast, at Boryspil airport, I stuck to just tea, while in sharp contrast, vodka and caviar, in the restaurant overlooking the runway at Sheremetyevo 2, was far more pleasurable. However, the one thing that was pretty constant, was the total lack of health and safety. On a flight back from Tbilisi to Moscow, despite knowing that Georgians were called the "Italians of the Soviet Union", I was amazed to see people queueing in the aisle to get off the plane, at least ten minutes before landing. Another time, on a mid-winter flight from Tallinn to Kyiv, we had a near vertical take-off, as no de-icing machines were available and so, the only way to dislodge the ice, was to dramatically increase the trajectory of our ascent. It's no surprise when the Russian for, 'Have a good flight,' is to wish the passenger, 'Soft landings.' One of the strangest things that happened to me was when, on a flight over the Caucasus Mountains, it literally started to rain on me, the condensation in the "supposedly" pressurised cabin, having got so bad. The memory of one of my fellow passengers putting up an umbrella, will stay with me for a long time. To take my mind off the genuine risk of flying in the Soviet Union, I would always have some soothing music playing on my indispensable *Sony Walkman*. However, on long flights there's only so much Sinead O'Connor you can listen to and so, another form of entertainment was required. Naturally, *Aeroflot* didn't show in-flight movies but they did rent out a hand-held video game, which for some reason involved a monkey catching cherries dropping from a tree. Over time I became quite proficient at the game, having decided to buy my own handset from a friendly air steward. On one particularly long flight back from eastern Siberia, I managed to set a personal record of 3,000 apples. Feeling pleased with myself, I asked the air hostess on arrival, if this was possibly a "world record", only to be told that one of her male colleagues had managed to get to 100,000.

Although I passed many hours on *Aeroflot* planes and waiting for them in airport departure lounges following delays, the time spent in the air dwarfed into insignificance, when compared with my time travelling by train.

14

A Close Shave

From a young age I always enjoyed trains. In my early teens, I used to travel independently from Leeds, to my grandmother's in north Wales, taking the *Trans-Pennine* service to Manchester Victoria, where I would change on to the Holyhead bound train, which stopped at Colwyn Bay. During my time based in the French Alps and being carless, I relied on trains to get me to the various competitions I entered across the continent, often taking an overnight train, to avoid the cost of a night's hotel accommodation. Journeys of up to 18 hours, were not unusual for me but nothing I had experienced so far was on the scale of the *Trans-Siberian*. Built between 1891 and 1916 and with a length of 5,772 miles, it is the longest railway line in the world, connecting Moscow with the Russian far east. Taking eight days to complete the journey, it spans a record eight time zones, although as I was to discover later to my cost, the buffet car always sticks to Moscow time. When I found out that the newly launched "Grand Russia Tour", comprising Leningrad, Tallinn, Kyiv, Tbilisi, Moscow and Irkutsk was also going to include four days on the train, I was genuinely excited and immediately purchased *The Trans-Siberian Handbook*, by Bryn Thomas, considered at the time, to be the most comprehensive guide to the train. It was already two weeks into the first "Grand Russia Tour", when me and my group reached Moscow, where we were to spend three days exploring the city, before catching the *Trans-Siberian* to Irkutsk. This meant I would have some time to prepare for the epic journey that lay ahead. Having read Bryn Thomas's excellent book and having spoken to fellow tour directors, who had already made the trip, I had come to realise that, although the journey may be epic, the sights along the way were certainly not. Given that the train roughly follows the same line of latitude, the topography basically doesn't change. For example, the point at which you cross the Ural mountains, moving from Europe to Asia, looks very similar to the previous thousand miles covered since leaving Moscow. In addition, for much of the journey, mile-long locomotives, carrying coal and iron ore, would chug slowly past your window in an endless chain, blocking out your view. I had heard that the section between Irkutsk and Khabarovsk was far more scenic, taking you around Lake Baikal, through the Buriat Alps and the Yablonovy mountains, however, we already had a return flight to Moscow from Irkutsk, booked and so would not be experiencing this. Given the above, the prospect of spending four days on a train, with nothing to do or see, was starting to seem less alluring. Clearly, some form of "on-board entertainment" was going to be required. I already had my *Masterteam Quiz Book*[23] with me and I thought after-dinner pub quizzes might be a way of relieving the boredom. By this stage, I had got to know my group quite well. Many were ex-colonial types, who had spent time in the Indian sub-continent and Africa. I had already had to move our evening meal back an hour, to allow time for the obligatory pre-dinner G&T and so, I knew they would be up for a party. The problem was I had been told that no alcohol was served on the train. The only answer and, coincidentally another way for me to make money, was to stockpile enough alcohol to last four days. With a group of around thirty, this wasn't an easy calculation to make and I didn't want to be left with a load of unsold booze. In the end, I decided that ten bottles of gin, ten bottles of vodka and three cases of beer, should suffice and so on the morning of our departure and while the group was visiting the Kremlin Armoury

---

23 *Masterteam Quiz Book* – published by BBC Books and edited by Rosalind Gold in October 1987.

Museum, I went with my new coach driver friend, Sergei, to one of the few hard-currency supermarkets selling the branded spirits I needed. Although the bottles of *Stolichnaya* and *Gordons* I bought were a bit more expensive than I would have liked, there being no discount for bulk buying, at least they had enough in stock and the ubiquitous *Heineken* cans were relatively cheap. There did, however, remain a problem, namely "no tonic water". With basically no choice and time running out, I had to settle for a few cases of rusty old cans of *Coca-Cola*, along with *Sprite* to serve as my mixers. Returning heavily laden to the coach, a bit down-hearted, I explained to Sergei about the tonic water drought and asked him if he knew of anywhere certain to be selling it. Luckily, he had heard about a supermarket that had just opened on the "Garden Ring"[24], which apparently, was the best stocked, in the whole of the city. The problem was we wouldn't have time to go there now, as we had to pick the group up from the Kremlin, in order to take them back for lunch at the Hotel Cosmos. Now, at the time, the *Trans-Siberian* departed from Yaroslavl Station, situated slightly to the north-east of the city centre, once a day, every day, at precisely 3 p.m.. Quickly doing some calculations in my head, I worked out that if I could get the group on the coach by 2 p.m. after lunch, I would have enough time to pick up the tonic water on the transfer to the station. Sure, it would be cutting it a bit fine but the thought of drinking gin and *Sprite* for four days, wasn't at all appealing.

As it was my last day in Moscow, I had arranged for Juliyanna to come for lunch at the Cosmos. I quite often asked her to come and mix with my groups, partly thinking it added to my credibility of being one of the locals. She was also a true Muscovite, born and raised in the city, the daughter of an aeronautical designer, responsible for the *Sukhoi Su-27* jet fighter[25]. Over lunch, along

24 Moscow Inner Ring Road, their version of the North Circular in London.
25 A twin-engine supermanoeuvrable fighter aircraft, entered service in 1985.

with Lara, my Intourist guide, for the whole "Grand Russia Tour", we discussed my plan for getting the all-important tonic water. Juliyanna, who already knew about the supermarket thought it was feasible but Lara clearly had her doubts, saying that the Garden Ring was notorious for traffic jams and we should stick to the original itinerary. However, based on my experience, the "Intourist itinerary" usually meant sitting around at stations and airports with nothing to do but wait. Despite a few years earlier, having caught a TGV[26] transfer from Geneva to Paris, with a minute to spare, accompanied by a group of fifty bemused Americans, I decided everything would be fine. So, at precisely 2 p.m., as per the "Geri itinerary", our coach pulled out of the Cosmos parking lot and started to head south, down Prospekt Mira, in the direction of the city centre. The road was relatively quiet and after less than ten minutes, we hit the intersection with the Garden Ring. With Lara looking decidedly uncomfortable, but Juliyanna smiling confidently, I instructed Sergei to turn right onto the Garden Ring and to head west, rather than east, in the direction of Yaroslavl Station. At first everything went smoothly. In fact, there was hardly any traffic on our side of the road and it looked like we were going to have plenty of time to spare. However, after a couple of kilometres, I started to become aware of traffic building up on the eastbound side of the road and then suddenly, everything heading in that direction was at a standstill. Now this presented a problem, as this was our only route back to Yaroslavl station. I think most "responsible" tour directors, would have at this point, abandoned "project tonic water" and told their driver to turn around. Needless to say, encouraged by Sergei and Juliyanna telling me that we still had time, we carried on. It was already 2.20 p.m. when we pulled up outside the recently opened, glass-fronted, Finnish-backed supermarket, with me jumping out and sprinting inside, desperately hoping that after all this, there

---

26 Train Grande Vitesse.

84

would be some cans of *Schweppes* available. Luckily, the place was deserted and just as Sergei had predicted, there was indeed plenty of tonic water. Grabbing three cases, I shoved a twenty-dollar bill into the hand of the cashier and not waiting for any change, headed back to the coach. The next thirty minutes were to prove the longest and most stressful of my working life. Rather than improve, the eastbound traffic jam had actually got worse. It turned out, an old *ZAZ Zaporozhets*[27] had broken down, causing the original snarl-up and then, the sheer volume of traffic had magnified the problem. We were now in serious danger of missing our train and I didn't relish the prospect of having to explain to my bosses back home, the reason why. I might realistically never work for the company again. With just seven minutes to spare, we eventually pulled into Komsomolskaya Square[28], to be met by an extremely worried-looking Intourist station rep, who had been expecting us three quarters of an hour earlier. Leaving Lara and Juliyanna to sort out the group and promising fistfuls of dollars to the circling porters, I headed for the platform, indicated by the huge departures board, located in the station's entrance hall. Now, the *Trans-Siberian* is not the shortest train in the world and the sleeping cars we had been allotted were all at the front. Thinking that the only way I might have time to get the group on board would be to "negotiate" with the driver, or even lay down on the track in front of the locomotive, I sprinted down the platform dodging past the numerous people, who had come to wish their loved ones a fond farewell. Arriving at the front of the train with just three minutes left to departure time, I turned to look back down the platform and was relieved to see that Lara and the group were starting to board the train, via the restaurant car situated to the rear. It looked like we were going to make it but I

---

27 Rear wheel-drive city cars, built from 1958 in the ZAZ factory in Soviet Ukraine.
28 Informally known as Three Station Square after the rail termini, Leningradsky, Yaroslavsky and Kazansky.

needed to stay where I was to ensure the train didn't leave before everyone was on board. With just thirty seconds remaining I saw the last of my group clamber aboard and suddenly remembered I needed to pay off the porters for their sterling efforts. I needn't have worried, for zooming towards me now on the empty electric powered luggage trolley, was the head guy. With a big smile on his face he shouted, *'Uspekh'* ('Success') as I gratefully shoved a fifty dollar bill into the palm of his hand and turned to jump on to the footplate of the train-carriage door, which was just starting to edge forward. In the distance, I could see Juliyanna waving madly and shouting something along the lines of, 'You lucky bastard!' It took over an hour to move all the luggage from the restaurant car, through the train, to our allotted compartments but everyone seemed in good spirits, exhilarated by the close shave we had just experienced. Lara was, however, more downbeat, muttering under her breath, 'never again.' Indeed, this was to prove our only tour together, although, whether this was a coincidence or not, I never got to find out. Over thirty years later, I still have a recurring nightmare about the day I nearly missed the *Trans-Siberian*, for the sake of a G&T. Of course, in the nightmare the train always leaves without me!!

15

Life on Board

It's amazing how quickly life slips into a routine when you're on a train for days on end. When travelling as a group, everything revolves around meal times i.e., breakfast, lunch and dinner, which are all included. I always made it a priority to "incentivise" the restaurant-car manager from the word go. This was to enable us to maximise our time, in the relatively spacious dining area, rather than spend all our time cooped up in the sleeping compartments. I was lucky, in that my company paid for me to have sole use of a four-berth cabin, however, some of my clients wouldn't have paid the high supplement to ensure this "exclusivity" and so, often ended up sharing with Soviet citizens. This could present big problems. For example, one time, I had to rescue a recovering alcoholic, from a drunken Red Army colonel, who simply couldn't understand why his fellow passenger wouldn't join him for a vodka, to celebrate the fact we had been allies during the Second World War. It was of course, up to me to down the vodka in one and the next, while I explained that my English friend had a medical condition that made it impossible for him to drink alcohol, actually not too far from the truth. With little to see out of the filthy compartment windows and the only entertainment being playing, 'I Spy – something beginning with – S,' (usual answers, 'seat', 'snow', 'silver birch', or, as a last resort, 'Siberia') the restaurant car was a place of sanctuary. It also gave me an opportunity to off-load the alcohol I had brought along. If there's one thing I learnt during my time on the *Trans-Siberian*, it is that you can never pre-buy too much booze. Although many of my group would have had the foresight to keep some "Duty Free" back for this epic journey, I could guarantee that by day two, they would have all run out. I literally had clients offering me back-handers to keep them "topped up". To preserve some semblance of professional responsibility, I only "dispensed" alcohol openly with the evening meal, while we played the ever-popular pub quiz. However, many was the occasion when I would get a visit to my compartment during daylight hours, with a request for a "little snifter".

Having alcohol available, definitely helped you forget the fact that the only meat served on the train, seemed to be boiled chicken. Now, I like chicken, but six meals in a row is a bit much. To vary their dietary intake, some of my more adventurous clients would buy food from the street sellers, who used to appear on the platforms during the numerous stops we made. Sometimes, these stops would last for up to twenty minutes, so there was plenty of time to peruse the produce. I remember, one woman being particularly pleased to have obtained a large jar of pickled mushrooms, she was less pleased when she spent the next three days sitting on the loo! I preferred to spend the longer platform stop-overs, perched on the shoulders of one of my taller clients, cleaning the compartment windows. It always looks good to be seen to be proactive. I even started taking *Windolene*[29] along with me!

As per our Intourist tour itinerary, we had set mealtimes. However, dependent on the previous evening's partying, breakfast was something of a movable feast. I would normally agree a time of around 10 a.m. with the group but after one particularly boisterous night, I pushed it back to 11 a.m.. Now, this would have been fine, so long as everyone was working to the same time zone. I preferred to move my watch forward as we headed

---

29 Windolene, first launched in 1922 as 'Windo', is the window cleaning product that makes glass and other shiny surfaces perfectly clean and clear.

east, whereas the restaurant car stuck to Moscow time. As usual, I was last to leave the restaurant, having "settled up" with the manager, for our extended stay and agreed the time for breakfast, which given the current location, just west of Perm, meant 9 a.m. Moscow time, i.e., 11 a.m. "local time". As I tucked myself into bed and set my two alarm clocks, I congratulated myself on a successful evening's entertainment and, on the fact that I had managed to secure a much-needed lie in. I shouldn't have been so smug. The next thing I knew, I was being woken up by a bucket of water thrown over my head, with a big cheer rising from the group of clients clustered at my door. It turned out that during the night, we had moved into a new time zone and some of the group had been more assiduous than I, in keeping up to date with "local time". They had, therefore, arrived early for breakfast, only to be told it wouldn't be served for another hour. Not best pleased and no doubt supporting a bit of a hangover, they had decided to get even with their smooth-talking, tour director, still blissfully asleep, in his own private compartment. Needless to say, I never made the same mistake again, with watches only being moved forward when the whole group was all together, rather ironically, at breakfast.

After the restaurant-car manager, the next most important person on the train was the *provodnik* (attendant or conductor in English, or as I came to call them, "inattendant"). Each carriage had a *provodnik*, in theory, responsible for checking tickets, letting down the carriage steps at stations and dispensing scolding tea, from the samovar, located by their two-berth cabin, surely a health and safety disaster just waiting to happen. I had already come across *provodniks* on my numerous journeys between Moscow and Leningrad. They were invariably male, smelt of vodka and always open to a bribe. Given that it was only an overnight train between Moscow and Leningrad, my company expected me to "muck in" with my group and so, it was up to me to make the journey more comfortable. This involved me "borrowing" the aforementioned two-berth cabin for the night, while the *provodnik* sat on one of the flip-down chairs in the corridor. For me, this was the best $5 I ever used to spend. Sleeping on the top bunk and using the lower bunk as a repository for my luggage and large overcoat, I was cocooned in my own little world, as the train rattled its way through the night. It also had the advantage of being situated closest to the toilet, found at the entrance to every carriage, very useful after a night on the *shampanskoye*.

No matter where I was in the Soviet Union, the trains I travelled on, were always the same. As early as 1927, the Soviet Union Railways (SZD) had started to electrify the network. Czechoslovakian-built *Skoda* electric locos, predominated, while the carriages were of East German origin, all furnished in an identical fashion. They say that familiarity breeds contempt, but I learnt to love these beasts of the *zheleznaya doroga* (literally "iron road"). A lack of bathing facilities, was a common criticism of westerners, taking the *Trans-Siberian*, however, with a bit of know-how and the help of a *provodnik,* willing to stoke up the boiler, it was possible to convert the bathroom, containing lavatory and basin, into a perfectly acceptable wet room, complete with shower attachment. I hasten to add, that I kept this particular bit of information to myself, not wishing to replicate the queues for shower blocks, I had experienced on European campsites.

Unlike the numerous delays I experienced when flying, the trains I used were invariably on time. There was, however, one epic exception and of course, it had to be on the *Trans- Siberian*. It was day three and we were about two hours east of Novosibirsk[30], when I suddenly heard a shrill blast on the train's hooter and the screeching of brakes, as we juddered to a standstill. Luckily, all my luggage was on the bunk below and so I avoided the fate of many

---

30 Most populous city in Asian Russia, 1.6 million inhabitants.

of my fellow passengers, who had assorted cases and bags rain down on them. Seeking out the carriage attendant, appropriately named "Pavil the *provodnik*", I tried to find out what was going on, but he just shrugged and started to mop up the glass beaker of tea, he had just spilt over the corridor floor. Now, I know that in the UK, when a train breaks down, you are not allowed on to the track and are told to remain in your seats. I remember, I once spent an incredibly frustrating two hours stuck on a train, 500 metres from the main platform at Leeds City Station, until a replacement engine could be found. This, however, was the land that "Health and Safety" had forgotten and so, leaving Pavil to his mopping up duties, I opened the carriage door and jumped on to the embankment, at the side of the track (even I knew it was a good idea to keep off the rails!) As usual, my carriage was close to the front of the train and so it was immediately apparent, what had caused us to come to a grinding halt. A little more than 100 metres further down the track, the overhead power lines, which provided electricity for the train, had completely collapsed. Clearly, we were going to be here for some time and pretty soon afterwards, I wasn't the only person soaking up the late September sun. In total, we were stuck, literally in the middle of nowhere, for over eight hours. This was the time it took for engineers to come from the small junction town of Taiga, 150 kilometres further down the track and to painstakingly, re-instate the 200 metre section of power lines, that had apparently been brought down by an inopportune landslide. Luckily, the weather was good, with many people deciding to make the best of a bad job and setting up impromptu picnic tables along the trackside. I, however, decided to console myself with a bit of late-season sunbathing and a group evening meal, in the restaurant car where, to compensate for the delay, all the drinks were for once, on Geri.

16

I'll Take St Petersburg

While I generally enjoyed my train journeys, the same couldn't be said for my experience of road transport. As previously mentioned, the roads were littered with potholes, largely a result of the freeze-thaw action, that occurred in mid- to late spring. Drivers were constantly swerving to avoid these "mini craters", particularly dangerous, when the road itself might be covered in black ice. The danger was heightened in Moscow, by the fact that, although the main thoroughfares, like Gorky Street, were often eight lanes wide, there were no central reservations. Head-on collisions were, therefore, commonplace. Having spent time in Italy, I was used to crazy driving but Moscow taxi drivers took the biscuit. For a start, they all drove *Volga Gaz M24s*. These were much bigger and more importantly, faster than the *Lada 2101s* (the Soviet take on the *Fiat 124*) that predominated at the time. Undertaking the vehicle ahead, was considered the same as overtaking and often, as we sped through the streets of Moscow, I felt I was in a Soviet version of *"The Wacky Races[31]."* In truth, I think sometimes, the drivers were deliberately trying to scare me. This was because all fares were agreed before the start of the journey, the taxi meters were completely redundant. With my blond hair and fluent Russian, I could quite easily be taken for an Estonian and so, I got quoted "local" prices, instead of the inflated fares paid by westerners. Once into the journey, however, the driver would quickly realise where I actually came from and some, feeling a bit cheated, would decide to show me just how

---

31 1968 Hanna-Barbera cartoon series with a large ensemble of assorted competitors and their uniquely designed vehicles that matched their personalities.

fast they could go. Nevertheless, Moscow taxis were preferable to flagging down private vehicles, as in general, you could be pretty sure the driver hadn't been drinking. In theory, there were fines and bans for drink driving, in practice, it was a complete free for all. This was due to the totally corrupt city police, who supplemented their meagre salaries, by taking bribes for turning a blind eye. The levels of corruption had got so bad, that although Juliyanna drove her father's *Lada* around the city, she hadn't actually passed her test. This was because, if she was stopped, it was cheaper and easier to pay the bribe "on the spot", rather than go through the lengthy and expensive process, of booking a driving test, which in any case, would require a hefty bribe at the end, to ensure you passed.

I never got to see whether Juliyanna's driving skills would have merited a pass. She lived with her parents and brother, in an apartment close to Gorky Park and it was easy for her to get the Red *Metro* Line (*Sokolnicheskaya*) straight into the city centre. We usually met up in the evening, at the Spanish Bar, located in the basement of the Hotel Moskva, close to Red Square. The bar was a joint venture with Venezuela and it was great to drink a beer, that for once, wasn't *Heineken*, namely, *San Miguel*. I normally had at least a couple of hours of free time, as I would have dropped my group off at the *Bolshoi*, only a five-minute walk away, for the evening's ballet or opera performance. If Juliyanna wasn't available, I sometimes would accompany my group, but only if it was a ballet. I'm definitely not an opera fan. One of the most boring nights of my life, was in fact, my first visit to the *Bolshoi*, when I had to endure three hours of the Georgian National Opera's interpretation of Mussorgsky's, *Boris Godunov*. In contrast, over the years, I became something of a ballet aficionado. My favourite performances, were those of, *Sleeping Beauty*, by Tchaikovsky and *Don Quixote*, by Minkus, both staged at the *Marinsky Theatre*, in St Petersburg. In fact, for those in the know, the *Marinsky* or *Kirov*, as it had been previously known, had a better reputation for ballet, than the more famous *Bolshoi*. For example, Rudolph Nureyev, perhaps the greatest ballet dancer of all time, trained at the *Kirov*. I also preferred the more intimate atmosphere of the St Petersburg theatre. Unlike the *Bolshoi* (literally "big" in Russian) where the dancers could be little more than specks in the distance, at the *Marinsky*, you really felt close to the action. I also liked the fact that it was much easier and quicker to get a glass of champagne during the frequent intervals. As a former sportsman, I appreciated the sheer athleticism of the dancers and I also marvelled at the beauty and complexity of the set designs. I remember once being blown away, by the sudden appearance of a train, centre-stage, at the finale to *Anna Karenina*, when the despairing heroine takes her own life, by throwing herself under its wheels. Clearly, I was spoilt by the level of ballet I experienced in Russia. A few years later and back in Leeds, I attended a performance by *The Ballet Rambert* at *The Grand Theatre*, only to be disappointed by, what I deemed to be, "lazy" dancing.

It wasn't just the ballet I preferred in St Petersburg to Moscow, it was everything. Although one couldn't fail to be impressed by Red Square and the Kremlin, in truth, that was just about it. St Petersburg on the other hand, with its beautiful imperial palaces and myriad of canals, was a constant source of unexpected delights. I remember once having tea with a friend, who was the head of languages at *The Pioneer*[32] (formerly Anichkov Palace) on Nevsky Prospect, only to be told that the small wood-panelled room we were in, had in fact, been the secret hideaway, where the emperor Alexander II, "entertained" his various mistresses.

The general atmosphere in St Petersburg was also much more relaxed. After its foundation by Peter the Great, in 1703, it was

---

32 Soviet era version of boy scouts and girl guides.

known as *"The Window on the West"* and its citizens certainly regarded themselves as culturally superior to their Muscovite compatriots. The presence of the secret police also loomed less large. In the centre of Moscow, I would frequently pass the imposing Lubyanka building, the headquarters of the KGB[33], with the statue of its founder, Felix Dzerzhinsky, outside, literally keeping an evil eye on the population. It is interesting to note, that this despised monument, was the first statue to be toppled, following the failed military coup of August, 1991, and the establishment of the new Russian state, under Boris Yeltsin. With over 400 miles, separating St Petersburg from Moscow, it was easy to see why people felt less under the yolk of the KGB. For example, while in the dining room of the Hotel Prebaltiskaya, located on the shores of the Gulf of Finland, I was openly able to exchange money with the waiters, whereas in Moscow, I was still required to go to the laundry room of the Cosmos.

Of all the hotels I stayed in during my time in the Soviet Union, my favourite was the Prebaltiskaya. Although it had been built at the same time as the Cosmos[34], the contractors had been Swedish and so everything was to a much higher spec. With 1,200 rooms, it was still on a large scale but when taking the lift to the upper floors, you could guarantee there wouldn't be any unscheduled stops, unlike the Cosmos, where you often felt your life was literally "hanging by a thread", as the lift ground to a halt, somewhere near the 25th floor. The food was also much better, with abundant amounts of black caviar available (Note that black caviar is vastly superior to red). When later I travelled on personal business, it was my hotel of choice and I spent many happy evenings in the lounge bar, chatting to fellow westerners, who like me, were attracted by the perceived fortunes to be made, in Yeltsin's new Russia.

---

33 Main security agency for the USSR.
34 Late 1970s.

17

Going Back to School

Unfortunately, in my early days of tour directing, the Prebaltiskaya was most definitely "off limits". Just like any other job, you were expected to work your way up from the bottom, which in my case, meant numerous back-to-back school tours, staying in budget hotels, the worst of which, was undoubtedly the Hotel Sevastopol, in south Moscow. Resembling one of the blocks of council flats found in my native city of Leeds, its only redeeming feature was that it had a *Metro* station, bearing the same name, right on the doorstep. Students of the Second World War history will no doubt recall the "Siege of Sevastopol (1941-42)" where Soviet forces suffered one of their worst defeats, with 118,000 men killed, wounded or captured, in the final German assault. It sometimes seemed to me, that the hotel was trying to recreate those bleak times. The lighting in the bedrooms, could best be described as "dim" and the tiny bathrooms, seemed more interested in catering to the needs of cockroaches, rather than paying guests. The food took me back to my days in Bulgaria and the difficult to locate hotel bar, had extremely erratic opening hours. It was at this time, that I came up with my list of three minimum requirements for a room. First, it had to be warm. Second, the telephone must work and third, the loo must flush. Anything else was a bonus. Sometimes I would have to try out three or four rooms, before finding the right one. Over the years, I got to know the idiosyncrasies of choosing a room. For example, when staying at the Hotel Intourist, at the bottom of Tverskaya (originally Gorky Street) on arrival in the depths of winter, I would check which way the wind was blowing and if it was an easterly wind, I would make sure I got a room on the west side, to avoid having to wear thermals in bed. Similarly, room location was vital when I stayed at the Hotel Rossiya, located opposite St Basil's cathedral and affording spectacular views of Red Square and the Kremlin. At the time, it was the largest hotel in the world with 3,000 rooms, a post office, a nightclub, a barber shop and a cinema. It even had its own police station, with jail cells, behind unmarked black doors, close to the barber shop. Given the sheer scale of the place, if you got the wrong room, you could literally be looking at a ten-minute walk to breakfast, a slight problem if you were running late, after a night on the town. I remember one time, coming back slightly the worse for wear and taking nearly thirty minutes to find my room, not realising I had entered the hotel from the opposite side to normal.

Although working with school groups wasn't particularly profitable, it did have its compensations. In general, the teachers were good company and left the kids to do the complaining. Also, the Intourist guides were more my age and often up for a good time. I became fond of one girl in particular, Inga from Leningrad. Her mother had been an English teacher and she had been a star performer, while studying at the Moscow School of Languages. When Ronald Reagan visited Leningrad, on a private trip, following his departure from office, it was Inga who acted as his interpreter. Pride of place on the bookcase in the small one-bedroom flat she shared with her mother, was given over to a signed photo of Inga with the former president and his wife Nancy. It wasn't however Inga's linguistic ability that most impressed me, more the fact that she was in the process of securing an entry visa to the USA. For me, the problem with Russian girls, even Juliyanna, was that I could never be sure they weren't more interested in my passport than me. Inga, on the other hand, had managed to convince some dumb American tourist, that she was in love with him and he, totally besotted, had asked her to get married. With the "passport" issue not on the agenda, it was perhaps inevitable that Inga and I would get together, for the period she remained in the USSR. I got on well with her mother, who seemed happy to let us have sole use of the one small bedroom and we worked effectively as a team, even finding ways to make some money out of the school groups that predominated at the time. It was through Inga, that I met Igor, who became my ticket supplier for the *Kirov*, never once letting me down, also the Ilyich family, who came to play a pivotal role in my future Russian adventures. At first, my affair with Inga seemed straightforward. We both knew it was going nowhere but why not have a bit of fun? Things, however, were about to get a bit more complicated. With just a couple of weeks left before her departure to the USA, Inga came to my room in the Hotel Karelia, to tell me she thought she was pregnant. She was already ten days late with her period and with hindsight, we had perhaps not been overly careful with our preventative measures. It seemed like her whole future in the USA was in jeopardy, as clearly, her "fiancé" wouldn't be best pleased to find out she was carrying another man's child. It was then that she said she would have to have an abortion. Now, I knew that obtaining an abortion was relatively simple. The Soviet Union's revolutionary leadership had seen women's access to safe legal abortion, both as an essential component for women's liberation and as a means to end the tragic consequences of illegal, back-street abortions. As early as 1920, the Bolsheviks had made the practice legal and, in some respects, it had come to be regarded as a form of birth control, albeit a rather extreme one! It turned out Inga had already had an abortion but I'd had previous experience of girlfriends missing periods and I suggested it was better to wait. I was also slightly reassured when I did the maths. Having been with Carmen, a semi-devout

Catholic for over a year, I was familiar with the "rhythm method" of contraception and I knew that we hadn't had sex between the 12th and 16th day of Inga's menstrual cycle (the time when she was most likely to be ovulating). It took me a little while to convince her that it would be better to wait a few more days and, slightly reluctantly, she agreed. I'll never know exactly what happened but three days later, Inga called to say that her period had come and that I was "off the hook". The following week, she boarded her *Aeroflot* flight bound for New York and her new life in the USA. I did see her again the following year, when she was visiting her mother and I could tell the "promised land" had been something of a disappointment, a loveless marriage and a job in a supermarket, way below the status she had enjoyed as a top Intourist guide. Unsurprisingly, the marriage lasted as long as was needed for Inga to get permanent residency and as far as I know, she remained childless, a sad reminder of the crazy times we lived in.

Partly due to Inga, I always had something of a soft spot for the Hotel Karelia. In Martin Walker's guide book, it was described thus: "Student groups are sometimes put up here, and do not speak well of it." I, however, liked the place, particularly when compared to the Sevastopol, which allegedly had the same rating. The staff, who I got to know well, were friendly and the bar was always open in the evening, serving *shampanskoye* for the equivalent of 25p a bottle. It also provided me with an opportunity to showcase my ability to get things done. Checking-in with a school group, one late afternoon in early February, I immediately became aware that the hotel lobby was unusually cold. I asked the receptionist if there was a problem, only to be assured that, although the lobby was cold, the rooms were fine. Slightly sceptical, I made my way up to the fifth floor and headed for the *dezhurnaya's* desk, to pick up the key. As soon as I saw her, I knew we had a problem. Instead of sitting in her chair reading a book as normal, she was walking up and down the corridor, stamping her feet, wearing a thick winter coat, furry hat and gloves. Clearly, there was no heating in the hotel and the *dezhurnaya*, who I knew, confirmed that this had been the case for the past few days. Given that the outside temperature was -15 °C, we were obviously in for an uncomfortable stay. Feeling annoyed that we had been allowed to check-in, to what was effectively, a "freezer", I got straight on the phone to Lara Karlina, the Intourist Operations Director, in Moscow and demanded that we be moved to a hotel with heating. Lara was apologetic but said that given the size of the group, it was too late to find an alternative and we would have to wait until the next day, when she might be able to come up with something. Putting on a brave face and getting a bottle of *shampanskoye* from the bar, I explained the situation to the three teachers, accompanying the sixth form group. Luckily, they didn't seem overly-concerned, perhaps subconsciously thinking, that the cold might dampen down the male teenage hormones, that had led to them having to "stand guard" at night, outside the girls rooms, during our time in Moscow.

They say there is no such thing as bad weather only inappropriate clothing and given my skiing background, I had all the right equipment to survive the cold. Nevertheless, I can't say I had the best night's sleep, especially when there was no guarantee that Lara would be able to come up with something. The next morning I was straight on the phone at 9 a.m., only to be told by Lara that all the Intourist hotels in Leningrad were full, apart from the Prebaltiskaya and this was too expensive for a school group. Realising that even the teachers' patience would wane, if we were forced to spend another three nights in the "freezer", I asked Lara to get in touch with my office in Leicester, to see if they would agree to pay for an upgrade. Half an hour later, she called back to say that, given the small margins made on school groups, neither Intourist nor my tour operator, would bear the extra expense.

She did, however, have a contact on Leningrad City Council, who might be able to help. Not quite understanding how a councillor was going to help fix a hotel's heating system, I left with the group on the morning's city tour. At least the coach was warm and I had already got Anna, our national Intourist guide, to book us lunch at the Hotel Oktyabraskaya, just off Nevsky Prospect, with me footing the bill. Given that we already had an afternoon visit to the Hermitage Museum, included in the itinerary, I reckoned I could keep the group warm until at least 5 p.m.. In fact, it was nearly 6 p.m. when our coach drew up outside the Hotel Karelia. For once, I had a school group that actually enjoyed their visit to the Hermitage[35], staying much longer than normal. One of the teachers was head of the art department and a number of the students were studying Art at 'A' Level. They were, therefore, blown away by the sheer extent of the paintings on display, including works by Monet, Renoir, Matisse and Picasso and plied the knowledgeable museum guide with numerous questions, taking copious notes of her answers.

Pushing through the revolving door, that formed the entrance to the hotel, I suddenly felt a waft of warm air and was relieved to see that the receptionist was dressed in her usual uniform. By some miracle, the heating had been fixed. It turned out that a fractured gas pipe had meant the whole of the local district had been without heating for six days. In normal circumstances, the problem could have persisted for weeks but due to my loud complaining and Lara's council contact, who was actually head of the works division, the pipe had been fixed in a matter of hours. Rather big-headily, I initially thought the local residents might like to erect a statue to their "foreign saviour" but on reflection, there were already too many statues of flawed heroes, on the streets of Russia!

---

35 The second largest art museum in the world after The Louvre in Paris.

18

Changing Times

A freezing night, tucked up in bed, in the Hotel Karelia, couldn't be in greater contrast to lounging by the roof-top pool of the Hotel Iveria in Tbilisi, Georgia. I first visited Tbilisi[36] (literally "warm location") in the late summer of 1990. The temperature was pleasant, in the high 20s and the air, after the pollution of Moscow, beautifully clear. The hotel, although rather basic in structure, had large rooms with parquet flooring and balconies, looking out on to a majestic water fountain, in the square below. Then there was the roof-top pool, 20 metres in length and with stunning vistas of the Caucasus mountains in the distance. Of all the places I have swum, only the view from the Olympic diving pool in Barcelona, can compare. However, looking back, it's not the stunning location I remember most but the surreal events that took place on, 22nd September, 1991. With great weather and already a week into an exhausting tour, the group and I had decided to forgo the chance of visiting a mediaeval church, in the foothills of the mountains, preferring to spend the afternoon lazing by the pool. I was probably only into the second song on my *Walkman,* when I heard some commotion in the square below and then suddenly, a shot rang out. On the city tour in the morning, I had been aware that some demonstrations had been taking place and we had had to make a couple of deviations from the normal route. In fact, opposition to the authoritarian government, of Zviad Gamsakurdia, had been growing for the

---

36 The Old Georgian word meaning warm was "Tbili" and the city was therefore given the name Tbilisi, "warm location" because of the area's numerous sulfuric hot springs.

past three months. For the first time, barricades had appeared in the streets of Tbilisi; opposition leaders had been arrested and pro-opposition newspapers closed down. Now things had turned decidedly ugly. For the next three hours, a pitched battle was fought in the streets below, while we watched on, in our designer swimwear and sunglasses. The next day, a state of emergency was declared and I found out from our local guide, that a number of anti-Gamsakhurdia protesters, had been killed. Naturally, we were confined to the hotel, with the small consolation that we would still be able to use the pool. With Gamsakhurida's crackdown a success, the day passed relatively peacefully and lying on my sun lounger, it was easy to forget that any bloodshed had occurred.

The following morning, we drove straight to the airport and boarded the plane, for the seven-hour flight to Kyiv. Unfortunately, this was to be my last time in Tbilisi. Over the next few years, a bitter civil war was fought, with thousands of people losing their lives. Even the Hotel Iveria didn't escape, subjected to a bomb attack by pro-Gamsakhurdia terrorists, as he sought to regain control, from the democratically elected government of Eduard Shevardnadze.

The events I witnessed in Georgia, were symptomatic of what was occurring across the whole of Eastern Europe, as the "Iron Curtain" started to disappear. On 9th November, 1989, I remember watching the TV news in amazement, as young East Germans, literally tore down the Berlin wall. Just over a month later, Christmas Day in fact, I was in a hotel room, close to Zurich airport, waiting for a group of Americans to fly in, early the next morning. I was going to be taking them for a week's skiing in Wengen and had therefore, for the first time in my life, flown out from the UK, on Christmas Day. The hotel was modern and well-appointed, with free satellite TV available. After dinner, I settled down to watch the news on *CNN*. Suddenly, the programme was interrupted and Nicolae Ceausescu, President of Romania and his wife Elena, appeared centre screen. While in the UK, I had already seen footage of Ceausescu being booed by a huge crowd, that had gathered in the centre of Bucharest and his grip on power, was clearly weakening. However, what I was now witnessing, was a show trial, convened in a small room in the town of Targoviste, 80 miles north of Bucharest, to where the Ceausescus had fled by helicopter, following the loss of army support for their regime. Although the footage was clearly not live, more edited highlights, it quickly became apparent, that the Ceausescus were being sentenced to death. I will always remember the image of them protesting, as their hands were tied behind their backs, in preparation for facing the firing squad. They simply couldn't understand why the soldiers would no longer submit to their command. After the execution, the camera lingered for a while over the faces of the two motionless corpses, just to prove to the long-suffering Romanian population, that they were finally free. For my part, I thought back to Florin, the Romanian boy I had beaten at table tennis, nearly fifteen years ago and wondered if he would have been part of the demonstrations, that finally toppled one of the world's cruellest dictators? With hindsight, probably not!

It is one of the ironies of my life, that when the defining event of the period occurred, namely, the attempted coup against Gorbachev, I was not actually in the country, instead I was on holiday in Italy, visiting friends and family, with my then Italian girlfriend. Sitting in the Piazza Santa Maria Novella in central Florence, I saw a man reading a copy of *La Republica*[37], with the headline *"Golpe a Moscou"*, emblazoned across the front page. Over the years, my grasp of Italian has always been a bit hit and miss but I never forget that, *golpe* is the word for "coup". It

---

37 Left leaning Italian daily newspaper.

transpired that the coup had begun the previous day (i.e., 18th August, 1991) when communist hardliners, including the heads of the army, KGB and police, had placed Gorbachev under house arrest, at his holiday home in the Crimea and declared a state of emergency. The plotters also had control of the airwaves and Soviet television had started broadcasting regular condemnations of Gorbachev's policies. Like many Kremlinologists of the time, I took the view that what had happened was inevitable and I had been naïve to believe that a better future was in sight. Totally deflated, I resigned myself to the fact that I would probably never see Russia again. Luckily, me and the "so called" experts were proved spectacularly wrong. The coup was, in fact, poorly planned and disorganised. Its leaders spent as much time bickering among themselves and drinking heavily, as they did on trying to win popular support for their actions. The other factor was the rise of Boris Yeltsin, the Russian Federation president, who denounced the plotters and organised strikes and street protests, with his fellow Muscovites. One of the defining images of the three days, that the coup lasted, was when Yeltsin stood on a tank outside the Russian parliament building and addressed his supporters, symbolically showing, that the majority of the rank and file in the army, were on his side. The collapse of the coup, brought a temporary reprieve to the Gorbachev regime but in western diplomatic circles, he increasingly started to be viewed as incompetent and a failure. Policy makers started to discuss what a post-Gorbachev situation would look like and they began a slow but steady tilt toward Yeltsin. In retrospect, this policy seemed extremely prudent, given that Gorbachev resigned as leader of the Soviet Union, in December 1991, signalling the end of one of history's largest ever empires.

19

A New Beginning?

With my Italian holiday over and a whole autumn season of tours reconfirmed, after the short-lived coup, I couldn't wait to get back to work and to see how things had changed. Luckily, my first trip was the "Grand Russia Tour", comprising St Petersburg, Talinn, Kyiv, Tbilisi, Moscow and Irkutsk. This meant I would now be, in effect, visiting four different countries, Russia, Estonia, Ukraine and Georgia. Starting in St Petersburg, at first everything seemed pretty much as before. Perhaps people were a bit more smiley but they still had to queue for food and in fact, inflation was on the rise. It wasn't until I got to Tallinn, that I realised how seismic the changes would prove to be. Everywhere you looked, the streets were draped with the blue, black and white striped flag of Estonia. On August 20th, during the coup attempt, Estonia had declared itself independent and this had been recognised by the Soviet authorities on 6th September, literally the day before my arrival. Our local guide, Agnesia, was friendly towards me but had a "frosty" relationship with our national guide, Sveta, from St Petersburg. I could see them constantly bickering about what could be paid for, with the old Intourist vouchers and what would now incur a supplement. Occasionally, I would have to step in, with some hard currency, to make sure everything ran smoothly. Following the city tour, I remember Sveta complaining to me, that Agnesia had been too nationalistic in her commentary and that she was re-writing history. The antipathy between the two was understandable.

Estonia had experienced a brief period of independence in the 1920s and 1930s, following the end of the First World War and had adopted a new, highly liberal constitution, establishing the country as a parliamentary democracy. However, the advent of the Second World War, brought occupation by the Red Army and on 6th August, 1940, Estonia was annexed by the Soviet Union as the ESSR[38]. When the German Operation Barbarossa, started against the USSR, in June 1941, around 34,000 young Estonian men, were forcibly drafted into the Red Army, fewer than 30 per cent of whom, survived the war. With the Nazi invasion proving unstoppable, the Soviets introduced a "scorched earth" policy. Many Estonians went into the forest, starting an anti-Soviet, guerrilla campaign. In late August, 1941, the USSR evacuated Tallinn, with massive losses and the capture of the Estonian Islands, was completed by German forces, in the October. A collaborationist administration was established, leading to the formation of the Estonian Waffen-SS division, which fought the Red Army, on the eastern front until it's eventual surrender, at the end of the war, in May, 1945. Thousands of Estonians opposing the second Soviet occupation, joined a guerrilla movement known as the "Forest Brothers". The armed resistance was heaviest in the first few years after the war, but Soviet authorities gradually wore it down through attrition and resistance effectively ceased, in the mid-1950s. The Soviets initiated a policy of collectivisation[39] but as the peasantry refused to accept it, a campaign of terror was unleashed. In March, 1949, about 20,000 Estonians were deported to forced settlements in Siberia. At the same time, the Soviet Union began the "Russification" of the country, with hundreds of thousands of Russians and people of other Soviet nationalities, being induced to settle in Estonia, which eventually threatened to turn Estonians into a minority in their own land. In 1945, Estonians formed 97 per cent of the population, but by 1991, their share of the population, had fallen to 62 per cent.

---

38 Estonian Soviet Socialist Republic.
39 The integration of individual land holdings and labour into state-controlled farms.

Given the above, it was clear that Agnesia thought that now was payback time for nearly fifty years of Russian occupation, while Sveta was angered by the Estonians' Nazi collaborationist past. As a neutral, I could see that both sides had a point but was a little annoyed, when the receptionists in the Hotel Viru, where I always stayed, now refused to reply to me in Russian, preferring to answer in English. Still, even if the receptionists had decided to act superior, nothing could put me off the Viru. Built in 1972, by a Finnish construction company, it was the first high-rise building in Estonia, offering superb views over the nearby Gulf of Finland. Officially, as the elevator displayed, there were 22 floors. The 23rd Floor, housed the KGB radio centre, where agents were stationed, to intercept radio signals and relay information back to Moscow. In addition, parts of the third floor, were used to listen in on the hotel's most prominent guests, including foreign dignitaries and journalists. Interestingly, many of the hotels I stayed in, didn't in effect, have a third floor i.e., in the lifts, there was never a number three button. I had originally been told that the reason for this, was that the space was reserved for the mechanical functions of the building, including the boiler room, however, with the benefit of hindsight, it's clear there was a more sinister explanation. Occasionally in the night, I would see hotel guests being frogmarched down the corridor, by men in dark leather overcoats (the KGB fashion must!) and I now assume floor three, was the destination. With regard to the KGB, Agnesia had proudly told me that they had been forced to leave the Viru in a hurry, only two weeks previously, following the declaration of Estonian independence.

Unlike most of the hotels I stayed in, the Viru easily measured up to western standards. The restaurant had plenty of choice on the menu, with particularly tasty seafood options. In addition, there was a large nightclub in the basement, where every evening there was a cabaret performance. Before coming to the Viru, my experience of hotel-based entertainment, had largely been confined to me running pub quizzes. However, the show put on by the artistes at the Viru was hugely enjoyable. The dancing was of an exceptionally high quality and the skimpy costumes, worn by the female members of the cast, left little to the imagination! After the performance, the *valyuta* (hard currency) bar, would turn into a disco, where some of the performers would re-emerge in normal attire, to chat and sometimes dance, with the drunk Finnish men, who formed the majority of the audience. Although I have no formal training, I have always managed to impress women with my dancing skills and so I would often "take to the floor", in the hope of finding a female partner, who was just a dancer and not a part-time prostitute. It is one of life's ironies, that the one person I danced with, who went on to become my friend, was actually a guy called Eddy. One night, I was "strutting my stuff", when I noticed that the good-looking guy, who had been the lead dancer in the evening's show, was mimicking my moves. Being the competitive animal that I am, I started to "up my game", throwing in a few spins and pirouettes. What followed can best be described as a "dance off", with the bar's clients forming a circle around us and clapping along to the thumping disco beat. At first, I managed to hold my own but when Eddy suddenly threw in a back flip, I knew the game was up. Rather short of breath, I asked my conqueror if I could buy him a drink and he readily agreed. For the next couple of hours the conversation flowed freely. At twenty-seven, he was the same age as me and had been classically trained at the *Kirov Academy of Ballet*, where he had been one of the star students, until a serious knee injury had ended his hopes of becoming a lead performer. Forced to leave the *Kirov* he had returned to his home town of Tallinn to live with his parents, originally from Moscow, who had been part of the wave of Russians that had come to Estonia in the 1950s. Like most of the young people I met, he was desperate to emigrate to the "West" and with his knee now much stronger, allied to his *Kirov* training, he was sure that he would have no problem getting work. At the time, he was only earning a small wage for his cabaret performances and although he had the looks, he definitely wasn't prepared to supplement his income by working as a male escort. In any case, his long-term Estonian girlfriend would never have agreed to it. It wasn't only financial considerations that were behind Eddy's desire to leave. As the son of Russian immigrants, he feared for his future in the newly independent Estonia. There was already talk of a language test being introduced, in order to gain Estonian citizenship and it was clear that when applying for any job, ethnic Estonians would automatically be at the front of the queue. The former colonists were now destined to be "second class" citizens. I felt really sorry for Eddy. From the way he had lifted, with consummate ease, his elegant dance partner high above his head during the show, I knew he was a talented guy and it seemed such a shame that in all probability, this talent was going to go to waste. On my return to the UK and between tours, I started to make enquiries as to how I could invite him over to stay. This proved to be a very complicated and drawn-out process, as Eddy was now effectively "stateless". Of all the former Soviet republics, Estonia moved the quickest to assert its new-found independence. As early as 1992, they re-introduced the kroon, their own currency, which hadn't been used since 1940, in the process, replacing the hated rouble, at a rate of one kroon to ten roubles. I still have a one kroon banknote, from the first ever issue, bearing the picture of Kristjan Raud, the Estonian symbolist painter and illustrator. After a while, it became clear that the only way to get Eddy and his girlfriend, Darja, over to the UK, was for Eddy to take the language test and to gain an Estonian passport. Now this shouldn't have been a problem, as Darja was an ethnic Estonian and Eddy was practically bi-lingual. However, just like any test at the time, it wasn't down to your ability to perform on the day, more your ability to come up with enough money, for the obligatory bribe.

I was now visiting Tallinn much less frequently than before, so Eddy and Darja took the night train from Tallinn to St Petersburg and came to the Hotel Karelia, where I had arranged a room for them. I hadn't seen Eddy for about four months and the first thing that struck me was that, although it was only 8 a.m., he was drunk. Now I was used to drinking on trains but Eddy had clearly decided to just keep on going. Anyway, I showed them to their room and said we would meet up for dinner in the evening, hoping that by this time Eddy would have sobered up. I am afraid I was to be disappointed. As a rather embarrassed Darja explained, instead of going to bed, Eddy had carried on knocking back the bottles of vodka secreted in his suitcase. It emerged that over the winter, he had twice failed the Estonian language test, simply because he couldn't afford the bribe. Deeply frustrated, he had taken to drink and now things had got even worse, as he had just lost his job in the cabaret for being drunk while performing. The only way out of the situation, was for Eddy to get $200 together, to ensure that he passed the test. I now knew why he had been drinking all day. His pride was telling him not to ask me for the money but deep down, he knew there was no other choice. Of course, I was happy to help out but I made certain to give the money to Darja, who assured me that it would only be used for its designated purpose. Early the next morning, a very hungover Eddy and rather sombre Darja, left to catch the day train back home. I was never to see them again. Tallinn disappeared from my tour itineraries and I was becoming increasingly pre-occupied with various business opportunities that were presenting themselves to me. I did speak with Eddy one more time, by phone, but he was evasive about his current status and I suspected the $200 had ended up in liquid form. When I look back on my time in the Soviet Union, the vast majority of my memories are happy ones but when I think of

Eddy, a supreme athlete, reduced to a gibbering alcoholic, I feel only sadness.

The second "new country" I visited on the post-coup "Grand Russia Tour", was the Ukraine. Arriving in Kyiv, just like in Tallinn, I was struck by the number of national flags that had appeared since my last visit, two months earlier. As was often the case, the weather was good. Never as cold in winter, nor as humid in summer as Moscow, the city is filled with parks and trees and summer stretches well into September. Its huge student population, also makes Kyiv a young city and a friendly one. With a free afternoon, following the five-hour flight from Tallinn and hoping to get some cheap tickets for the evening performance, at the National Opera House, I set off for a stroll along Kreschatik, which the more fanciful locals described as their version of the Champs Elysees, in Paris. Almost exactly a mile long, it is a wide and grand boulevard and has been the main street of Kyiv since the 1830s, when the wealthy moved from their traditional quarter, because the army was building a vast barracks there.

After walking for about ten minutes, I came across a large crowd, mainly students, which had gathered outside the central *Metro* station. Many of them were carrying the blue and yellow striped flag of the newly, independent Ukraine and they were being addressed by a young guy using a loud hailer. It transpired that they were debating what to do with the large statue of Karl Marx, situated at the *Metro* station entrance. Most people seemed to want to pull it down but there was little agreement as to how best to achieve this. Leaving them to their deliberations, I continued on to the National Opera House, where I was able to get, for a few roubles, thirty tickets for that evening's performance of Tchaikovsky's, *Queen of Spades*. Retracing my steps and pleased that the opera was one of the more accessible ones, with a relatively simple plotline, I was surprised to see that during my absence, a crane had arrived in the square, in front of the Kreschatik *Metro* Station and an iron cable, in the form of a noose, was being placed around the neck of the Karl Marx statue. Clearly, they were going to try and emulate the felling of Felix Dzerzhinsky's statue, outside the KGB headquarters, in Moscow. For once, I wished I had a camera with me, as the crane struggled to topple the granite monolith, cheered on by the youthful crowd. However, having dominated Kreschatik for over sixty years, "Old Karl" was not going to go without putting up a fight. It soon became evident that the crane was not powerful enough to bring the statue down, so discussion turned to blowing it up, until someone pointed out, that this might result in the total collapse of the *Metro* station. In the end, they contented themselves with cutting off one of the hands, using an acetylene torch.

One couldn't help but be impressed with the students' enthusiasm for change. It was therefore, slightly depressing when three months later, on 5th December 1991, Leonid Kravchuk, who had been the Communist Party boss before the attempted coup, won the Ukraine's first presidential election. Notoriously corrupt, Kravchuk was responsible for plunging the country into a deep recession, during which its GDP[40] decreased by 60 per cent. When I next returned to Kyiv in the spring of 1992, September's youthful optimism was nothing but a distant memory. The government had introduced a new currency, the Ukranian coupon, which was basically worthless, given the five digit inflation rates and in any case, there was nothing to buy in the shops anyway. It struck me that being "free", didn't automatically mean you got to drive a *Mercedes Benz*. In fact, the Ukraine's experience was mirrored across many of the other former Soviet republics, with

---

40 Gross domestic product (GDP) is the standard measure of the value added created through the production of goods and services in a country during a certain period. It also measures the income earned from that production, or the total amount spent on final goods and services (less imports).

the rulers simply swapping a communist hat for a nationalist one and "feathering their own nests", while the living standards of the people continued to fall.

After Kyiv, my next stop was Tbilisi, where I spent a couple of uneventful days, blissfully unaware of the rising resentment that would manifest itself so violently, a couple of weeks later (see previous chapter). And so, on to Moscow, where only three weeks earlier, the world had held its breath, as the Gorbachev reforms seemed destined for the scrapheap of history. As usual, I met up with Juliyanna at the Spanish Bar and she told me she had taken part in the street demonstrations that had been pivotal in stopping the coup in its tracks. She seemed genuinely enthused by the populist Boris Yeltsin, saying he was the future and Gorbachev the past. Although I was sure that Juliyanna had played her part, about others, I had my doubts. I remember, in particular, our Moscow guide, coincidentally also called Boris, waxing lyrical about how he had been on the barricades with Yeltsin, during the showdown outside the Russian White House (primary office of the Russian government and official workplace of the prime minister) on the 19th August. This struck me as a bit strange, as I already knew that his wife was the daughter of a senior Red Army general and the chances of Boris putting his "head above the parapet", were virtually zero. However, Boris was insistent and described in great detail how events had proceeded. I think most people are familiar with the expression, "he doth protest too much" and so it proved with Boris. We had just finished the morning's city tour at Gorky Park and Boris asked if we could drop him off at his home on the way back to the Cosmos. Imagine my surprise, when "home", turned out to be a block of flats, directly opposite the Russian White House. Clearly, Boris had witnessed all the drama from the safety of his apartment balcony. It reminded me very much of my time in France, when everyone I met of a certain generation, professed to have been part of the Resistance, when in fact, most people had adopted a form of passive collaboration with the Nazis.

Still if people like Boris were now "*za Yeltsin*" (for Yeltsin) then at least it meant there was no turning back. On December 25th, President Mikhail Gorbachev resigned, declared his office extinct and handed over its powers, including control of the nuclear launch codes, to Yeltsin. That evening, at 7.32 p.m., the Soviet flag was lowered from the Kremlin for the last time and replaced with the Russian tricolour flag. Watching the events on TV, back home for Christmas in the UK, I thought of all the friends I had made over the past three years and hoped that this really was the dawning of a new era.

20

Una Bella Donna

There can't be many men who meet their future mother-in-law before they meet their wife but I'm one of them. All my groups were told to come to check-in 72, Terminal 1, Heathrow Airport, to pick up their visas before flying out to either Moscow or St Petersburg, with *British Airways*. For once, I had a relatively small group, just twenty-six in number and I was expecting to be done and dusted relatively quickly, enabling me to grab some breakfast, before the 10.30 a.m. flight to St Petersburg. By 8.30 a.m., I had handed out all the visas bar one, a certain Miss Corrina, who given the passport style photo on the visa, I was looking forward to meeting. It was very rare for younger women to travel alone. The vast majority of my clients were either married couples or friends travelling together. By 8.45 a.m., fifteen minutes past the deadline for handing out the visas, I was forced to put a call out over the airport public address system, asking Miss Luisa Corrina to come immediately to Check in 72, to pick up her visa. A couple of minutes later I was relieved to see an attractive redhead walking briskly towards me, smiling brightly and so I called out, 'Miss Corrina, over here,' and waved the visa in the air. Her reply came as something of a shock, 'I'm not Miss Corrina, that's my daughter.' I immediately thought something was very wrong here, there's no way I'm taking an unaccompanied ten-year-old on a three-week tour of the Soviet Union. And then suddenly, Luisa appeared, rushing across the airport concourse. She was even more beautiful than her mother, with flowing auburn hair and a winning smile. Looking at the two of them together, they could never have been taken for mother and daughter, much more likely

116

sisters. Apologising for being late, she had been in the women's' loos when my call had gone out, she asked if I knew which hotel we would be staying at in St Petersburg, as she had been doing some research and she had read that the Pribaltiskaya, was very good. I had learnt by this time never to commit to naming a specific hotel, as Intourist often changed my itinerary at the last minute, but given that we would only be in St Petersburg for two nights, I suspected it would probably be the Hotel Moskva, as it was more central. I could see Luisa was a bit disappointed with my non-committal answer but she still smiled and said she had been looking forward to the trip for the past couple of months. Realising I was in danger of missing a much-needed breakfast, I said we would meet up once through passport control, at St Petersburg airport and turned to go. Just as I was about to leave Judy, Luisa's mother, said, 'You better take care of my daughter!' Little did I realise at the time, was that it was going to be Luisa who took care of me, for the next twenty-seven years!!

On the flight out to St Petersburg, I took my usual aisle seat at the rear of the *BA Boeing 737* and scanned around to see if I could spot Luisa. Normally, I tried to avoid any contact with my clients but hadn't her mother asked me to take care of her? Unfortunately, she had taken a seat right at the front and given that the plane was virtually full, I realised there would be no chance of striking up a conversation. In fact, for once I did talk to some of my clients, as a couple of older ladies, who were travelling together, were smokers and they were seated in the row diagonally behind me. They were called Angela and Pauline, ex-colonials, who had become friends in Kenya during the 1950s and were clearly up for a good time. The G&Ts were already flowing well before midday. Unable to join them for an alcoholic drink (I only ever drank on the flight back to the UK) I was, nevertheless, entertained by their tales of "the empire" and the three-hour flight passed relatively quickly. It transpired that one of the reasons for the early drinking session, was that Angela had a fear of flying and so she was rather taken aback, when I told her that there would be four internal flights during the tour. She had apparently thought we would be taking the train everywhere. The early morning flight from Kyiv to Tbilisi, would prove a particular challenge, as there was nowhere to get a drink at the airport and certainly, no alcohol available on the plane. I remember her ashen-faced, with hands gripped tightly to the armrests, as we taxied down the runway, at Boryspil International airport, 18 miles east of Kyiv.

Arriving late afternoon in St Petersburg, I was pleased to find out that our national guide for the three-week tour, was to be Yelyena, a short, rotund, middle-aged woman, who had a great sense of humour. I had already worked with her before and loved the way she described Russia as, "'The Land of the Evergreen Tomato.'" The other good thing about Yelyena, was that I knew she wouldn't provide any romantic distraction, in my pursuit of Luisa. As I had suspected, our two nights in St Petersburg were to be spent in the Hotel Moskva, a relatively modern hotel, located right beside the Nevsky Monastery and overlooking the upper part of the River Neva. At check-in, just two of the group had paid the single room supplement, Luisa and Johann, a South African heart surgeon, who had been extremely worried going through passport control, as the Soviet Union had only recently normalised relations with South Africa, following the release of Nelson Mandela and he was concerned he might be refused entry. Having ensured that Luisa got a room close to mine, I went through the tour itinerary with Yelyena, pointing out opportunities for some "optional" ways of making money. Unfortunately, there were no performances at the *Kirov* during our two-night stay, so following dinner, I suggested the group might like to join me for a drink in the well-stocked, hard-currency bar. Most declined the invite, following a long day of travelling but Luisa, Johann and of course Angela and Pauline, were up for it, along with a couple of ex Royal Navy sailors, coincidentally, both called Jack, accompanied by their wives. Given that we were three hours ahead of the UK, I always preferred to stay up late on the first night and pretty soon the conversation was flowing freely, with me giving an impromptu lesson on the Russian alphabet. It turned out that the reason why Luisa was travelling alone, was that when the holiday had originally been booked, she had been going out with a US naval pilot called Grant, who was on attachment to the US Embassy in London. He had, however, subsequently "cheated" on her, with one of her best friends and the relationship had ended. Perhaps feeling guilty, Grant had agreed to pay for Luisa's trip, no doubt using the money he would have received back, following his own cancellation. However, the one thing he wasn't prepared to pay for was the single room supplement (around £300 at the time) and so Luisa had had to pay it. All I got for the next three weeks was the recurring complaint, why were tour operators victimising single people? In truth, I actually thought the single room supplement was good value. On one tour, I had an elderly woman travelling with her middle-aged son. She liked to go to bed early and so didn't want her son coming in late and waking her up. They had therefore decided to have separate rooms but didn't want to pay two single-room supplements. Opting to share can be a bit of a lottery, as although tour operators try to match similar people together, you can never guarantee you won't end up with an oddball. On this occasion, the son was fine, instantly bonding with his new room-mate, however, his mother wasn't so lucky. It turned out the woman she was sharing with had OCD and was driving her crazy. Of course, she now wanted to pay the single room supplement, which for a ten-day tour, would have been £150. Unfortunately, not having pre-booked a single room, meant having to pay the standard rate of £70 a night i.e., £700 for the whole tour. I'll always remember the look of despair that appeared on her face when I gave her the bad news. Needless to say, she couldn't justify the extra money, for what was already an expensive tour, instead, having to resort to late night drinking with her son and new friends in the hotel bar, in order to spend the maximum time out of her room, which had become like a prison cell.

As usual, our first full day in St Petersburg involved taking in all the major tourist sites, including the Peter and Paul Fortress, St Isaac's Cathedral and the Winter Palace, which housed the world-famous Hermitage Museum. I immediately noticed that Luisa was a keen photographer. She had an expensive Nikon camera and was constantly snapping away or asking me to take a photo of her in front of some monument or other. Now, anyone who knows me will tell you, I'm the world's worst photographer. To this day, I've never owned or wanted to own a camera. I've always thought that by seeing the world through the view finder, you miss all the other stuff that is going on around you. Looking back through family albums, nearly thirty years later, it is easy to see the photos I took, as they are invariably slightly out of focus or badly composed.

That evening, more of the group joined me for a drink in the bar of the Hotel Moskva, including a young couple from London, called Holly and Simon. She was a journalist, originally from New Zealand and he was "something in the city". As they were a similar age to Luisa and I, it was natural that we would be drawn together as the evening progressed. Talk turned to our lives in the UK and I discovered that Luisa was half-Italian, hence the surname Corrina and the unusual spelling of her first name. At the time, she was working as a radiographer in the London Clinic, a private hospital on Harley Street, in the centre of London. Maybe because Holly was a journalist, she was great at eliciting information from people and I overheard Luisa telling her that following Grant's act of treachery, she was definitely "off men". Clearly, this was going to be a tougher challenge than I had originally thought.

The following morning, we had an included excursion out to Pushkin Palace (also known as Catherine's Palace) located in Tsarskoye Selo (literally tsar's village) 15 miles south of St Petersburg. As Yelyena led the group through the Great Hall, designed by the Italian architect Rastrelli, I couldn't help but notice, that every time a painting was pointed out, Luisa would take a pair of glasses out of her jacket pocket and put them on. She was obviously a bit short-sighted and possibly a little vain! Having returned to the hotel for lunch, the group was given the afternoon off, which seemed like a perfect opportunity for me to get to know Luisa better. Having spent the past couple of days inside various museums and palaces, she said she was keen to stretch her legs and to get some fresh air. I therefore suggested a walk down to the summer gardens, originally laid out by Peter the Great, with lakes, fountains and pavilions, to echo the formal French gardens of his day. After a pleasant stroll along the banks of the Neva and through the Summer Gardens, we ended up at the Literary Café, on Nevsky Prospect, for a spot of afternoon tea. This was one of my favourite places in St Petersburg. During the nineteenth century, it had been the haunt of famous writers such as Pushkin and Dostoyevsky and it retained some of the grandeur of those former days. I also, by this time, knew that Luisa had a sweet tooth and the Literary Cafe was the only eatery in the city, where edible cake could be guaranteed. As usual, the place was packed but I knew that a $5 bill, slipped into the hand of one of the waitresses, would guarantee us a table. Feeling a bit like the character, *Henry Hill* in *Goodfellas*[41], when he first takes his future wife Karen on a date to a swanky nightclub, I walked straight to the front of the line of people queuing outside, nodded at the

---

41 1990 Oscar nominated film by Martin Scorsese.

121

doorman, who recognised me and whisked Luisa into the café. Hoping she would be impressed with the ease with which I got us a table in a secluded corner, I started to tell her about the history of the café, including how the poet, Alexander Pushkin, had met his second, Konstantin Danzas, there, on the way to his fatal duel with George D'Antes, in 1837. However, as was to prove the case frequently over the course of the tour, she already knew much of what I was telling her, having done her research prior to leaving the UK. At least I could claim to have studied Pushkin's *The Gypsies*, for 'A' Level Russian Literature and so, trying to move the conversation in a more romantic direction, I told her of the great love of the Russian nobleman, Aleko for the gypsy girl Zemfira. Quick as a flash Luisa said, 'Didn't he end up killing her?' Which obviously put a bit of a dampener on the moment! Things improved with the arrival of tea and cake and on the *Metro* ride back to the hotel, the quickest way "home" as we were in danger of being late for dinner, I began to think, *'she might be warming to my idiosyncratic charms.'*

21

Geri The Dancer

Later that evening, we left the Hotel Moskva by coach, for the short transfer to the station, to get the overnight train to Tallinn. At dinner, I had allocated the sleeping arrangements for the four-berth couchettes, Luisa already having told me that she was going to share with a married couple and their sixteen-year-old son. I had Johann down for sharing with me, in my pre-reserved, four-berth, so as to avoid him ending up with some locals, although he didn't seem particularly concerned. The rest were all couples, who seemed happy to share, apart from one elderly gentleman and his wife, who approached me after the meal, saying they had paid a supplement to avoid sharing. Now, I knew they were confusing the supplement for the *Trans-Siberian* with the overnight to Tallinn, but they were adamant and to keep things running smoothly, I agreed to "sort it out". This involved a $10 "donation" to the *provodniks'* "benevolent fund", with me and Johann crammed into the attendant's two-berth cabin, at the entrance to our carriage, while the elderly couple enjoyed the comparative luxury of my four-berth cabin. Luckily, it was only for one night and I got on well with Johann, who was, unlike *The Spitting Image* song[42] "a nice South African". As was always the case in Tallinn, we were staying in the Viru and again, I ensured that Luisa's room was close to mine.

With a population of under half a million, Tallinn was over ten times smaller than St Petersburg and had a completely different feel. It was, and still is, despite it becoming the destination of

---

42 1986, B side, to the chart topping, *The Chicken Song*, called *I've Never Met a Nice South African*.

choice for raucous stag parties, in the early 2000s, one of the best preserved of the old north European Hanseatic[43] towns. At the time, it was one of the few Soviet cities where you could be woken by church bells and stroll through the delightful old town, following the smell of fresh pastries and real coffee, until you reached a delightful café. My favourite place to hang out, was at the Maiasmokk, Tallinn's oldest coffee house, dating back to 1864 and located diagonally opposite the Church of the Holy Ghost, in the heart of the old town. It was therefore only natural, that Luisa and I would end up there during the "free afternoon" we had to enjoy, following the morning's city tour. We had already spent a couple of hours together, wandering through the streets, with Luisa frequently stopping to admire the work of the various artists, who were offering views of the city for sale. It later turned out that she was a talented artist herself. Of course, as we all know, artists aren't great at business and so it had been up to me to do the haggling, to ensure she got a fair price for the small number of paintings she bought. Over coffee and the Estonian version of a Danish pastry, the conversation flowed freely and when I mentioned that there would be a show that evening, in the hard-currency bar of the Viru, she was keen to come along, especially when I told her that I was good friends with the lead dancer Eddy. She was sure Holly and Simon would also like to come and in the end, there were about ten of us who made our way down to the hotel basement, following the group's evening meal. I think the best way to describe the show would be like the film *Cabaret*, starring Liza Minelli and Joel Grey i.e., lots of sexual inuendo and risqué dancing. After the performance, the older members of our small group, including Angela and Pauline, said it was getting late and time for bed but I was keen to stay

---

43 A medieval merchant guild or trade association. The Hanseatic League was a medieval commercial and defensive confederation of merchant guilds and market towns in Central and Northern Europe.

and show off my dancing skills to Luisa, knowing the floor space was about turn into a nightclub. At first, it looked like I would be staying on my own, but Holly managed to convince Simon to "let his hair down for once" and not wishing to seem a killjoy, Luisa, rather reluctantly, agreed to delay bedtime. There must have been about fifty people left, from the show's audience, mainly middle-aged businessmen, who clearly knew the way the evening usually developed and sure enough, after about ten minutes, various members of the cast started to filter into the room, having changed out of their costumes, into their normal clothes. Unfortunately, for me, although the bar was filling up and the music was good, the dance floor remained deserted. I asked Holly if she would like to dance but she politely declined and I could see from the look on Luisa's face that there was no point asking her. It looked like, not for the first time, I was going to have to get the party going, all on my own.

The previous year, I had been leading a group of Canadian girl high-school students, on an extensive coach tour of continental Europe. After two weeks together, we had arrived in the beach resort of Lido di Jesolo, which was to serve as our base for visiting Venice. For once, we were going to spend two nights in the same hotel and with the prospect of a relatively late start in the morning, some of the older girls asked their teacher whether they could go out clubbing. He was extremely dubious but as some of them were over eighteen and had already graduated, he effectively couldn't stop them. A compromise was therefore reached, whereby all the group, about thirty in number, could go but they had to be back by midnight and they had to have me accompany them. I immediately didn't like the idea. First, Italian nightclubs never get going until way after 1 a.m., so the place would be deserted and second, any Italian boys who were out, would be drawn to my group like bees to a honeypot!! Despite my concerns, at 9.45 p.m., the girls gathered in the hotel lobby, all dressed for a night out, with skimpy tops and short skirts. It was about a twelve-minute walk to the club and like most places, the doors opened at 10 p.m.. As was the common practice, entry was free between ten and midnight, as long as you had one of the flyers, which were handed out in large numbers, by "pluggers" during the daytime. Of course, all the girls in my group already had their "free ticket". Wanting to get the whole thing over as quickly as possible, we set off for the club, the girls chatting away excitedly behind me. The streets were relatively quiet, too late for elderly tourists to be out but still way too early for any self-respecting clubber to be seen. Nevertheless, after about five minutes, I started to sense we were being followed. Sure enough, a group of thirty single girls walking noisily through the Miami-style streets of the Lido, was starting to attract attention. Pretty soon, I started hearing the familiar cat calls of *'Sei molto bella,'* ('You are most beautiful,') and *'Comme ti chiami?'* ('What's your name?') The majority of the girls' new admirers were young teenage boys, chancing their luck and with no hope of getting into a club. However, as we neared the nightclub, I started to notice that some of the later ones to join, what was now a procession, were older and the call outs were becoming a bit more risqué. As predicted, there was no queue at the club entrance and we walked straight in, the doorman giving me a knowing smile, no doubt thinking this was good for business. I had already spent a lot of time in European discos and the scene that greeted me was a familiar one. A cavernous hall, with balconies in the upper reaches and a huge dance floor, encircled by a wall of full-length mirrors. The gigantic, spangly ball, spinning over the centre of the dance floor, completed the picture. Given that we were the only customers, it almost felt like you were in a cathedral, as our voices echoed around the place. Needing a drink I headed for the bar, where the girls, some for the first time no doubt, were already ordering a selection of exotically named cocktails. The two guys behind the bar, must have thought Christmas had come early and when I explained to them, that all the girls were with me, they gave me a nod of respect and said all my drinks would be "on the house." Finding a table, pint of *Peroni* in hand, I sat down and started to count the minutes to quarter-to-twelve, when we would have to leave. Pretty soon I was joined by Carrie, the unofficial leader of the group and a few of her older friends, who could best be described as "the cool kids". The younger girls preferred to keep their distance, huddled round corner tables, away from the dance floor, enjoying their first taste of illicit alcohol. Although I had previously warned Carrie that the place would be dead, she still seemed surprised by the lack of clients. By eleven o'clock, I think she started to realise that I hadn't been exaggerating. Yes, a few of the older boys who had been following us, were now hanging around, in small groups on the balconies overlooking the dance floor but despite the pounding disco beat, emanating from the huge speakers, no one was dancing. With less than an hour left, I said to Carrie that if she wanted a dance, then now was the time. Emboldened by her second tequila sunrise, she said she would go round all the girls and then we would make a mass entrance onto the dance floor. A couple of minutes later she was back and said everyone was up for it. Hearing the first bars of one of my favourite songs, *Don't Leave Me This Way*, by *The Communards*, starting to play, I grabbed Carrie's hand and started to walk towards the floor, expecting all the other girls to follow. However, Carrie had been over optimistic and I immediately sensed the girls were hanging back. Just as we reached the floor, Carrie lost her nerve, released my hand and shrank back into the shadows, leaving me alone, literally "under the spotlight". At that point, one of the boys on the upper balcony shouted down, *'Che cazzo fai?'* (What the fuck are you doing?') and that's when I thought,

'*I'm going to show you what real dancing is, not that poncy, mirror-loving stuff you guys do.*' Inspired by the music and fuelled by three pints of *Peroni*, I launched into one of my routines, with lots of spins and jumps and even included a bit of *Michael Jackson Moonwalking*. With the Canadian girls now clapping along and shouting out words of encouragement, I managed to keep going for two more songs, by which time all the balconies were filled and even some of the local boys were smiling appreciatively. As I started to drag myself exhausted from the floor, I suddenly saw a wave of girls coming towards me, with Carrie in the lead. This time she grabbed my hand and said I had to keep going. 'Just one more song,' I gasped and, luckily for me, it was more of a mid-tempo number. Of course, with thirty attractive Canadian girls strutting their stuff, I didn't remain the only male on the dance floor for long. By the time I reacquainted myself with my *Peroni,* there must have been at least fifteen local boys on the floor and over the next twenty minutes, the number steadily grew. Now, I know teenage girls are meant to be more mature and sensible than their male counterparts but these girls were from a rural community and I don't think they were used to having so much attention from dark-haired, olive-skinned Italian gigolos. They were loving every minute of it and in some cases, leading the boys on. It quickly became apparent that I was going to have difficulty making the midnight curfew. Not for the first time, my ego was creating problems. If only I'd resisted the temptation to show off, then the dance floor would have remained empty, with no chance for Canadian-Italian intermingling. At 11.40 p.m., I decided now was the time to start rounding the girls up. Despite the inevitable protests and some murderous looks from the local boys, I managed to get everyone out of the club in under ten minutes. However, I couldn't help noticing that as we left, some of the girls were pushing pieces of paper into the hands of their recent dancing partners. Determined to make the midnight deadline, I had used this as a bargaining chip, when persuading the girls to leave, implying that if we made the curfew, then the teachers might allow them to do the same thing in Rome, which was our next destination! We set off, on the short walk back to the hotel. Almost immediately, I knew we were being followed but at least the girls kept together, only occasionally looking back wistfully over their shoulders. Reaching the hotel, bang on midnight, it was with some relief that I handed over responsibility to the lead teacher, who thanked me profusely for getting the girls back on time. Saying it was no problem, I headed for bed, safe in the knowledge that it wasn't going to be me who was going to have a sleepless night. I heard the first boy, shinnying up the drainpipe outside my bedroom window, after about twenty minutes and more were to follow. It was evident that some of the girls had been giving out hastily scrawled room numbers, on those pieces of paper and given "the green light", no self-respecting Italian boy, was going to leave it at that. I found out the next morning that things had finally quietened down about 4 a.m., with the teachers having to literally "repel" a testosterone fuelled Italian invasion. Needless to say, the girls never got to sample the delights of Roman nightlife!

I was thinking about the above episode, as I downed the last dregs of my pint of *Heineken* and headed for the dance floor of the Valuta bar, in the vague hope that I could get the party started. However, for once, I needn't have worried because just as the first bars of, *The Only Way is Up*, by Yazz kicked in, suddenly Eddy was there beside me. Encouraged by his presence, I launched into one of my set routines, with him enthusiastically following my lead. Soon, we were joined by some of Eddy's fellow dancers and before long Holly, Simon and most importantly, Luisa, were also on the floor. From that point onwards, the night seemed to fly by. In truth, Luisa wasn't the greatest dancer in the world, most of her rhythm seemed to be in her shoulders, but she gamely stuck at it, probably helped by frequents sips from the free-flowing champagne I had ordered and I even managed to get a slow dance with her, as the DJ started to wind the evening down. It must have been past three in the morning, when I finally went to bed, which made it a bit of a struggle making the 9 a.m. breakfast. Still, I knew I would be able to skip the morning's excursion out to the Gulf of Finland, including visits to the Olympic Centre, used for the yachting and rowing events at the 1980 Olympics, also, to the Tallinn Song Festival Grounds, where three years earlier, Estonians had gathered to sing patriotic hymns, in what became known as: "The Singing Revolution". There was definitely no need for three guides to accompany the group, on what was simply an opportunity to take some panoramic pictures and to promote Estonia's new found independence. Explaining I had some admin to do, I returned to my room, had a leisurely bath and then read a copy of the $2 *International Guardian* I had bought the previous day, in the hotel lobby.

22

Gamblers Never Win

For the first two years of my time in the Soviet Union, it had been virtually impossible to get hold of any foreign press but now things were changing and luckily for me, *The Guardian* was in the forefront of these changes. I would avidly read the paper from cover to cover, particularly interested in how the events I was experiencing first-hand, were being reported in the West. There is an old saying that, "'A journalist never lets the facts get in the way of a good story,'" and many was the time I felt the truth was being mis-represented, particularly by TV journalists. For example, in the period following the collapse of the Soviet Union, it is true that there was a lot of economic hardship. However, the Moscow correspondent for the BBC, decided to declare that there were massive food shortages and that a famine was imminent. To illustrate this, he showed images of bags of food, hanging outside peoples' balcony windows, evidence, he said, of the stockpiling that was going on. What he failed to mention, was that given it was January, the outside temperature was -20 °C and Russians were simply doing what they always do, namely, using the outside as additional freezer space. On the back of this mis-reporting, I had one school group bring out food parcels, to be distributed among the needy. For some reason, Lara Karlina had arranged for us to visit a hospital, where a very embarrassed female doctor explained to me that, *'My ne takiye bednyye,'* ('We aren't that poor,') as she reluctantly posed for photos, with the teachers who had organised the collection back in the UK.

Given that it was a 4 ½ hour flight to Kyiv, we left the Hotel Viru straight after lunch and made the short transfer to the airport, located 3 miles to the south-east of the city centre. It was a beautiful day for flying, with clear blue skies and virtually no wind. As the *Tupolev 154* left the ground, I leant across Luisa, who was sitting in the window seat next to me, to point out where we had been staying, accidentally brushing against her breast. She would later claim that at the time, she didn't think the action was "accidental" but I still struggle to remember! On arrival in Kyiv, I was pleased to find that our accommodation was going to be in the recently-built and aptly-named, Hotel Intourist. This was definitely a step up from the Hotel Lybid, where I normally stayed and had the added attraction of having a casino in the basement. That evening, after the usual chicken kiev (or as it was known post-Chernobyl "Atomic Rooster") me and a group of the "usual suspects", made our way downstairs, to check out this new addition to the tourist experience. The Soviet government had only lifted its ban on all gambling two years previously and this was, therefore, going to be my first time in a casino. I come from a card playing family and so I was pleased to see that the only game available in the deserted room, was *Blackjack*, or as I knew it better, *Pontoon*[44]. Although so far, I had not had any opportunity to earn any extra money from "Geri optionals", I knew that Tchaikovsky's *Swan Lake*, was on at the *Bolshoi*, during our upcoming stay in Moscow and I'd already pre-booked seats through my ticket man, Misha. This meant I would conservatively be making $500, on one night's performance and so I felt I could easily justify gambling a few dollars, particularly as no one else seemed in a hurry to play. In addition, the dealer was a friendly guy and eager to practice his newly-acquired skills. At first, things went swimmingly, with me winning hand after hand, aided, I thought, by the fact that the dealer was forced to stick on sixteen or below. Clearly, I was teaching this novice card player a lesson and so I started to increase the size of my stake. They say, "'pride

---

44 British version of the French game originally called *Vingt-Un* or Twenty-One.

comes before a fall,'" and in this case, never a truer word was spoken. Suddenly, I started to lose, going "bust" a number of times in succession and pretty soon, I had gone from being comfortably in profit, to being $100 in the red. Too late I realised that playing second, meant the dealer never went bust. Unlike me, playing on emotion, the "house" simply played the odds, the basis for all forms of organised gambling. A bit poorer but a lot wiser, I decided to cut my losses and head back upstairs to the main hotel bar, where I hoped Luisa might join me for a nightcap, but she said she was exhausted and going to bed. Was she starting to tire of my constant showing-off?

The next couple of days gave me very little time for any extra wooing of Luisa. This was the tour when I nearly got shot by the lock guard on the River Dnieper and after losing $100 at *Blackjack*, I resolved to recoup my losses by getting tickets for a Ukranian dance troupe, who, for some reason, were performing at the National Opera House, in the centre of town. As it turned out, they were spectacularly good, displaying all the athleticism of traditional Cossack dancing and from that time on, they became a fixture in the list of "Geri optionals".

The thing I most remember about Luisa in Kyiv, is that she got really upset when she got "short-changed", when exchanging money on the street. It was the usual sleight of hand trick of swapping ten-rouble notes for one-rouble notes, at the last second. I always discouraged my groups from changing money on the "Black Market", partly because of the aforementioned trick but mainly because it was "illegal" and could create problems for me, if the exchange was a KGB set-up, which would require a large bribe, to ensure my client didn't spend the night in a police cell. I was therefore, rather less than sympathetic, when Luisa complained that she had been conned, pointing out that at the end of the day, she had simply obtained what was the official exchange rate at the time. I did add, that if she needed more roubles I would be happy to get her some through my usual contacts but with her pride injured, she said that wouldn't be necessary and walked briskly away.

With a 7 a.m. flight booked to Tbilisi in the morning, our last evening in Kyiv was a quiet affair, with everyone going to bed straight after dinner. I did notice that Angela had managed to get herself a small bottle of vodka from one of the waiters, which hopefully was going to help her survive the flight down to the Georgian capital. We left the hotel at 5 a.m., for the 20-mile transfer out to Boryspil airport, which I thought was way too early, but Yelyena was old enough to be my mum and she was insistent. A lesson in life, "Always listen to your mother", as the old coach we were on, managed to break down half-way into the journey. It took thirty minutes of the driver "banging around" inside the engine, before we were on our way again and so, breakfast at the airport and the subsequent allocation of flight seats, was more rushed than normal. This meant, that for once, I didn't get to sit next to Luisa, instead, ending up next to a guy from Tbilisi, who it turned out, had a friend who had just started making souvenir T-shirts. This seemed like a good contact, so I took his telephone number and said I would call to arrange a meeting the following day. Everywhere I travelled in the Soviet Union, tourist memorabilia of varying quality were available to buy, from *matryoshki* (Russian dolls) to furry hats and lacquer boxes. However, a recurrent complaint from my groups, was that there were no T-shirts available, to act as mementos for the incredible places they had visited. This was particularly true for the *Bolshoi* and *Kirov*. It is, therefore, no surprise that my first idea for doing business in the Soviet Union, was to produce *Bolshoi* ballet T-shirts in the UK and to sell them through the ticket touts I knew, who operated outside the theatre.

My new Georgian friend, Ilia, was good company for the six-hour flight, but I couldn't help occasionally glancing backwards over my shoulder, to catch a glimpse of Luisa, sitting three rows behind me. She, however, was in deep conversation with the mother of the family she had shared a compartment with, on the overnight train from St Petersburg to Tallinn and whether deliberately or not, she showed no desire to make any eye contact. I was beginning to think my best chance of female company in the next couple of weeks, was going to be meeting up with Juliyanna, once we got to Moscow.

23
Wooing Luisa

With blue skies overhead, we landed at Novo Alexeyevka airport, in the early afternoon and made the short transfer to the Hotel Iveria, where we were due to stay for three nights. As usual, more in hope than expectation, I made sure Luisa and I had adjacent rooms and with the city tour not due until the following morning, I suggested the group might like to spend the time before dinner, chilling out by the roof-top swimming pool. Given the beautiful weather, everyone thought it was a good idea and so they retired to their rooms to change into their swimwear. I had got Luisa and I rooms on the 16th floor, affording great views up the valley, toward the massive Caucasus mountains, looming in the distance. Hoping to get some brownie points, I asked Luisa if she had any washing she needed doing, as I knew the *dezhurnaya* would be more than happy to help out, for a couple of packets of *Marlboro Red*. After a week on the road, she said that would be useful and disappeared into her room, emerging a couple of minutes later, with an assortment of tops and some rather expensive looking lingerie. Blushing slightly, she asked me how much it was going to cost and when I replied it was "on-the-house", she gave me one of her beautiful smiles. Having added Luisa's washing to the plastic bag full of socks and pants, that was constantly at the bottom of my suitcase, I headed off to find the *dezhurnaya,* who gave me something of a knowing look, as I handed over the "mixed" bag of washing. Perhaps she thought I was a transvestite!? A few minutes later, I was sitting by the pool in my skimpy black speedos, applying the last of some factor-four sun cream, to my already-brown torso. Suddenly, Luisa appeared, wearing a fetching, red and white, striped bikini that didn't leave much to the imagination. I gestured for her to come over and told her that the washing would be ready in the morning. Again, she thanked me and asked if there was anywhere she could buy sun cream, as she hadn't thought to bring any with her. I said, 'no,' but given her olive coloured skin, inherited from her Italian father, I told her she was welcome to have some of my factor four and asked if she would like me to rub some on her back and legs. Blushing for the second time that day, she declined my "gallant" offer, saying she was only going to be tanning her front and so, could quite easily manage herself. Even though it was already 4.30 p.m., the temperature was still in the mid-twenties and most of the group were already in the pool. I spotted Holly and Simon swimming in the deep end and waved over to them. They waved back and shouted for me and Luisa to join them. Luisa immediately got up from her sun lounger and asked me if I was coming too. Having just applied a load of sun cream, I was in no hurry to go in the water, which gave me the idea of playing a practical joke. 'I can't swim,' I said, 'and I don't want to make myself look a fool in front of the group.' A puzzled look appeared on Luisa's face but as I was to find out, over the next few years, she had a gullible side to her. In fact, I once told her that gullible wasn't in the dictionary and she actually believed me! Leaving me to my sunbathing, she did an elegant dive into the pool and struck out in the direction of Holly and Simon. After about twenty minutes, Luisa was back sitting on the sun lounger beside me. Now was the time to put my plan into action. Telling Luisa I was going to get a bottle of water from my room, I headed for the door, that acted as the entrance back into the hotel, which was located by the deep end of the pool. Just as I neared the door, I feigned a slip and tumbled into the water with a huge splash. I immediately swam to the bottom and started to breaststroke my way back towards where Luisa was sitting. Surfacing a couple of metres away, I could see that she was standing at the pool edge, an anxious look on her face, a look which suddenly turned glacial, when she saw me treading water and laughing out loud. 'You bastard!' she screamed, 'I thought you were going to drown.'

'Come on in,' I shouted in reply, but she was having none of it and pointedly lay down on her lounger and started to read the *Baedeker* guide book, she always carried with her. Realising I'd probably been a bit too clever, I thought it best to leave her alone and instead, contented myself with a few leisurely lengths of the pool, followed by a couple of back-flips into the water, for "showing off" purposes.

That evening at dinner, as was always the case in Tbilisi, the food was far better than anything we'd experienced during the past seven days. The local speciality was various types of meat served as kebabs, not on sticks, but on what can only be described as small swords and for once, you could actually taste the meat. In addition, Georgian red wine was served with the meal and although not on a par with a good *Bordeaux*, it was eminently drinkable. For once, everyone seemed happy to stay in the restaurant long after the meal had finished, some ordering extra bottles of wine to have at their table. It must have been nearly midnight when people started to head for their rooms and as if by chance, I ended up in the lift with Luisa, as we headed for the 16th floor. She was a little bit tipsy and seemed to have forgiven me for my swimming-pool antics. There was nothing planned for the following afternoon, so I asked her if she would like to go for a walk in the hills that surround the city and she said that would be nice.

The next day, the weather was cloudy but still warm, as the coach pulled away from the front of the Iveria, with the local guide, Mariam, at the microphone. I hadn't worked with Mariam before and we'd already had a bit of a falling out, as she couldn't understand why my group didn't want to go to see the performance of traditional Georgian dancing, that had been laid on for us at the circle-shaped, glass-fronted concert hall, in the centre of town. I just said, '*Ne volnuysya*,' ('Don't worry,') having already made contact with the concert hall director the previous year and come to an Anglo-Georgian arrangement, which cut out the "Russian imperialists from Moscow" i.e., Intourist. Compared to Yelyena, with her quick wit and sense of irony, Mariam was very much "old school" and I had this perverse idea, that she might be directly descended from Stalin[45]. She even had a bit of a moustache on her upper lip! Still, nothing could take away from the beauty of the old town, nestled on the banks of the River Kura. A particular highlight, was a visit to the Orbeliani sulphur baths, where Luisa was insistent on recreating an image she had seen in *Paris Match*[46], of Caroline of Monaco, standing astride two of the brick domes, that formed the roof of the building. While preparing to write this book, I came across the photo in an old family album and given that I took the picture, it is, of course, out of focus! However, you can still make out that Luisa was equally as good looking as the Monegasque princess.

The city tour complete, over lunch I arranged to meet with Luisa at two o'clock, to go on our afternoon walk, with romantic visions of seducing her in the woods. I was, therefore, a little disappointed, when she appeared in the hotel lobby, accompanied by Holly and Simon. However, I could hardly tell them to get lost and so, the four of us set off in the direction of an observation platform I knew about, located high in the hills above the city. It took us nearly an hour to reach the platform, with both Holly and Luisa stopping frequently, to take panoramic shots across the valley. A small café was situated next to the platform and thirsty after the climb, we each ordered a bottle of the locally produced

---

45 Born in the Georgian town of Gori in 1878.
46 French language weekly news magazine.

lemonade, with its unique tarragon flavour. Conscious that time was moving on and already having arranged to meet Ilia's T-shirt producing friend, Giorgi, outside the sulphur baths at 4.30 p.m., I suggested we start heading back to the hotel. Both Luisa and I were wearing trendy brown deck shoes, unlike Holly and Simon, who had decided to wear more sensible footwear. Given my skiing background, I'm pretty sure-footed but Luisa wasn't so adept and during the descent, she managed to slip quite badly, thereby allowing me to hold her in my arms for the very first time, as I broke her fall.

Once back in town, I explained that I had a friend to meet and I would see everyone for an early dinner, before our "Geri optional", to watch the Georgian dancing. However, being a journalist, Holly was naturally inquisitive and liked the idea of meeting a real Georgian, while Luisa said she was keen to come, probably suspecting that I was going to catch-up with an old flame. As we approached the entrance to the sulphur baths, it was easy to spot my "friend", Giorgi, as he was wearing one of his T-shirts with the Georgian national flag (large red cross with four smaller red crosses in the quadrants) emblazoned across the front. I was already a bit uneasy about having clients with me during "business" negotiations and I started to worry that Giorgi might be an English speaker. Luckily, he only spoke Georgian and Russian, so all Holly's questions had to come through me. She seemed particularly interested in the civil unrest that was starting to break out in the country, but clearly Giorgi was a businessman, pure and simple and to my relief, he said he had little time for politics and was only interested in selling his wares. Having negotiated a sale or return deal, for $5 a T-shirt, he handed me a large plastic bag containing twenty items and accompanied by Luisa, Holly and Simon, I headed back to the hotel. Unfortunately, this was to prove one of my less successful deals. The quality of the cotton was pretty poor and worse still, there was only one size, namely XS. I did manage to sell a couple of shirts that evening at dinner, as one couple said they would probably fit their two grandchildren, but the rest had to be returned the following day, when unusually for me, I didn't have the heart to take my 50 per cent commission. In truth, I wasn't that bothered, as the Georgian dance evening was always a nice little earner. I simply paid the normal rouble price on the door and then, while the group were getting seated, I went to the director's office, to hand over the pre-arranged symbol of Anglo-Georgian friendship, namely, 200 *Marlboro Red*. I used to charge my group $15 a head (half the Intourist price) and the high-leaping, dagger-throwing, male dancers, with their knee-length black leather boots, never failed to disappoint.

It was late when we got back to the hotel after the evening's performance and given that we had an early start in the morning, as we were going to be spending the day in the Caucasus mountains, everyone headed straight for bed. I accompanied Luisa back to her room, thinking, '*she might invite me in for a night cap,*' but unlike the previous evening, she wasn't at all tipsy and simply said, 'Goodnight,' as she closed the door firmly behind her.

The next day, the weather was overcast, which was a shame, as we were going to be travelling along one of the most stunning roads in the world, the Georgian military highway, the historic route connecting Tbilisi with Russia, first carved out by traders and invaders alike, in the first century BC. Even before visiting Georgia, I knew about the road, as it features in, *A Hero of Our Time* by Mikhail Lermonov, one of the set works for my Russian Literature 'A' Level. Our first stop was at the Jvari Monastery, which stands on a rocky mountaintop, at the confluence of the Mtkvari and Aragvi rivers, overlooking the town of Mtskheta, the former capital of the Kingdom of Iveria, from where our hotel got its name. By sheer chance, a religious service was taking place and it was impossible not to be moved by the sound of the Georgian chant[47], that was emanating from inside the stone-walled temple. In some ways, it reminded me of a Welsh, male voice choir, no music, just pure singing. Our next stop was at the Ananuri Fortress, which dated back to the thirteenth century, when the region's leaders built two defensive castles on the bank of the Aragvi river. Lunch was pre-booked at a restaurant in Pasanauri, a town known as the "home of khinkali[48]", the signature dish of Georgian cuisine, where we also got to sample some of the local wine. The day's touring finished at Kazbegi, a small town from where fabulous views of the imposing Mount Kazbek (5033m) and the mountaintop Gergeti Trinity Church, were normally available, but the weather had failed to improve and so the group had to content themselves with buying cheap postcards of the views, that Mariam was trying to describe. It took us over two hours to drive back from Kazbegi to Tbilisi but I was in no hurry, as the day's intermittent drizzle had, by now, turned into a steady downpour and so rooftop swimming was not going to be on the agenda. As we approached the hotel, I took the microphone from Mariam and rather half-heartedly, thanked her for being our guide in Tbilisi. I know it wasn't her fault that the weather had been poor but she was so boring that, for her, even valium would have acted as a stimulant! She definitely wasn't getting a *podarok* (gift).

With no organised evening entertainment available and a relatively late flight to Moscow in the morning, I thought now was the perfect opportunity for the first "Geri Quiz" of the tour. Everyone was keen and so, after dinner, the group divided themselves up into teams of four, Luisa, choosing to play with the family she had shared with on the overnight train from St Petersburg to Tallinn.

---

47 A form of monophonic, unaccompanied sacred song in Latin.
48 Dumplings stuffed with meat and spices.

In truth, it was a rather strange combination. Angela had, for no other reason than the father was called Bruce, nicknamed the family, the "Brucie bonuses" and it was something of a running joke that in the family it was the wife, Elspeth, who "wore the trousers". They were usually the first to go to bed after dinner but Elspeth had obviously decided that it was time to be a bit more sociable, or maybe, she was good at quizzing. The latter proved to be the case and suddenly the nickname seemed appropriate. With a bit of help from Luisa, she got an Italian cookery question correct, the family easily won but they said Luisa was to have the winning prize, as they didn't drink much. With the "Brucie bonuses" already heading for bed, I sat down at Luisa's table and asked if she needed any help drinking the bottle. She said that would be nice, while at the same time, gesturing to Holly and Simon to come over and join us. For once, my luck was in, as Holly said she was feeling a bit under the weather and that she and Simon were going to bed. I thought now might be a good time to impress Luisa with the breadth of my literary knowledge and so, I started to tell her about the concept of the *lishniy chelovek* (superfluous man) as detailed in, *A Hero of Our Time*, the only book I had enjoyed studying at 'A' Level. Given my background of always being a bit different, I easily identified with the lead character, Pechorin, an individual, perhaps talented and capable, who does not fit into social norms. Luisa seemed genuinely interested in the concept or maybe she was starting to get a bit drunk. After a little over an hour, we had managed to polish the bottle off and remembering I still hadn't returned her washing, I suggested we retire upstairs, so she would be able to pack her case, before she went to bed. We took the lift to the 16th floor and I went to my room to retrieve the plastic bag, which had been delivered the previous day. Returning to Luisa's room, I noticed that she had left the door open and so after a gentle tap and not waiting for a reply, I entered the room. Luisa was standing on the balcony with her back to me, staring out over a panoramic view of the illuminated city, with the mountains in the distance. 'Isn't it beautiful?' she asked and walking up to her side, dropping the bag of clothes on the floor, I replied, 'Yes, magnificent.' Although I was talking more about Luisa than the view. Suddenly, as if pre-ordained, all the lights in the room and the city beyond went out, clearly the result of a massive power cut. For a moment I thought of the broken gas pipe in St Petersburg, which had caused me no end of problems and hoped we were not in for a night without electricity. Luisa though, didn't seem at all concerned. She just smiled at me and said, 'You're the tour director, you can fix anything.' As a sign of bravado I replied, 'I'll just click my fingers then,' which I did, only to be amazed when instantly, all the lights across the city came back on. 'You really are amazing,' Luisa said wistfully. Who was I to disagree and thinking, *now is the moment,*' I moved to kiss her lips, only to be astonished, when she pulled herself away. Trying to cover my embarrassment, I mumbled something about the inadequacies of the Georgian power grid and made my exit, reminding her that her washing was in the bag on the bedroom floor.

24

Don't Blame the Photographer!

1 - The Hotel Cosmos

2 - Being Woken on the Trans-Siberian Train

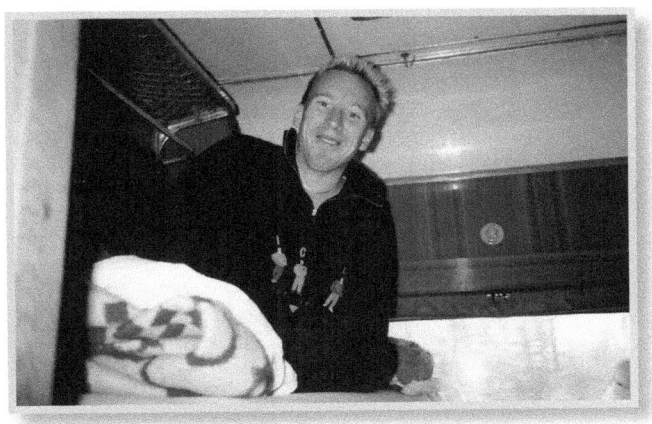

3 - Observation Platform in Tbilisi with Holly and Simon, Sept 1990

4 - Luisa re-creating the Princess of Monaco pose on the domed roof of the Orbeliani sulphur baths, Sept 1990

5 - Juliyanna and Geri - Spanish Bar, Hotel Moskva, Oct 1990

6 - Luisa, River Neva, the Winter Palace (Leningrad) in the background, Sept 1990

7 - Geri and Lara (Intourist guide) and her daughter on a Moscow Metro Tour, Sept 1991

8 - Luisa and Geri 'playing as tourists' at Catherine's (Pushkin) Palace, July 1992

9 - Geri standing outside the Hotel Astoria in his signature, mustard-coloured raincoat, May 1993

10 - Cristian standing next to the River Neva in the pouring rain, July 2016

11 - Cristian and Geri at the Bolshoi having interval drinks, July 2016

12 - Cristian and Geri, Bolshoi auditorium, July 2016

13 - *Cristian and Geri at Petrodvorets Palace. A view of the palace and gardens. More beautiful than Versailles, July 2016*

14 - *Thanks to Tolya, a decent pool table in Russia, July 2016*

25

Playing Not So Hard to Get!

The next morning, nursing a bit of a hangover, I decided to pretend as if nothing had happened and catching sight of her, sitting alone at the breakfast table, I called out, '*Ciao, bella!*' Big mistake. 'You're not Italian,' she said, 'stop pretending you are.' Not wishing to cause a scene in front of some of the group, who were starting to enter the restaurant, I simply nodded, resolving as I did, to spend as much time as possible with Juliyanna, during our upcoming stay in Moscow.

Arriving at the airport a couple of hours later, I made sure, for the first time, that Luisa and I would be kept well apart during the flight, instead, choosing to sit with Johann. For once, on an internal flight, we weren't the only westerners, as during the previous week, Tbilisi had been hosting an international juggling festival and these guys just couldn't stop juggling, be it in the departure hall, on the transfer bus out to the plane and even on the flight itself! Their enthusiasm was infectious and slowly my mood began to lighten, especially with the prospect of seeing Juliyanna again in a few hours.

It was early evening by the time our coach pulled up outside the Hotel Cosmos, so following check-in, it was straight to the dining room for our evening meal. As usual, on the first night anywhere, Yelyena and I sat apart from the group, so we could discuss the programme for the forthcoming days. After about fifteen minutes, Juliyanna breezed into the room and sat down at our table. We hadn't seen each other for over a month and so we had a lot of catching up to do. Occasionally, I would look over to where Luisa was sitting but she seemed to be making a deliberate attempt not to catch my eye, preferring to remain in deep conversation with Bruce and Elspeth. After dinner, Juliyanna and I went for a drink in the *Heineken* bar and were soon joined by Holly and Simon, who were keen to meet my mysterious friend. I asked them if they thought Luisa would be coming but they said that, complaining of a headache, she had gone to bed. Interesting, I thought, as she had never struck me as the sickly type.

For the next few days Juliyanna effectively became the assistant Moscow guide, accompanying us on all the tours and sharing mealtimes with us. She was always great for having the most up-to-date information. The big news was that the hard currency supermarket, where I got my liquor supplies, for the *Trans-Siberian*, was closed for refurbishment and the only other place with a decent selection of booze, had consequently doubled its prices. I was therefore, going to have to find another source of alcohol, if I was to maintain my profit margin. Luckily, one of my favourite drivers, Valodya, was working with me that week and with his help, I was able to get two cases of Azerbaijani cognac, for the equivalent of $10, from a backstreet vendor, close to the souvenir centre of Arbat Street[49].

Feeling confident I had enough "essential supplies" for the four-day journey to Irkutsk, I was in a good mood, as our coach pulled into the forecourt outside Yaroslavl station, with plenty of time to spare before our 3 p.m. departure. As the luggage was loaded on to the electric baggage trolley, I spotted the head porter, who had "saved my bacon" the previous year and gave him a knowing smile, to indicate he wouldn't be getting $50 this time, for his team's work, rather $10 and a few packs of *Marlboro Red,* which was the going rate for a normal baggage transfer. With the cases nearly loaded, I went to say goodbye to Valodya and to arrange

---

49 Dating back to the 15th century, one of the oldest surviving streets in Moscow.

with him an extra evening's work, for when we returned to Moscow. I had managed to get tickets for a performance by the *Moscow State Circus*[50], on Tsvetnoi Boulevard, in the city centre and thought it would be a good way to end our three-week tour. I always really enjoyed my evenings at the circus but I realised they weren't everybody's cup of tea. The previous year, I'd had a group of school children walk out of a performance, complaining about animal cruelty. Now, I'm no great animal lover but maybe it's true that bears aren't meant to ride motorbikes!

Re-joining the group, I noticed that Luisa had struck up a conversation with Juliyanna and for one horrible moment, I thought that, in an act of sisterly solidarity, she was telling my Moscow girlfriend about my attempted "Georgian pass". However, as usual, Juliyanna was smiling brightly and once we were back together, it was clear that, thankfully, Luisa hadn't "spilled the beans". With departure imminent, I gave Juliyanna a farewell hug and arranged to meet her in a week's time, outside the circus theatre. As the train slowly pulled away from the platform, I mouthed the words, *'Ya tebya lublu,'* ('I love you,') and in return, she gave me one of her dazzling smiles. Although I really liked Johann, I couldn't help wishing it was Juliyanna that I would be spending the next four days with, cooped up on a train.

Given that the vast majority of the group had paid the supplement to ensure dual occupancy of a four-berth compartment, we were split between two carriages. In my carriage, were Angela and Pauline, Holly and Simon, the "Brucie bonuses", plus Luisa and of course, Johann. The rest of the group were with Yelyena, in a carriage two removed, toward the front of the train. That evening at dinner, in the restaurant car, I decided to introduce a new innovation, whereby everyone told their favourite joke.

---

50 There are two sites, the other is known as the *Bolshoi* Circus, opened in April 1971, on the south side of Moscow, with a seating capacity of 3,400.

154

Of course, it was up to me to get the ball rolling and perhaps, unwisely, I decided to tell a rather risqué joke, where the punchline was 'Welcome to Barbados, have a nice day,' at which point, the "Brucie bonuses" decided it was time for another early night. Luisa however, along with the rest of the group, perhaps fuelled by Azerbajani cognac, seemed to be enjoying the evening and it was approaching midnight when the party started to break up. Returning to our carriage, Johann asked Luisa if she would like to join us for a nightcap and seeing that Holly and Simon had already closed their compartment door, she accepted the invitation. The best way to utilise the space in a dual occupancy, four-berth compartment, is to both sleep on the top bunks, with the lower bunks reserved for cases, toiletry bags, books and games. There is storage space under the lower bunks but during the daytime, these become your seats, while the aforementioned items are moved onto the top bunks for easy access. At this late hour, we were in night-time mode and so the simplest solution, was for us to sit on the top bunks, with our legs dangling over the edge. Luisa naturally chose to sit next to Johann, who was in his late fifties and therefore, unlikely to become flirtatious. He was a really interesting guy, a paediatric cardiothoracic surgeon, appropriately from Johannesburg and despite his Afrikaans background, clearly no fan of apartheid. After a while, the conversation turned to Israel, which Luisa said was operating a form of apartheid, in the way it treated the Palestinians. She revealed that she had met a guy a few years previously, while travelling in Israel with a fellow radiography student, called Elizabeth. He was a Palestinian and at least ten years older than her. A relationship had developed, in which, Luisa's eyes had been opened to the injustices inflicted on the Palestinian people, by the Israeli government. Never overly political, this would remain the one constant in the way she looked at the world. It transpired that on one occasion, she had been questioned for over two hours, by *El Al* security staff, when trying to board a flight from Heathrow to Tel Aviv, carrying a parcel destined for her Palestinian boyfriend. Stupidly, she had pretended that the parcel contained a present for an English female acquaintance, living on the coast at Jaffa, but not believing her, the questioning had become increasingly aggressive, with Luisa ending up in tears and admitting the truth. With the parcel confiscated and warnings to her future conduct, she was allowed to fly; although the relationship would prove to be short-lived, her enmity towards Israel would be enduring.

With my "Chardonnay socialist" background, I was with Luisa on the "question of Palestine" and it did seem we had more in common than I had originally thought. We had both spent a lot of time abroad from an early age. Luisa had lived in Italy between the ages of five and seven and she had already travelled widely, across mainland Europe, including visits to Croatia, Bosnia and Sicily, three places I had never been. In addition, since our arrival in Moscow, the antipathy she had displayed before our morning flight from Tbilisi, had disappeared. I couldn't help thinking that this might have something to do with the appearance of Juliyanna. From past experience, it always seemed that I was automatically more attractive to the opposite sex, when I already had a girlfriend in place and the following days were going to prove the point, once again.

Although she got on well with the "Brucie bonuses", it was hard work, sharing a four-berth compartment and consequently, during the daytime, Luisa would flit between different compartments, spending time in particular with Angela and Pauline, Holly and Simon and most importantly me and Johann. On the third day, she had just left our compartment, having spent the previous couple of hours playing vanishing whist, a perennial Bowen family favourite. 'Such a lovely girl,' Johann said, about to return to his second detective novel of the trip. 'I know,' I replied, 'I really like her and I think she's starting to warm to me, but I feel guilty about Juliyanna back in Moscow.' It was then, that he uttered, what was to become our family motto, 'No one said it was going to be easy!'

That night was our final one on the train before reaching Irkutsk, at 9 p.m. the following evening, where we had three night's accommodation booked at the Angara Hotel, located in the city centre. I had already realised that, unsurprisingly, not everyone in the group had the same sense of humour, so communal joke telling had been replaced by the ever popular quiz night. With a bottle of Azerbaijani cognac as the prize, yes, I did still have some left, play commenced after the evening meal, with the same team line ups from the previous week in Tbilisi. Again, it was Luisa's team that won and just for once, Elspeth said it was ok for Bruce and their son Jonathan, to stay up and have a taste of their winnings, probably because even she was beginning to tire of the joys of travelling on the *Trans-Siberian Express*. However, when a bit later, talk turned to setting up a poker game, they politely made their excuses and headed for bed. Of the others, the two Jacks, with their navy background, were up for it and as usual, Angela and Pauline were up for anything. Luisa said that she didn't know how to play but was happy to watch, while the rest, including Johann, possibly suspecting I was a bit of a hustler, said they were quite happy to take a "rain check". With Luisa sat close beside me and having pushed two tables together, to accommodate the six of us, the game of *Texas Hold'em* started. In truth, I'm no great shakes at poker, whist is my forte but at least I was able to explain the rules to Luisa, as the game progressed and it was nice to have her close to me and peering over my shoulder, to see which cards I was choosing. After an hour's play, we were the only ones left in the restaurant car and, with everyone about even, we decided to call it a night. The two Jacks headed off to their carriage, where no doubt their two wives were complaining about how ex-sailors never changed, while me, Luisa, Angela and Pauline went back to ours. Ever the party animal, Angela asked if we would like to join her and Pauline for a quick nightcap and we both readily agreed. True to form, a bottle of half-drunk cognac was sitting on the table in their compartment, which soon disappeared, accompanied by stories of sexual impropriety during the final days of the "Empire". It was already well past midnight when Luisa and I made our excuses and wished Angela and Pauline a heart-felt goodnight. They really were great company but during our conversation, I was sure that Luisa had started to play footsie with me under the compartment table and it looked like now might be a good moment to test the water, for a second time.

As we made our way down the corridor, towards our respective compartments, with Luisa in front, I suddenly reached out and wrapped my arms round her waist. Slowly she turned and this time I knew I wasn't going to be rebuffed. She was smiling and whispered, 'Are you really allowed to touch your clients?'

'Depends who they are,' I replied and kissed her on the lips. Suddenly, everything happened very quickly, as three days of pent-up sexual frustration were released. Realising both our compartments were "out of bounds" and still in a passionate embrace, I started to lead Luisa towards the exit door of the carriage, knowing that the space between our carriage and the next one, would be empty at this time of night. Here, in a scene reminiscent of when Phil Daniels seduces Lesley Ash, in a back alley in the film, *Quadrophenia*[51], we got to know each other intimately. With the railway couplings moving around under our feet and the natural swaying of the train, it was a bit of a struggle to gain purchase but in the end I was successful and, at least for Luisa, the earth literally moved! Returning to our carriage, I gave Luisa one final kiss and whispered, '*nos da*,' (the Welsh for 'goodnight,') and crept into my compartment, hoping not to wake

---

51 British film from 1979 about mods and rockers in the sixties.

Johann. I needn't have bothered, as he was sitting up in his bunk with the light on, reading his third detective novel of the journey. 'I wondered how long it would take you,' he said, with a slight smirk on his face.

'What do you mean?' I replied, but I knew the game was up. 'I'd be grateful if you could keep it to yourself.'

'Of course,' he said and went back to his book.

Although I had slept with a number of clients while tour directing in Europe, I knew it was rather frowned upon in the industry and so I'd always been very discreet. Clearly, over the next few days, I was going to have to be very careful, especially as I didn't want to look like a "love rat" in front of the group, with Juliyanna waiting for me back in Moscow.

26

Dangerous Liaisons

The next day, the fourth on the train, always seemed to drag the most and this time it was even worse. I couldn't help but think about being alone with Luisa again, but this time, in the more comfortable confines of a hotel bedroom. However, even I couldn't make the *Trans-Siberian Express* go any faster and so, it was with some relief, when we pulled into Irkustk station, at the scheduled time of 9 p.m.. After a short transfer to the Angara Hotel, everyone headed straight to their bedrooms, desperate for a shower and a good night's sleep, for the first time in four days. I had already arranged with Luisa to come to her room, adjacent to mine, at 11 p.m. and having checked that the coast was clear, gently tapped on her door. There was a slight delay and for a moment I feared that she might be having second thoughts but then sure enough, the door swung slowly open and there she was, dressed only in a simple cream-coloured nightdress and beckoning me to come in. It was nearly six o'clock, when I literally crawled back to my room, in the hope of getting a couple of hours sleep before breakfast. I had already slept with a few Catholic girls and it did seem that the innate guilt they felt about pre-marital sex, made them better lovers, when they finally let themselves go.

For the morning's city tour, I was pleased to see that our local guide for the next couple of days, was going to be Olga. In fact, it always seemed to be Olga, when I was in Irkutsk. She was a serial networker and desperate to "escape" to the West. She had already asked me to buy some designer swimwear for her that she had shown me, in a copy of *Vogue*, on my previous visit, so I

160

went back to my room and returned with the costume wrapped up in a *Monsoon* bag my sister had given me. Just as I was handing over the bag, Luisa appeared in the hotel lobby and I suddenly thought, *'maybe this didn't look too good.'* Thinking it better to be up-front, I therefore called her over and introduced her to Olga, explaining that Olga would be paying me $50 for the costume, as it was impossible to get anything similar in Irkutsk. Now Olga was an attractive looking blonde in her mid-twenties but there was nothing going on between us, as I was definitely not the kind of husband she was looking for, to aid her passage to the West, far too poor. Rather predictably, a couple of years later, she ended up marrying a middle-aged, millionaire Irish beef producer and as far as I know, to this day, she continues to enjoy the life of a Dublin society lady. At the time, I'm not sure that Luisa was totally convinced about the $50 price tag, maybe she thought I would be looking for "payment in kind", but when Olga took her purse out of her handbag and counted out five ten-dollar bills, she seemed to relax, saying to Olga that she had a similar costume, back home in London.

After the hustle and bustle of Moscow and the ennui of the *Trans-Siberian*, I always enjoyed my time in Irkutsk. To begin with, there were no ways to make any extra money, as cultural events were few and far between, so I could simply relax and enjoy the scenery. With hindsight, I'm not sure where Olga got the money for designer swimwear from but at the time I didn't like to ask. Following the rather underwhelming city tour, no fault of Olga's, there really isn't much to see (the main reason for coming to Irkutsk, is to visit Lake Baikal, located about 50 miles away) we had a free afternoon, to get some much-needed fresh air, after four days cooped up on the train. I decided to take Luisa to the main department store in the city, *GUM*[52], where, although the

---

52 State Department Store.

choice was limited, prices were incredibly cheap. The previous year for the princely sum of 20 roubles (£2) I had managed to buy a perfectly acceptable black, full-length, winter overcoat, which meant that even in temperatures as low as -36 °C, I was never cold. I still wear that coat over a suit on winter nights out in Leeds, bragging that I bought it for less than the price of a coffee at Starbucks.

As we were leaving the hotel, we bumped into Holly and Simon, who were keen to join us on our "shopping trip". Once again, I was reminded that I was meant to be working, not romancing and that there would be no holding hands on this afternoon stroll. Luckily, *GUM* turned out to be something of a surprise hit with the girls, as there was a section devoted to lacquer boxes, which were equal to the ones found on Arbat Street but at half the price. While Simon and I loitered in the background, trying not to look too bored, Holly and Luisa engaged in a seemingly endless discussion about which boxes were the most beautiful, occasionally asking for a bit of male input, which elicited the usual response of, 'I don't know.' At least when it came to purchasing the four winners in the "Lacquer Box Beauty Contest", it was very straightforward, as unlike on Arbat Street, there was no haggling to be done. In this far flung corner of Russia, you simply paid the price on the ticket. Holly seemed particularly pleased with the bargains she had secured and maybe, as a reward for Simon's patience, she said they were going to head back to the hotel, for a pre-dinner nap, which I took to be a euphemism for a bit of *"Afternoon Delight"*, as per the song by the *Starland Vocal Band*[53].

With "Afternoon Delight" definitely too risky for me and Luisa and not over laden with souvenir purchases, lacquer boxes are incredibly light, I suggested we take a walk along the banks of the River Angara, which flows through the western part of the

---

53 Released in 1976.

city. The weather was unseasonably warm and we were one of a number of couples enjoying the late-afternoon sunshine. Suddenly, I became aware that we were being followed by a young man, dressed in a rather shabby, grey raincoat. Thinking this a bit strange, he certainly didn't look like KGB, I slowed down to see if he would walk past us. He, however, slowed too and then stooped down as if to tie his shoelaces, in the process managing to avoid my quizzical gaze. Determined to find out what he was after, I called out in Russian, 'Can I help you?' only to be surprised when he replied in perfect English, 'My name is Kolya, I just want to talk.' It transpired he had indeed been following us for the past half an hour, having overheard our discussion in *GUM* about the varying merits of lacquer box design. Since then, he had been trying to summon up the courage to speak with us, as he had just started studying English at Irkutsk State University but had never had the opportunity to converse with native speakers. Although his English was excellent, Kolya was very timid and he kept on doubting himself, often asking if his pronunciation was correct. He came from the town of Lensk, 700 miles north-east of Irkutsk and this was his first time away from home. Clearly, he was lonely and struggling to adapt to life, in what, for him, was the big city. Wearing thick rimmed glasses and with a mop of unkempt hair, he was the classic, classroom geek and I couldn't help feeling sorry for him. I was sure Luisa felt the same and so, with time moving on, I took a fifty rouble note from my wallet and said he was to get himself a new raincoat from *GUM*, as well as some decent boots for the harsh winter that lay ahead. To me, fifty roubles was small change but for Kolya, it was probably the equivalent of one month's student grant. At first he refused to take the money, saying it was far too much but I insisted, saying I too had been a language student and knew how difficult it was to survive on a grant, not entirely true. As we parted ways, Kolya said, 'I hope to see you in London one day.'

'Of course,' I replied, but unlike Olga, I suspected he was destined to spend his days stuck in the Siberian wilderness.

The next morning, after another night of passion with Luisa, keeping our relationship secret seemed to add to the excitement, we set off on the one-hour coach journey to Lake Baikal. One fifth of all the world's fresh water is in Baikal and in some places, it is over a mile deep. At 25 million years old, it is a one-off, geographic phenomenon, with over 1,000 living species, unique to its waters, including the *golomyanka*, a long-finned, translucent fish, that always appeared on the menu at the lakeside restaurant, where all Intourist groups ate. Personally, I thought it tasted horrible but there certainly was novelty value in eating a fish, through which you could see the plate underneath.

Arriving at the side of the lake and with the previous day's fine weather continuing, a few of the group were keen to take a dip and thus be able to say that they had swum in the world's largest lake. I, however, was less keen, knowing that the imperious snow-capped mountains that surrounded us, were an indication that the waters would be like the glacial lakes I had encountered during my time in the Alps, i.e., absolutely freezing. Despite my warnings, both Simon and Jonathan were determined to dive in and in anticipation, had already put swimming trunks on under their jeans, before leaving the hotel. Luisa, however, was going to follow my advice, having already experienced the "joys" of the traditional Boxing Day morning swim, in her home town of Eastbourne, when it had taken her the whole of the rest of the day to thaw out. I think the screams that both Simon and Jonathan emitted, as they hit the water, could have been heard back in Irkutsk and theirs must have been the shortest dip ever recorded.

After lunch, as per the normal itinerary, we were joined by a local guide, Sasha, who was there to lead us on a scenic walk through the forest and up into the foothills of the surrounding mountains. The allotted time was two hours and I did have to advise the group, that in some places, the going was a bit tough. It was usual for some of my group to opt out and this time a mother and daughter from Birmingham, called Diane and Shelley, decided they would prefer a leisurely stroll along the lakeside. Arranging to meet with them back at the restaurant in a couple of hours, we set off, with Sasha in the lead. I've always loved being in the mountains and with Sasha explaining all about the unique fauna and flora of Baikal, the time just flew by. At precisely four o'clock, we were back at the restaurant but of slight concern was the fact that Diane and Shelley were nowhere to be seen. By half past four and still with no sign, Sasha, Olga and I headed off in three different directions, while the rest of the group stayed at the restaurant drinking tea and coffee on the veranda. After three years tour directing, this was the first time I'd ever lost anyone and this included leading groups of fifty Americans through the London Underground. I simply couldn't understand where they could have gone. By five o'clock, I was really worried. I could already see the newspaper headlines "Birmingham mother and daughter lost in Siberia; tour director held responsible". Returning to the restaurant to meet up with Sasha and Olga, I decided the best course of action was for Olga to return to Irkutsk with the group, while me and Sasha continued searching. Just as the last person was boarding the coach, a car sped into the restaurant car park and out from the rear seats stepped Diane and Shelley, both looking a bit sheepish. It transpired that rather than stick to the shoreline they had decided to wander into the forest and had become a bit disorientated. On regaining the road, they had asked a local man, in their strong Brummie accent, 'Where is the *pektopah*?' thinking they were asking for the location of the restaurant. What they had failed to realise, was they should have said, '*restoran*,' (*pectopah* in Cyrillic!) and utterly confused, he had sent them in totally the wrong direction. After a couple of miles, it had become apparent, even to them, that they had made a huge mistake and, at least had the good sense, to flag down a passing car. Although the driver didn't speak any English, he did know that the only place in the vicinity, where westerners hung out, was at the lakeside restaurant and being a good Samaritan he had brought them back. Thanking him profusely and stuffing a couple of packets of *Marlboro Red* into his hands, I signalled goodbye to Sasha and re-joined the group on the coach. As we pulled away, I resolved to add *restoran* to the small vocabulary of, *privet* (hi) *do svidaniya* (goodbye) and *spasibo* (thank you) that I supplied to all my groups.

That night it was great to curl up in bed with Luisa and to relieve the stresses of the day! Now that we were getting along so well, I thought it was time to ask her why she had snapped at me in Tbilisi. In response, she said that she sometimes experienced quite severe PMT[54] and that she was just having a bad day. Quietly pleased with her answer, my thoughts turned to the next day and our flight to Moscow and then suddenly, I didn't feel so smug. What was I going to do about Juliyanna and our pre-arranged meeting at the circus?

Given that Irkutsk is five hours ahead of Moscow, we had a morning flight booked, which would mean an early afternoon arrival in the capital and therefore, plenty of time to have a meal, before heading off to the circus. Unlike the previous days, when the temperature had been in the mid-twenties, the weather had changed dramatically, with low-lying cloud and persistent rain. Having flown hundreds of times in my life, I almost had a sixth sense on arrival at an airport, if something was wrong and as we entered the departure hall, I immediately knew there was going to be a problem. All the phone booths to the right of the hall were

---

54 Premenstrual Tension.

occupied and each had a small orderly queue of people beside it, waiting their turn. Glancing up at the departure board, I could see that all five flights, scheduled before midday, including our own had, *zaderzhki* (delay) alongside them. We were clearly going to be in for a long wait. Yelyena went off to try and get some extra information and returned with the news, that there were violent thunderstorms over central-eastern Russia and planes were being diverted or not even allowed to take off. Our flight was due to refuel in Novosibirsk, so flying at the moment was apparently out of the question. 'Why can't we refuel in Omsk?' (400 miles further west) I asked. On previous flights, despite the fact we were meant to land at Novosibirsk, we had often ended up in Omsk (I often wondered what happened to the passengers for whom Novosibirsk was the final destination. It would have been a long bus ride back from Omsk!).

'No better,', replied Yelyena and using one of her favourite English idioms, said, 'You're just going to have to grin and bear it.'

Now they say "Every cloud has a silver lining" and for once, the expression couldn't have been more appropriate, for although I was going to lose around $250 on the missed circus performance, at least I now had a valid reason for not meeting up with Juliyanna. By this time, it was eleven o'clock and I realised, that if I called now, given the time difference, I would be able to catch her before she left for work. Luckily, Yelyena knew one of the girls in the *Aeroflot* office and so I didn't have to use one of the public phones, which were notoriously unreliable and where long queues had now formed. Amazingly, I got through first time to be answered by the slightly groggy voice of Juliyanna's father. 'What do you want?' he asked rather gruffly. I knew he didn't approve of our relationship, thinking, probably correctly, that it was doomed to failure. 'Is Juliyanna there?' I asked.

'Of course she is,' he replied and not wishing to continue the conversation any longer than was needed, went off to find her. Relieved to have got hold of her, we had a relatively short conversation where, given that she was working the next day as well, it was agreed that we would meet up again the next time I was in Moscow, which would be in two weeks. Just as I was about to put the phone down, Juliyanna asked, 'How was the train journey, anything exciting happen?' Grateful that she couldn't see my lying eyes, I simply said, 'Nothing out of the ordinary,' and ended the call, before my guilty conscience became too much.

It was eight in the evening, before the news came through that we would be flying and a further hour, before we took off. We had almost been at the point of returning to the Angara, for an extra night in Irkutsk but this would have meant missing our return flight to Heathrow, the next day, so it was with some relief, that we touched down at Domodedovo Airport, almost twelve hours behind schedule and yes, we did stop at Omsk!

It was approaching midnight when we finally checked in at the Hotel Cosmos, with me taking my usual room on the 20th floor and Luisa joining me, for what might be our final night together. I had enough experience of "holiday romances" to know that the vast majority never lasted and with me being constantly on the road, I thought our chances were slim at best.

The next day, following the habitually under-whelming tour of the Park of Economic Achievement (VDNKh) we made our way out to Sheremetyevo 2, for our flight back to the UK. Luckily, Juliyanna was no longer working in the duty-free shop. Tired of the long commute and with better prospects, she had got herself a job as a translator, in the recently opened *CNN* office, in the centre of Moscow. This was one of the reasons why she was so up-to-date with what was going on in the city.

Once through customs, most of the group met up in the Irish Bar for a final, communal drink. With the *Guinness* flowing readily, people started to re-live their own personal highlights of the past three weeks. Luisa, obviously choosing to be discreet, remained quiet. As usual, Angela was the most vocal and she seemed to have conquered her fear of flying, stating that, 'If you can fly on *Aeroflot,* then you can fly on anything.' It was a fairly well-oiled group of travellers, who boarded the *BA Boeing 757* flight to London and given that the plane was only a third full, we were able to sit where we liked and to carry on our farewell party mid-air. At the time, all drinks on *BA* scheduled flights, were complimentary and even though the air hostesses were often snooty, given that we weren't in Business Class, the drinks just kept on coming. With me finally "off duty", encouraged by the relaxed atmosphere and thinking no one was looking, I gently stroked Luisa's knee under the plane seat table, only to get a knowing look from Pauline, sitting across the aisle, who had clearly twigged long before what was going on.

Once through passport control at Heathrow and while waiting in baggage reclaim, I put a call through to Lyn, to check it was still ok to stay a couple of nights, before I next flew out to Russia. She had recently got married to an English guy called Andy and they had bought a flat in Wood Green, north London. Unfortunately, she had some bad news, as her mother had unexpectedly come down from Leeds and she was going to be staying over the weekend. I did have a back-up plan, which involved staying with one of my mum's old friends, Margaret, in Winchmore Hill, but I felt on the last occasion, I'd maybe over-stayed my welcome and so was keen not to over-impose. With the luggage from our flight starting to appear on the carousel, I returned to where I had left Luisa and was surprised to find she wasn't there. For a moment I thought she might simply of grabbed her luggage and in the old parlance, "Done a runner". But then I spotted her distinctive pale blue suitcase coming towards me and a couple of seconds later, she was standing alongside me. It turned out she too had been making a phone call, in her case, to her boss at the London Clinic, to check what time she was due into work the following morning. To her surprise, according to the staff rota, she wasn't due back until Monday and with it now being only Thursday evening, she had therefore, decided to head down to Eastbourne for a long weekend, to see her parents. With a note of hesitancy in my voice, I asked if there was any chance of me coming along, as at this point I didn't have a bed for the night. With a wry smile on her lips she said that would be ok but I would have to sleep on the floor and I could only stay a couple of nights. To be honest, I would have been happy to sleep on the beach if it had meant another night together, so straightaway I agreed. She said she would just have to confirm it with her mother and went off to make the call, while I loaded our luggage on to a trolley.

27
The "Costa Geriatrica"

At the time, before the Heathrow Express existed[55], the quickest way to get to Eastbourne by public transport, was to take the coach link to Gatwick Airport via the M25 and M23 and then catch a *Southern Line* train, down to the coast. We were lucky with our timings and by eight o'clock that evening, we were standing outside the door of Luisa's mother's house. It was Judy who opened the door to us and having given Luisa a big hug, she turned to me and smiling said, 'I know I asked you to take care of my daughter, but I never thought you would take it so literally!' Entering the hallway, I instantly became aware of noisy chatter coming from the dining room to my left. I did remember that Luisa had said something about foreign-language students but it hadn't really registered. Now the evidence was before my eyes. Judy was "hosting" five international students, ranging in age from nineteen to twenty-eight and from countries as diverse as Indonesia, Japan and Saudi Arabia. It was like walking into a session of the United Nations and explained why I would be sleeping on the floor. Luisa's parents had split up when she was eighteen and since then, Judy's main source of income had been from hosting foreign-language students. With a good business head on her, she had maximised the amount of rentable space and had converted the downstairs living room, into a bedroom for herself. It was in this room that Luisa stayed, when she was down from London for the weekend, sharing her mum's double bed.

---

55 Opened 1999.

While the students were finishing their evening meal, we went through to the kitchen, at the back of the house, where Judy had prepared some sandwiches for us. Sitting at the table and just about to go out clubbing, was Luisa's much younger sister, Monica and her Nepalese friend, Sue. I was starting to wonder how long the queue for the bathroom was going to be in the morning, as apparently, Sue often stayed the night in Monica's room, if they were late back from *Cloisters*, the most popular night club in town. By my reckoning, there were going to be ten of us in total and this normal-sized Eastbourne terrace house, was definitely no *Tardis*[56].

However, things started to quieten down after 9 p.m., as not only were Monica and Sue going clubbing but also all the students. It was free entry to *Cloisters* on a Thursday night and so this had become something of a ritual. Given that Luisa and I had been in eastern Siberia only two days earlier, we were both now starting to experience the inevitable jet lag and with the dining room now free, Judy offered to make up my "bed" for the night. This was a fairly simple process, as it involved putting three large settee cushions on the carpeted, dining-room floor and throwing a sheet and blanket over the top. Sensing that Luisa and I could do with a little time on our own, Judy said she was going to do some reading in her bedroom and that she would see Luisa later and me in the morning.

I can't say my first night in Eastbourne was the most comfortable one I've ever experienced. Luisa stayed with me for about an hour, as evidenced by the carpet burns I found on my knees, the next morning and I was woken at about 2 a.m., when all the students piled home from *Cloisters*. Fortunately, there was a lock on the inside of the dining room door, which meant Luisa and I had not

---

56 The time machine and spacecraft that appears in the British Sci-Fi TV series *Dr Who,* which was larger on the inside than outside.

had to worry about being disturbed, while "rolling around" on the floor and which now meant I wasn't going to be trampled underfoot, by a horde of inebriated foreigners, in search of a bit of late night TV.

The next morning, Luisa brought me tea in "bed" and told me I needed to get up sharpish, as her father was coming round to see her. Anxious to make a good impression, I went upstairs to join the bathroom queue that was already forming, had a shower and returned downstairs to get changed in my "bedroom" only to find Luisa's father, Marcello, standing outside the dining room door. They say that, "You never get a second chance to make a first impression," and with only a small towel wrapped around my waist and still dripping with water, I must admit, this was not the way I had envisioned meeting the man, who ultimately, was to become my father-in-law. However, Marcello didn't seem particularly interested in me, he was more concerned about the searing pain he was experiencing from an abscess on one of his back teeth and was in fact, on his way to an emergency appointment with his dentist. Having myself endured similar pain a few years earlier, at least I could say from day one, that we had something in common, other than Luisa.

Once dressed and having had breakfast in the kitchen, Luisa took me for a walk along the Eastbourne seafront, pointing out the spot close to the bandstand where she had braved the freezing waters of the English Channel, on Boxing Day, the previous year. As we walked past the famous *Carpet Gardens*[57], I couldn't help but notice how many elderly people were about and suddenly, I remembered the old joke about there being a sign outside the town, with the words, "Left for the Continent, Eastbourne for the Incontinent!" That evening, Luisa and I joined Judy and some of her friends for "party night" at *Cloisters*. Luckily, one

---

57 The centrepiece of Eastbourne's Promenade.

of these friends, Stella, was an enthusiastic dancer, so at least I had someone to dance with, as Luisa was distinctly apprehensive about joining me on the floor, other than for a slow smooch at the evening's end.

The next day, Judy drove us out for a pub lunch in Alfriston, a small village, in the heart of the Sussex Downs. On the way, we passed the towering cliffs of the Seven Sisters, including Beachy Head, where Phil Daniels rode his motorbike into the sea, at the end of *Quadrophenia*. Although totally different from the rugged beauty of Snowdonia and the Yorkshire Dales, I couldn't help but be impressed by the sweeping vistas of rolling hills and surging waves that appeared through the passenger window of Judy's aged *Citroen 2cv*.

After a pleasant lunch at The George Inn, it was time to head back to the house, for me to pick up my things, before taking the short walk to the station, as I was heading back to Heathrow, to spend the night in a hotel, before my morning flight to St Petersburg the next day. Although the accommodation had been a bit basic, I had received a really warm welcome from everyone I had met and Judy was a great cook, having lived in Italy as a young mother. On the walk to the station, I could sense that Luisa was a bit tense and so to lighten the mood, I decided to play another trick on her. Putting my case down, I took her by the hand and gazed into her eyes and in my most serious voice said, 'I've got something to tell you that's been bothering me for some time.'

'What is it?' she asked, her bottom lip starting to quiver slightly. Feigning a bit of a stutter I replied, 'I'm bi... I'm bi...,'

'Tell me,' she interjected, 'I'll understand.'

Finally, I said, 'I'm bilingual!' and started to laugh, knowing that just like at the pool in Tbilisi, I'd got her.

'You bastard,' she said, but her eyes were smiling, 'I really thought after I saw you dancing with Eddy and your obsession with sunbathing, that you might be bisexual but I was waiting for you to tell me.'

'If you come from Yorkshire, you're not allowed to be bisexual,' I said and taking her in my arms, gave her a deep kiss on the lips.

Being in no hurry to get to Heathrow and wishing to save a bit of money (the coach transfer between Gatwick and Heathrow was quite expensive) I took the train to London Victoria and then got the underground District Line, to south Kensington, where I changed onto the Piccadilly Line, for the journey out to the airport. With time to kill and some romantic music on my *Walkman*, my thoughts constantly returned to Luisa and what would happen next. We had parted on good terms, promising to meet up when I was next in London, but there was a problem. At the time, she was living in a shared flat near Royal Oak Tube Station, in the western part of the city. The rent was incredibly cheap but the reason for this, was that it was owned by a Christian housing association and therefore, females only, with no boyfriends allowed overnight. The two girls she was living with were following the rules "religiously" and Luisa had already said she would be uncomfortable rocking the boat. This to me, seemed a real shame, as Royal Oak is on the Circle Line with quick access to the Piccadilly Line at Hammersmith and therefore, an easy journey out to Heathrow. Deciding that after three weeks' separation, Luisa might be more prepared to push the boundaries, I had left the question of where I would be staying on my return, hanging in the air, simply saying I would sort something out. Of course, there was the strong possibility that during my absence, Luisa would decide that the idea of sitting around for weeks on end, waiting for me to show up, wasn't all that appealing and I hadn't, as yet, made any promises, regarding Juliyanna.

28

No Sex Before Marriage!

During my three weeks away, I managed to call at least four or five times. International pay phones had started to appear in hotel lobbies and a $24 phone card would get you four minutes of chat. It seems incredible to think that now, for a similar amount of money, you can have a month's limitless call time but in some ways, I preferred to keep the conversations short, as I didn't really want to go into too much detail about what I was up to. Somewhat inevitably, I was continuing to see Juliyanna, "hedging my bets" against a possible let down from Luisa.

A day before I was due to return to the UK, I phoned to check the "lie of the land" and was genuinely touched when Luisa said she was going to come out to Heathrow to meet me. No mention was made of sleeping arrangements but things seemed to be looking good. As usual, my *BA* flight from Moscow, landed back in the UK late afternoon and for the first time in many years, there was someone waiting for me at the airport, Luisa having finished work a couple of hours early, so as to be there. I'd had a very lucrative three weeks away and so splashed out on a taxi ride into town, so as to avoid the joys of the Piccadilly Line, with its countless stops, including my least favourites: Hounslow West, Hounslow Central and Hounslow East, which made it seem like you were going nowhere. It was already seven o'clock when the taxi pulled up outside a large, three storey, detached house in Notting Hill where Luisa was living on the first floor, with her two flatmates, Sandy and Helena. Luisa was good friends with Helena, as they had trained together at UCH[58] and it was through her, that she had found the flat. Helena meanwhile, had met Sandy while attending services at a local evangelical church, of which Sandy was a leading member and thus, with contacts in the Christian housing association, which had led to her securing the flat. During the taxi ride, Luisa had told me that it was Sandy who was keen on enforcing the "no boyfriend overnight" rule, while Helena wasn't really bothered. Meeting Sandy confirmed all my worst fears. She was very plain and way too serious for someone who was still in their mid-twenties. Apparently, she did have a boyfriend, which slightly amazed me and they were planning to get married the next year. However, sex before marriage, was definitely out of the question.

With Helena's support, Luisa had managed to get Sandy to agree to me staying the night, on the lounge sofa but had required assurances that there would be no "hanky panky". She even asked me to abide by the house rules and reluctantly, I agreed. I felt I was being addressed by a paranoid teacher, on some school trip from years ago and was only too keen to be on our way to the restaurant Luisa had booked, for our evening meal. We ate at Surinder's, a restaurant close to where Luisa worked at the London Clinic and one that would become our favourite, over the years to come. Returning late to the flat, I was pleased to see that Sandy and Helena had already gone to bed and that their lights were out. Luisa and I had already been getting quite intimate in the hallway outside the flat door and so, I guess it was natural that we progressed straight to her bedroom. To begin with, Luisa tried to stick to the house rules but in the end she succumbed to my charms, although for obvious reasons, she was a bit quieter than normal.

---

58 University College Hospital, London.

The next morning having spent the rest of the night on the pre-ordained sofa, I decided I was tired of skulking around in the dark and not sleeping in a proper bed. It being Friday and with me flying back out to Russia the following day, Luisa had already taken the day off work, so I suggested that following a day in London, we spend the night together, out at my Heathrow hotel and she readily agreed. Sandy in particular seemed pleased when we told her I wouldn't be staying another night, while of course, omitting to tell her of our plan of sharing a comfortable hotel bed, out at Heathrow. Luisa simply said she was going down to Eastbourne for the weekend.

Luisa had already been living in London for nearly ten years and so she knew how to get the most out of the city. We had lunch at the Grosvenor Hotel, near Victoria Station, which allowed me to leave my suitcase all afternoon with the hotel porter, while we went for a walk along the South Bank, followed by a visit to the Victoria and Albert museum, to see an exhibition of works by William Morris. Around 6 p.m. we caught the tube out to Heathrow, had a leisurely meal in the hotel restaurant and then retired for an early night. For the first time, we didn't have to worry about being caught together in the corridor or overheard by someone in the adjacent room and so it was a tired but very contented tour director, who stood at check-in 72 the next morning, ready to hand out visas.

The following day, I called Luisa, who was indeed in Eastbourne, from the lobby of the Hotel Prebaltiskaya, in St Petersburg. From the tone in her voice, I immediately sensed something was wrong. It turned out, that a suspicious Sandy had carried out an inspection of Luisa's bedroom, on her return from work on the Friday evening and, had somehow, come across a condom wrapper under one of the pillows. She had subsequently phoned the house in Eastbourne, only to be told that Luisa wasn't coming down until the following morning. Putting two and two together and unfortunately making four, Sandy had decided that Luisa's time in the flat was up and was going to invoke the clause in the tenancy agreement, which outlawed any form of co-habitation. Luisa had literally just had a phone call from Sandy to this effect and was obviously concerned about where she was going to live. I couldn't believe how Sandy could act in such a pious and devious way. What gave her the right to rifle through Luisa's bed linen? Were we living in some kind of theocracy? At the same time, I did feel a bit guilty about putting Luisa in a difficult position. I could easily have paid for a night in a London hotel, but it was early days in our relationship and I didn't want to appear as though I was taking things for granted. At least by the end of our conversation, Luisa was starting to sound a bit more positive, saying she had found being with Sandy a bit of a trial and that it was time to move on. By the time I was next back in London, she was living in a terrace house in Worcester Park, owned by one of her work colleagues, Gill and, although it was a longer commute, at least we didn't have to worry about the "thought police" anymore. Interestingly, we later heard through Helena, that Sandy's wedding, planned for the next year, had been cancelled as her "supposed boyfriend" was actually a conman, who had done a runner, having been loaned £10,000 by Sandy's mother, for some fictitious business venture. As I thought at the time, "What goes around comes around!"

29

A Change of Rules

As the Soviet Union collapsed around me, my tours became increasingly confined to Moscow and St Petersburg, with the occasional trip to Kyiv. In some respects this suited me, as I was away for shorter periods of time, which meant I got to see Luisa more regularly. As long as she was pre-warned, Gill was happy for me to stay in Luisa's large, south-facing bedroom, which, most importantly, had a king size bed. We even came to an agreement, whereby if I stayed for more than one night, then I would pay £20 for each subsequent night.

By the summer of 1992, I had been working for over three years as a tour director in Russia and had established a reputation for running successful trips. My client satisfaction ratings, gleaned from the CSQs[59], filled in by all my groups, were in the low nineties and despite there being fewer tourists, due to the economic downturn, we were experiencing at the time, I still had plenty of work. I was therefore, a little surprised when one morning I got a call in my hotel room at the Cosmos, from Lara Karlina, asking me to come into the Intourist office, as there was a bit of a problem. During the taxi ride into town, I struggled to think what the problem might be. Any complaint from a client would have come through my own company, so I thought it must be something administrative and so it proved.

As usual, Lara was all smiles as I entered her first-floor office. She was sitting at her desk, located by a window, through which there was a great view of the Kremlin walls and you really had the

---

59 Customer Service Questionnaires.

sense you were close to the centre of power. To begin with we just engaged in some small talk about family and mutual friends but pretty soon the purpose of the meeting became clear. In the new Russia emerging under Boris Yeltsin, companies like Intourist were expected to make a profit and Lara for the first time ever, was being asked by her bosses to maximise income. Traditionally, in the travel industry, the best way to make money is to sell optionals, however, of all the thousands of people who had been on my tours, not a single person had ever officially been on one. In contrast, *Thomson Holidays*[60] clients, readily bought optional excursions and they also bought tickets for the *Bolshoi* and *Kirov,* through Intourist. I said something about my clients being much more independently minded, which had a grain of truth to it, but I realised I'd been flying under the radar for too long and that it was time for a bit of "negotiation". It was approaching midday and so I suggested to Lara that we go for lunch, obviously on me, at the Spanish Bar, which was only a five-minute walk away. She agreed and while she went to get her coat, I mulled over my tactics. I did know that Lara was having an affair with the head of the Intourist office in London but he was ex-KGB and, in any case, I thought it would be a bit hypocritical on my part to play that card. Instead, I decided, as in all negotiations, it would be best to wait and see what Lara wanted rather than immediately make concessions.

After ordering tapas and a bottle of Rioja, the conversation turned to the large group of tourists (200 in number) that was arriving the following week. They were all members of the *Women's Institute*, the seven-day holiday, having been sold through the organisation's in-house magazine. Due to the size of the group, they were flying out on a *Thomson* charter plane, accompanied by an old friend of mine, Tom, who had, until recently, been working as a translator for the *CNN* office in Moscow, where Juliyanna now worked. I was

---

60 Original incarnation of TUI.

looking forward to welcoming the group, as although it was going to be a logistical nightmare, involving four coaches at a time and four different Intourist guides, the money-making possibilities were virtually limitless. I always gave the guides I worked with, a cut on any "Geri optional" they led themselves but ballet and opera tickets, were my preserve. It appeared that this was going to have to change. To make her figures look better, Lara wanted two optionals on the tour to be "official", namely the Armoury Museum in the Kremlin, which contained a collection of *Faberge* eggs and the visit to Petrodvorets Palace, on the outskirts of St Petersburg. In addition, I was to give a cut of the profits from any theatre ticket sales to Anna, who was going to be the lead Intourist guide throughout the whole seven-day tour. Now, I knew and liked Anna, having already worked with her a few times before but it was crystal clear, that on this occasion, she would be representing the personal interests of Lara, during our time together. I quickly did some calculations in my head and realised what Lara was proposing, was actually quite reasonable. It was always a struggle to get cheap tickets for the Armoury and two hundred would be virtually impossible. In addition, Petrodvorets had only recently re-opened, after a two-year restoration project and as yet, I hadn't run it as a "Geri optional". Lara was too coy to talk about percentages on theatre tickets but I was sure that Anna would tell me!

The next week I took a taxi out to Sheremetyevo 2 and met up with the four Intourist guides in the coach park and distributed the large signs I had produced the previous evening, WI1, WI2, WI3 and WI4 and asked them to put them in the front window of their respective coaches. I was pleased to see that as well as Anna, one of my favourite Moscow guides, Galya, was going to be working with us. The other two, I knew by sight but that was it.

As the group were arriving on the *Thomson* charter flight, the head rep from *Thomson's* Moscow office, James, had come out to the airport, to pick up some passenger lists, as the fax machine in their office wasn't working. When I say office, this is somewhat misleading. All they had was a small suite on the top floor of the Intourist Hotel, where it was difficult to distinguish what was bedroom and what was office. In my early days of touring, some of the school groups I led, used to "piggy back" on *Thomson* flights and the day before departure, I used to have to go to the "office" to pick up the boarding cards. The place was always a complete tip, with empty vodka bottles on the floor, unwashed dinner plates in the bathroom sink and there was definitely something growing in the microwave. None of the three reps living in this chaotic environment spoke Russian and they merely carried out airport transfers, leaving the day-to-day running of tours to the Intourist guides. I often thought that being a *Thomson* rep, was like being in the army, never knowing where you were going to get posted. At the time, there was only one rep in St Petersburg, a girl called Sarah, occupying one room in the Hotel Pulkovskaya, close to the airport, on the south side of the city. It was her first position with the company, having previously worked at *Euro Disney*[61]. With few guests and not speaking Russian, she was desperately lonely and I had tried introducing her to English speaking friends of mine, without much success. She seemed to prefer the company of a bottle of *Stolichnaya*[62]! With passenger numbers falling, the days of the Moscow and St Petersburg offices were to be numbered. A surprise visit by head office a few months later, revealed how "native" the reps had gone and the whole operation was closed down with disciplinary notices being issued to the team. Strangely, one of them, Philippa, took this as the push she needed to leave the company and instead of returning to the UK, stayed in Moscow with her Russian boyfriend and started selling timeshares in the Canary Islands, to the locals.

---

61 Re-branded as Disneyland Paris in October 1994.
62 Popular Russian vodka.

At the time, I thought she was mad but when the following year I passed through the arrivals hall of Tenerife South airport, the first thing I spotted was a sign offering pesetas for roubles. Maybe she hadn't been so crazy after all?

Usually, when meeting groups at the airport, I had to keep my wits about me, as people came through in dribs and drabs, the only indication they were with me, being the red and orange luggage labels they had been advised to put on their cases before departure. However, on this occasion there was no missing my group. With the editor of *Home and Country*[63], in the lead, suddenly the whole of the arrivals hall was invaded by a sea of English matriarchs, many wearing the unofficial *WI* uniform, of twinsets and pearls. Bringing up the rear, I spotted Tom, who for some reason was chatting away to two young English guys. It turned out that they had been "bumped off a tour"[64] earlier in the year and for some reason, had been offered this one as an alternative. Well, they were certainly in for a fun time, their combined ages being somewhat less than any other member of the party.

Once on my designated coach WI1, I took the microphone and introduced myself, explaining how I would be co-ordinating the tour. As usual, I went through a few basic Russians words for people to use including the word *nyet*, which then led me to tell my favourite joke, which I thought would be appreciated by this group in particular, given the age range. Throughout much of the post-war Soviet period the foreign minister had been Andrei Gromyko, who came to be known in the West as *"Mr Nyet"*, as the USSR was always saying, 'No,' in UN Security Council meetings. This led people to believe that he didn't have a sense of humour.

---

63 The in-house magazine of the Women's Institute.
64 Occurs when tours don't attract enough clients to be commercially viable and are cancelled.

However, as the story goes, he was once asked if it had been Nikita Krushchev, who had been assassinated in 1963, rather than John F Kennedy, then would it have made a major difference to subsequent world events? After a few moments deliberation, Gromyko apparently said he didn't think it would have made much difference but Aristotle Onassis, would definitely not have married Mrs Krushchev! True to form, the joke got a good laugh, although the two young English guys looked a bit perplexed.

On the transfer down to the Cosmos, I sat next to Lucinda, the magazine editor, who I'd been instructed to liaise with and went through the programme for the upcoming days. The main piece of news I had to impart, was that given the size of the group, we had been unable to get enough berths on the overnight train to St Petersburg and so, we would be taking the day train. I said something about it being a great way of seeing the Russian countryside but in truth, I knew it was going to be nine hours of utter boredom, with little to see or do.

That evening after dinner, Tom and Anna came to my room to discuss how we were going to run things. Unlike me, Tom wasn't overly interested in the commercial side of tour directing. Until recently, he had been living with his wife Maria, an assistant producer for *CNN*, in a Moscow apartment and he was definitely more of a native than me. They had only returned to the UK as Maria had certain health issues, relating to having been in Kyiv when the Chernobyl disaster[65] occurred and they were now both working for a Russian company based in London. For him, this was more of a holiday and a chance to catch up with old friends. Already with a salary he said he wasn't interested in, taking any cut on excursions and tickets, the only thing he wanted was a night out in Moscow, followed by the requisite morning off the next day to get over the inevitable hangover. Agreeing to his

---

65 26th April, 1986.

limited demands, I turned to the question of the *Bolshoi* ballet, which was performing *Giselle* the following evening. I had already pre-booked tickets, but given the number of tickets involved I'd had to use a couple of new suppliers, in addition to my normal guy Misha. Recently the "street price" had been on the increase but I was still clearing $15 a head, while easily undercutting the inflated Intourist prices. Turning to Anna I said, with a knowing smile, 'I understand we have a new system in place regarding tickets?'

'That's right,' she said, 'We'd like a third of the profits,' (i.e., $1,000). Relieved that this wasn't going to be the usual joint venture, with a 50-50 split, I nodded my head and started to go through the list of "Geri Optionals" I was proposing for our stay in Moscow, the main one being a trip out to Zagorsk, the first stop on the Golden Ring.

With the Moscow programme agreed, Anna said she would see us in the morning and headed off home for the night, from where she would no doubt be phoning Lara to give her the good news. With a lot of catching up to do, Tom and I went down to the *Heineken* Bar. He was a few years older than me and had studied Russian at university, back in the seventies. Somehow, he had ended up working for the Soviet Union News Agency TASS in Prague, during the late eighties, which is where he had met Maria. I myself knew Maria, from my days working with the American schools' tour operator. She had studied Greek at university but incredibly, simply because the alphabet was similar to Russian, she had ended up leading tours to the Soviet Union and had quickly become a fluent speaker. I was interested to find out about the Russian company Tom and Maria were now working for in London, but for once, Tom was a bit vague, saying it mainly involved looking after visiting Russians and showing them the sights. *Not a bad job,* I thought, little knowing at the time, that a couple of years later, I would be finding out for myself that it wasn't as easy as it sounded.

For the next couple of days I took a back seat, leaving Tom to socialise with the clients on the various tours, while I stayed in the Cosmos, "banking" the money I collected, in various hiding places in my room. Thankfully, the evening at the *Bolshoi* passed off without incident, although the tickets from my two new suppliers, were not as good as the ones Misha got me, including two dress-circle box seats, which I gave to Lucinda as a goodwill gesture.

As per my programme, day four was given over to the optional trip out to Zagorsk, while on the official itinerary, we were meant to be visiting VDNKh (The Park of Economic Achievement). Liaising with Lucinda, I explained about the inadequacies of the VDNKh tour but it was decided to give the group a choice. In the end, about fifty people chose to learn about post-war Soviet tractor production. This meant I would need three coaches to run my own optional. Of the four drivers that had been with us since the beginning of the tour, two were due to be doing VDNKh and both readily agreed to change to my optional for $30 and a pack of *Marlboro Red*. Of the other two, one was my favourite driver, Valodya, who was quite happy to forego his day off, so I now had my three coaches. Anna however, said that if we waited till the morning, she would simply tell one of the new drivers that the itinerary had changed and that we were now going to Zagorsk, thereby saving us $30. Sensing that Anna was starting to get a bit greedy, I expressed my reservations but she said the two older Moscow guides I hadn't worked with before, were starting to complain that they weren't making enough money and $30 would help to keep them quiet. Against my better judgement, I agreed to go along with her and went off to find Valodya to tell him that he wouldn't be needed after all. Big mistake!

30

The WI Army

The next morning dawned bright and beautiful, perfect for a day out in the country. At breakfast, I told the group that coach WI1 would be going to VDNKh, while the other three would be going to Zagorsk. Arriving in the coach park to see the group off, I was slightly concerned to see a number of the ladies, as well as Dan and Steve, the two young guys who had been "parachuted" into the WI army, milling around one of the coaches that had a new driver. Through the front screen window, I could see Anna remonstrating with the driver, who I didn't recognise, although he had a distinctive mop of red hair. There was clearly a problem, so I jumped on board and asked Anna what was going on. 'He won't go to Zagorsk,' she said, 'because it's not on the itinerary.' Guessing that Anna had probably been a bit off-hand with him, a lot of female Intourist guides looked down on the drivers, I said, '*kurite*?' ('want a smoke?').

'*Ya ney kuryu*,' ('I don't smoke,') he replied abruptly. It was then that I started to get worried, as I had just noticed, that as well as red hair, he also had green eyes. Now I'm not overly superstitious but I did remember my father saying to me when I was a child, never to trust a man with this colour combination. It probably dated back to some anti-Irish sentiment, on my Welsh grandmother's side of the family. Regretting ever having listened to Anna, I asked him how much he wanted to make the trip out to Zagorsk, to which he simply replied, '*Ya nay idu*' ('I'm not going,'). I had to accept, that after three years in the country, I had met my first incorruptible Russian. Maybe he had a chip on his shoulder, having been bullied at school or maybe he was simply scared, whatever the reason, he had put me in a very difficult position. Coach WI1 had already left for VDNKh and the other two coaches were ready to leave for Zagorsk. Quickly, I did a head count which came to forty, myself included and with no sign of any other coaches "to hire", decided I was going to have to take the dreaded taxi option. As previously mentioned, I had a slightly difficult relationship with taxi drivers, as once they found out I was a westerner, they resented having agreed to me paying a local's fare. However, for once, the boot was on the other foot. Heading for the taxi rank, I knew I was going to need ten taxis and that it was going to cost. Just like everything else in and around the Cosmos, taxis were a mafia-run operation. As I approached, I spotted the guy in charge, lounging in a chair at the head of the rank, smoking a cigarette and soaking up the morning sunshine. 'How much to get to Zagorsk?' I asked.

'Depends who it's for,' he replied and I instantly knew he'd got me over a barrel. I was wearing my signature, mustard-coloured raincoat and he obviously knew who I was. In the negotiations that followed, my main aim was to at least break even on the day's events and although the taxis cost me $500 (i.e., $50 each) at least I didn't incur a loss. With the other two coaches already departed, I split the group up into fours and we set off for Zagorsk, in what must have resembled some form of presidential cavalcade. I was in the lead taxi, along with Dan, Steve and Lucinda, who, ever the journalist, was keen to find out what the two Essex boys thought about being the only males in a group of two hundred. Luckily, they said they were having a great time, spoilt rotten by all these women with no one else to lavish their maternal instincts on. That evening, Anna came to my room to finalise the accounts, for the Moscow section of the tour. Naturally, she was a bit sheepish about the day's events but I decided not to rub it in, simply saying that at least we'd all learnt an invaluable lesson, namely don't trust people with red hair and green eyes!!

As expected, the following day's rail journey proved a real drag. We left at 10 a.m. from Leningradski station and settled down for nine hours of boredom. There is really nothing to see between Moscow and St Petersburg, other than the occasional lake and lots and lots of trees. We didn't even have the traditional sanctuary of the restaurant car, as due to the size of the group, we had been given packed lunches, which we ate in our individual compartments. At least we arrived on time in St Petersburg and as I stepped onto the platform, my spirits lifted. I always felt at home in the city and I already knew we were going to be staying in my favourite accommodation, the Hotel Prebaltiskaya. Suddenly, a cry went up and looking down the train, I saw that one of the more elderly ladies in the group, had fallen while alighting from the train and had gashed her leg on the carriage steps. Given the current obsession with health and safety, it is difficult to believe I could be in charge of leading a group of two hundred people, having had no first aid training and even worse, with no first aid box. Where blood is concerned, I'm not that squeamish but this looked like a particularly nasty wound, which was going to require hospital treatment. For me, this was a bit of a worry, as my only previous experience of a Russian hospital, had been when visiting Juliyanna, after she had had her tonsils removed and let's just say, the levels of hygiene didn't exactly inspire confidence. The general consensus was that hospitals made you worse, not better. It was at this moment that the WI sprang into action.

Suddenly, all sorts of compresses, antiseptic sprays and bandages started to appear from peoples' cases. It seemed as though being a trained first aider, was a membership requirement of the *Women's' Institute*. In no time at all, the flow of blood had been brought under control and the leg expertly bandaged up. Amazingly, Anna had managed to get hold of a wheelchair from somewhere and as I pushed the lady, whose name was Gladys, down the platform, she gave a smile and a little wave to the crowd of concerned onlookers. Although she remained in her room the following day, tended to by her travelling companion Mildred, there was no need for a hospital visit and by the end of the week, as she herself described it, she was, 'as right as rain.'

After the unexpected drama of our arrival in St Petersburg, the rest of our time in the city passed off uneventfully. Following the Zagorsk debacle, normal money-making operations were restored with a performance of *Swan Lake* at the *Kirov*, a riverboat cruise on the Neva and an evening's cabaret show at the Fontanka restaurant. I even got to visit Petrodvorets palace for the first time, following its restoration and couldn't help thinking it was even more beautiful than Versailles, with it's amazing cascading fountains and stunning location, on the shores of the Gulf of Finland.

It was a tired but happy tour director, who bade a fond farewell to Lucinda, just before she passed through security at Pulkovo Airport. Overall, the trip had been an outstanding success and she promised to send me a copy of the article she was going to write about the experience, including how *Home and Country,* for the first time, had two "Poster Boys", called Dan and Steve. Just then, I heard the familiar call of "Geri" and turned to see Natasha, one of my favourite Saint Petersburg guides, coming towards me. *No rest for the wicked!* I thought, remembering that the next group, was due to land in under thirty minutes.

31
School's Out

Looking back, I think the *Women's Institute* tour was the high point of my tour directing days but, in some respects, the writing was already on the wall. Now that it was no longer a crime to possess hard currency, everything was becoming more expensive. Gone were the days when I could commandeer a hydrofoil for 200 *Marlboro Red*. Station porters now wanted dollars and not cigarettes, while the new arrangement with regard to theatre ticket sales, became the norm. Also, the type of client started to change. In an effort to maintain passenger numbers, my company had started to offer discounted deals through newspaper promotions. I remember one particularly bad week, when ironically, a group of *Yorkshire Evening Post*[66] readers, were not remotely interested in any of the culture on offer but simply wanted to know which bars were selling the cheapest beer.

By this time, I was the only English freelancer working regularly in Russia. The married couple who had been based in the Hotel Rossiya, when I first arrived, had long since gone, unable to adapt to the changing times, also, because the husband had developed a drink problem. The new climate even started to impact on the school tours I ran. In the early days, every group attended an evening's social event at the Pioneer (formerly Anichkov) Palace, in St Petersburg. The pioneers were the Soviet equivalent of our boy scouts and girl guides, but membership was mandatory. I had become good friends with Irina, the rather formidable lady who ran the modern languages section, also with her mother

---

66 The local paper in Leeds.

Galya, who had survived the siege of Leningrad and her daughter, Oxana, who was studying Hungarian and Finish, at St Petersburg University. I had been to eat at Irina's flat on numerous occasions and when I saw that on my latest itinerary, there was no sign of the evening social, I gave her a call to find out what was going on. She explained that under the new system, the pioneers were expected to self-generate some of their income and so, very much against their will, they had been forced to ask Intourist to pay a commercial rate for the evening's entertainment. Lara Karlina, under pressure to cut costs, had refused and so there would be no more teenage dances with cans of flat *Fanta* and dodgy, Russian folk music. Irina was very much an old school communist, hence her position and she instinctively hated the capitalist way of doing things. However, I could see she was becoming something of a dinosaur in Yeltsin's "Brave New World".

The evening at the Pioneer Palace, had been replaced by "Visit to an English Club with disco" on my itinerary. This immediately seemed a bit strange, as the club, apparently from the address supplied, had its meetings in a Seamen's Mission, in the docklands part of the city. I asked my local guide, Ludmilla, if she knew the place and rather ominously, she said it was the kind of area where even the Alsatians walked round in twos! This particular school tour had been going rather well, as for once, I had been able to sell some *Bolshoi* tickets, the group being sixth formers from Cheltenham Ladies College, one of the top girls' boarding schools in the country. I was therefore anxious that our evening of "international friendship", was going to run smoothly.

There was a mood of excitement in the coach as we left the Hotel Karelia, for the short journey down to the docklands area. All the girls were wearing party dresses and were chatting animatedly about the prospect of meeting some Russian boys. As soon as we pulled up outside the Seamen's Mission, I knew I was in trouble.

Spotting a drunk slumped by the entrance door, bottle of vodka in hand, I told the teachers to keep the girls on the coach and went to investigate. The contact name I'd been given, was Vladimir and at least he was there, a small balding man in his mid-thirties. It turned out he was a lecturer in English and ran the "club" as a way of meeting fellow anglophiles. The problem was, it was a club for adults and as I scanned the sparsely populated room, I could see he didn't have many members! In fact, there seemed to be more sailors, than lovers of the English language.

Returning to the coach, I explained the situation to the lead teacher, Clarissa, expecting her to agree with me and call the evening off. However, she was one of those gung-ho, hockey sticks types and to keep the girls sweet, had promised to let them have a supervised drink. Having confirmed that the bar was open, it was, after all, a place where sailors hung out and that there was music playing, me, two teachers and thirty of the poshest girls in England, entered the room. The looks of incredulity that greeted us will last with me for a lifetime. We might as well have been aliens arriving from a different planet.

I introduced Clarissa to Vladimir and as teachers do, they automatically arranged the girls in tables of five each, accompanied by their very own Russian "buddy". As you can imagine, to begin with, the conversation was rather stilted but I got each table a bottle of *shampanskoye* from the bar, paying the equivalent of 25p a bottle and things started to liven up. In addition, the disco music wasn't at all bad and being the independent type, pretty soon some of the girls were strutting their stuff on the dance floor. Starting to relax and with Vladimir and Clarissa getting on like a house on fire, it wasn't long before I too was "popping some shapes". It took me back to the time in Lido di Jesolo, when I had danced with the Canadian girls but at least this time, I didn't have to worry about any local interlopers on the dance floor, Russian men, at the time, definitely didn't do disco.

The Cheltenham ladies trip turned out to be one of my final school tours. Increasingly difficult to organise, witness my experience at the Seamen's Mission and with margins having always been tight, they would shortly be pulled from the programme. This was a shame, as although they weren't very lucrative for me, they were usually pretty much stress free. Coming from a family of educationalists, my maternal grandfather had been a primary-school teacher, I invariably got on well with the group leaders and in the early days, they had allowed me to learn the ropes, while making the odd mistake. I remember the first time I took a group to the recently opened Moscow *McDonalds*[67], thinking that by 9 p.m. the queue would have died down, only to be confronted by a sea of humanity, in Pushkinsklaya Square, which indicated at least a two-hour wait. Needless to say, the teachers, unlike the children, were not interested in standing around for ages, in temperatures of -20 °C, for something that tasted exactly the same as what you could get back home.

By mid-1993, it wasn't only school trips that were disappearing but also my "bread and butter" work. Russia was starting to get a reputation for extreme violence. Western news outlets were carrying regular reports of mafia killings on the streets of Moscow and for once, they weren't exaggerating. I too, was becoming distinctly aware of the mafia's growing influence.

---

67 Opened January 31st 1990, the first fast food outlet in the USSR.

32

A Night at the *Bolshoi*

My groups would invariably arrive at Moscow Sheremetyevo mid-afternoon and on the transfer down to the Cosmos, I would explain what performances the *Bolshoi* was putting on during their stay. If I was lucky, there would be a couple of ballets but more usually, it would be one ballet and one opera. Unsurprisingly, ballets were much easier to sell than operas, which often required me going through a detailed explanation of the storyline before the evening's performance. Payment for all theatre bookings was taken at dinner on the first night and I would then meet up with Misha the next morning, to confirm numbers and prices. By this time, I had been working with Misha for nearly four years and he had never let me down. He was originally from the far east of Russia and had come to Moscow to study mathematics in the early eighties. Like most students, he was always short of money and so he had come up with an ingenious way of supplementing his meagre student grant.

The queue to see the embalmed body of Lenin, in the mausoleum on Red Square was, during the Soviet era, probably the longest one in the world. All visits to Moscow by Soviet citizens, from outside the city, were on organised tours and a mandatory part of any itinerary, was a visit to pay one's respects to the leader of the Bolshevik Revolution. The head of the queue was at the entrance to Red Square, beside the State Historical Museum. From there it wound its way back, past the Tomb of the Unknown Soldier and the Eternal Flame and through the Alexander Gardens, following the outer walls of the Kremlin. Given that opening times were restricted, waits could be anything up to six hours, ironically, similar to when *McDonalds* first opened in Moscow. To avoid Red Square becoming clogged up with people visiting the mausoleum, groups of fifty at a time, would be taken from the head of the queue and escorted the 200 or so metres, from the State Historical Museum, to the tomb entrance. It was this that gave Misha his opportunity. Arriving early in the morning, long before the mausoleum opened, he would get himself a position ten rows back from the front and then wait. There is an old tradition in Russian society of saving a place for someone in a queue and Misha played on this to maximum effect. When the mausoleum opened he already had a friend back in the Alexander Gardens who would sell Misha's place in the queue to anyone willing to pay the twenty rouble asking price. With impeccable timing this individual would arrive just as the group of fifty left for the tomb entrance, replacing Misha in the process. Misha would then simply drop back ten rows and the process would repeat itself. No one ever complained about what Misha was doing, as he was moving backwards through the line and therefore couldn't be accused of queue jumping. The operation became so successful, that Misha soon abandoned his maths studies and went into "business" full-time. Soon, he had branched out into *Bolshoi* ticket sales, originally sourcing his tickets through a friendship he had developed with a member of the theatre's orchestra. In the closed circle of Moscow's black marketeers, he had become something of a legend, the kid from the far east who, with his shabby black raincoat and lank hair, had literally revolutionised the scene. However, by the summer of 1993, his days would prove to be numbered.

I had just seen my group off on their city tour and with an order for forty tickets, for that evening's performance of the *Nutcracker*, went to find Misha at our usual meeting place, outside VDNKh *Metro* station. As I neared the station entrance, I was approached by a man calling out my name. Not recognising him, I immediately asked him what he wanted. He said that Misha was poorly and that I was to give him the money for the tickets. Now, this struck me as unusual. First, Misha wasn't the sickly type and second, on the rare occasions he was unable to make it, he sent one of his trusted lieutenants, Boris or Dima. In addition, this guy who said his name was Artem, was asking for payment, when everyone knew my "Golden Rule", no tickets, no money. He was able to show me a couple of tickets for that evening's performance but they were high up in the gods and in any case, I needed another thirty-eight. Telling him to wait, I went back to the coach parking lot at the Cosmos and spotted a couple of touts I knew, chatting to a Japanese tour director. Once the tour director had left, I asked them if they had seen Misha recently, but they replied in the negative. Reluctantly, I asked what would be the going rate for forty *Nutcracker* tickets but they said they didn't have any tickets left, having negotiated a good deal for supplying the large Japanese group. Given that the *Nutcracker* was almost certainly going to be sold out, I decided I was going to have to take a chance on Artem and returned to the *Metro* station. At the time, the usual price for a black-market *Bolshoi* ticket, was $10 but certain performances such as *The Nutcracker*, could command $15 and "surprise, surprise" this is what Artem wanted. In the end, I agreed to pay $15 a head, with the proviso that none of the tickets were "restricted view", like the two he currently had in his possession. I also insisted that I would only pay for ten tickets up front and that I needed to have all the tickets by 2 p.m.. With a smug grin, he agreed and begrudgingly, I counted out $150.

Four hours later, I was back in the same place, only to be told by Artem that there was a slight problem and that he wouldn't have the tickets until 6 p.m.. This was cutting it fine. All *Bolshoi* evening performances started at 7 p.m. and I liked to have my groups there by 6.40 p.m. at the latest, to give people time to find their seats in the huge auditorium. I had already arranged for my group to have an early dinner at the Hotel Intourist, a ten-minute walk away from the *Bolshoi*, so I agreed to meet Artem there at 6 p.m.. Over dinner, everyone was chatting excitedly about the upcoming spectacle, while I shifted uncomfortably in my seat, not wishing to tell them that, although I had their money, I didn't as yet, have their tickets. While the group finished their meal, I made my way to the hotel lobby, fingers crossed that Artem was going to turn up, needless to say there was no sign of him. By 6.20 p.m. and with the group starting to congregate for the short walk to the theatre, I knew I'd been had. There was only one thing for it, dash over to the *Bolshoi* and try and magically get hold of forty tickets. Telling my clients there was a small problem, I explained to one of the married couples, how to get to the theatre via the labyrinthine underpass and they agreed to lead the group over. With my heart pounding, I sprinted out of the hotel and headed straight across the ten-lane highway that is Tverskaya (formerly Gorky) Street, dodging cars, as drivers blasted their horns at the crazy westerner, zigzagging his way across the road. In under two minutes, I was standing outside the colonnades of one of the world's most iconic theatres but for once, there was no time to admire the neoclassical architecture, I had forty tickets to find. Suddenly, I spotted Gennady, one of the touts who had helped with tickets for the WI group the previous year and I called out to him. Although I thought his tickets were usually over-priced, now was not the time for haggling. For $200, he agreed to let me have his last ten tickets and then headed off, to try and find some more. By this time, a couple of other touts had noticed my rather agitated state and approached me with similar offers of $20 a ticket. The problem was, they only had a few tickets each. It looked like about half my group were going to be disappointed and I had no idea how I was going to decide who the unlucky ones were going to be. Gradually, the crowd that always forms outside the *Bolshoi* in the half hour before the evening's performance,

199

started to thin and I could see that time was running out. In the distance, I caught sight of my group emerging from the underpass exit and I redoubled my efforts to get the requisite tickets. Increasingly, I was buying single tickets, not from touts, but from normal theatre goers, who were keen to cash in on this unusual occurrence. With my group now watching on, I was dishing out dollars left, right and centre, while at the same time, trying to make sure I wasn't being sold bum seats. With ten minutes to go till the curtains rose, I was still six tickets short, when suddenly, a smiling Gennady appeared in front of me, waving some tickets in the air. I was saved.

With the last of the tickets handed out and all my group now in the theatre, I asked Gennady if I could buy him a drink and he readily accepted. I was keen to relax after the stresses of the day but I was also anxious to find out what had happened to Misha. Over a couple of pints in the dimly-lit bar of the Hotel Intourist, Gennady explained, that with more and more western companies setting up offices in Moscow, suddenly there was a demand for corporate entertainment at the *Bolshoi* and this was pushing up prices. With increased prices, had come increased interest from organised crime, who were now trying to create a monopoly out of, what up till then, had been something of a cottage industry. He didn't know what had happened to Misha but he suspected that he wasn't "poorly". I later found out that Misha had in fact been kidnapped by the mafia gang that was trying to take control and, unwilling to divulge his ticketing source, had been badly beaten up. The gang were still amateurs in the procurement of tickets and that was why Artem had failed to get the forty I needed, instead, in true mafia fashion, contenting himself with keeping the $150 I had paid up-front. I never got to see Misha again. The word on the street was that fearing for his life, he had returned back to his family home, in the far east of Russia but I was never able to confirm this.

Sitting alone in the coach with my driver Valodya, waiting for *The Nutcracker* to finish, I couldn't help thinking the good times were coming to an end. Although I had managed to make a small profit on the evening's entertainment, it was clear that pretty soon, all decent *Bolshoi* tickets would be mafia controlled. There was also something of a moral dilemma. Guys like Artem didn't conform to the norms of society and I had no desire to help "feed the beast". At least the group were happy with the tickets I had procured. In fact, strangely, they seemed more appreciative of my efforts than usual, having witnessed at first-hand, my frantic street bargaining. Feeling slightly buoyed up, I contented myself with the thought that in a couple of days I would be back in my "hometown" of St Petersburg, little knowing that here too, things were changing rapidly.

33

The Good and the Bad

A couple of years earlier, I had been flying out to St Petersburg to stay with my friend Tolya, with whom I was trying to set up an import-export business. As usual, I had purchased a "bucket shop"[68] ticket for the *BA* flight, which had cost me £250. During the three hours in the air, I had struck up a conversation with the guy sitting next to me. His name was Mahesh and he was going to be the general manager of the recently restored Grand Hotel Europe. The hotel was due to open in three months and he was coming to St Petersburg for the first time to oversee staff recruitment and training. Originally from India, he had married an English girl called Janet, whom he had met while managing a boutique hotel in London and they had recently had a baby son called Oscar. Janet and Oscar would be joining him in St Petersburg once the hotel was open. He obviously knew a lot about running hotels, the Grand Hotel Europe was due to be the premier hotel in the city, but he didn't know much about travel. It turned out, he had paid £800 for his flight, over three times more than what I had paid. He was therefore extremely grateful when I gave him the number of the "bucket shop" I used and he invited me to come and have a drink with him, at the hotel the following day.

Over the next few months, the Grand Hotel Europe became my new home in the city. It was ideally situated, on the corner of Nevsky Prospect and Arts Square and had an amazing atrium over its central courtyard. It also incorporated a bistro called "Sadkos", where for the first time ever, you could get a decent

---

68 Scheduled airlines would off-load unsold seats through them.

lunch for roubles. A joint Swedish-Russian venture, all the staff were locals, who under Mahesh's expert tutelage, were starting to develop a reputation for excellent customer service, a totally new concept for the Russian hospitality industry. When Janet and Oscar arrived, I quickly developed a good friendship with Janet. Mahesh had found a reasonably modern flat for the family to rent but he spent most of his time at the hotel and Janet, with a young baby and friends and family thousands of miles away, was always keen to invite me over for a large G&T and a chinwag.

Over the next eighteen months, things slowly improved for Janet on the social front, as international companies started to relocate staff to St Petersburg. She set up a mothers' group, for the small expat community, arranging meetings in playgrounds across the city where, in freezing temperatures, the conversation no doubt turned to when the first soft play centre would open in the city.

Back in St Petersburg, after the drama of the *Bolshoi* tickets, I gave Janet a call and she invited me over for a drink that evening. This suited me fine as Igor, my *Kirov* supplier, had already got me tickets for the opera, *Eugene Onegin* and so I would have a good couple of hours to catch up on all the local gossip. As soon as I arrived at the flat, I knew that something was wrong. The jug of G&T standing on the dining room table was larger than normal and Janet already had a half-empty glass in her hand. I asked what was wrong and she said that Mahesh had had a major problem at work. A couple of days before, he had dismissed the hotel's head of security for being drunk while on duty. That evening while driving home from work in his *Lada Niva*, he had turned into the road leading to the apartment, only to find the road blocked by two large black *Mercedes*. Skidding to a halt, to avoid a collision, he had then been summarily dragged from the car by four men wearing balaclavas and forced to sit in the back seat of one of the *Mercedes*, where it was explained to him, that if the head of security was not re-instated, then the consequences for Mahesh and his family, would be dire.

The next morning, after a sleepless night, Mahesh had gone into the hotel, determined to stick with his original decision, only to find the supposedly disgraced head of security, sitting at his desk, glass of vodka in hand and smiling smugly at him. With his authority totally undermined, he had phoned his bosses in Sweden, only to be told that security was the preserve of the Russian partner in the joint venture and there was nothing they could do. After two years of continuous work, which had resulted in the Grand Hotel Europe becoming not only the best hotel in St Petersburg but in the whole of the former Soviet Union, Mahesh found himself in an impossible situation and promptly resigned on the spot. He, Janet and Oscar were due to fly back to London at the end of the week. For Janet, it was a cruel blow, as despite the difficulties of living in the city she, like me, had fallen in love with St Petersburg and now the future was very uncertain, with no jobs waiting for them on their return to the UK.

I was destined to have a further six months of tour directing but work was becoming spasmodic and dried up totally, when it was decided that it was no longer economic to have a UK tour director accompanying groups, instead relying on the perfectly capable Intourist guides, to lead the tours on their own. In some respects, I wasn't overly upset. Luisa and I had recently got married and bought a flat in London and aged nearly thirty, after half a lifetime on the road, I was starting to think about settling down. I was also hopeful that some of the business projects I had been nurturing over the past five years would start to bear fruit. I wasn't done with Russia just yet!

34

A Bit of Business

From the very beginning, I thought I was in the right place at the right time. The meeting of the Supreme Soviet, which coincided with my original visit in 1989, paved the way for the societal reforms that made business possible, for the first time in over seventy years. The first idea I came up with was inspired by a mother and daughter, travelling on one of my earliest tours. They were the types who went to *Tom Jones* concerts together and possibly threw their knickers at him but what they really wanted was a T-shirt, to act as a record of what they had seen. They were, therefore, mortified to find out that there were no *Bolshoi* ballet T-shirts on sale and the same thing applied for the *Kirov*. Clearly, there was a hole in the market and I determined to fill it. A couple of weeks later on a separate tour, I was explaining my idea to a member of my group and he said he might be able to help. His name was Dave and he had originally trained as a graphic designer. By now, he was running a successful print and advertising business, with a large factory on the outskirts of Manchester. It had been his wife's choice to come to Russia, to celebrate her fortieth birthday and to a certain extent, Dave was simply along for the ride. However, he had a keen eye for business and he said that on his return to the UK, he would come up with some designs. Dave was as good as his word and on a break between tours, I went up to the north-west to visit his factory and to stay with him and his family. The designs were really good and production would be relatively straightforward. The problem was going to be distribution and that would be my responsibility. I had initially thought about taking a suitcase full of T-shirts, each time I flew out and selling them on through Misha, but as Dave patiently explained, this wasn't really a serious business model, I would need to do some more research.

I soon discovered that exporting to the Soviet Union from the West was fraught with difficulty, unless you were part of a joint venture and there was no way I, on my own, was going to meet the criteria. Dave, on the other hand, with his successful UK based limited company, would be a different proposition. I had recently got to know a family friend of Inga's, a guy called Tolya, who had just returned to Leningrad, from a three-month trip travelling around the USA. God knows how he had managed to get hold of a visa or get hold of the money to fund the trip. He was clearly a resourceful guy and unlike Inga, he saw his future in Russia. We were the same age and although totally different characters, he definitely wasn't a disco dancer, we got on well. More importantly, we both wanted the same thing. Unusually, Tolya spoke French, having spent some of his childhood in Guinea, west Africa, where his geologist father had worked as an adviser to the newly independent government[69]. This would prove useful over the next few years, when we wanted to be sure not to be overheard.

Tolya had numerous ideas about how to make money in the "new" Russia. Strangely though, *Bolshoi* ballet T- shirts weren't on his agenda – too small scale. On his trip to the USA, he had seen the tools required to run a market economy: business cards, brochures, advertising hoardings etc. and when I told him about my visit to Dave's print factory, it seemed the perfect fit. At the time, quite a few western companies were getting their "fingers burnt", in dodgy joint venture deals and when I suggested a business trip to Russia, Dave was, at first, rather sceptical.

---

69 Gained independence from France in 1958.

However, I said everything would be done through Tolya and I was happy to vouch for his integrity.

And so it came to pass, that on a sunny July afternoon, mine and Dave's plane touched down at Pulkovo airport. I was in a relaxed mood, as for the first time I was flying into Russia, unaccompanied by any tourists and had therefore taken advantage of *BA*'s complimentary bar service. Tolya and his father Sergei, were there to meet us, Sergei at the wheel of his *GAZ-M20 Pobeda*, which dated back to the early 1950s (*pobeda* means victory in Russian). Given a free choice, I had decided to stay at the Hotel Prebaltiskaya and with Sergei's rather cautious driving style, it was a good half-hour before we were checking into our room. That evening, we were invited to eat with Tolya and his parents, in their small flat, just off Moskovsky Prospect, on the south side of the city. Tolya's mother, Kira, was an amazing cook and she had prepared a fabulous spread. I had taught Dave a few rudimentary Russian expressions and he totally nailed, '*O-chen pri-yat-no*,' ('Pleased to meet you,'). In fact, to this day, he still pronounces it perfectly. Returning to the hotel and still on UK time, we decided to have a drink in the hotel bar. Although it was already 11 p.m., it was still as light as day outside. My company never ran tours to Russia in July and so, this was my first proper experience of the *belyye nochi* (white nights) when it always seems too early to be going to bed. There were only a few people in the bar and so it wasn't difficult to spot the two girls, who were clearly eyeing us up from across the room. By this time, I was fairly tipsy, Sergei having insisted on numerous vodka toasts, to Anglo-Russian friendship and so, slightly against my better judgement, I motioned for them to come over. Their names were Sveta and Marina and they said they had just finished their shift working as waitresses in the restaurant, on the top floor of the hotel, with its panoramic views over the Gulf of Finland. Given the clothes they were wearing, I was slightly dubious about this but then, maybe, I was just getting cynical and in any case, Dave seemed to be enjoying the female attention. Trying not to appear over virtuous, I said to them that, unlike the Cosmos in Moscow, it was nice to be able to have a quiet drink in the bar and not to be propositioned by prostitutes. To which they smiled demurely and started to sip on the cocktails I had ordered for them. Sveta didn't speak any English but Marina had a reasonable command of the language and so it was natural for her and Dave to strike up a conversation. This suited me, as it had been quite tiring having to translate everything for Dave over dinner. I was just beginning to think that the girls might be the genuine article, when Marina said that a friend of theirs, who was one of the hotel porters, was great at drawing caricatures and would Dave like to commission one as a memento of the evening. It was only going to cost $10 and Dave, with his graphic design background, thought it was a great idea. In next to no time, the guy, whose name was Yuri, was sitting across the table from us, drawing pad and pencil in hand. For the next fifteen minutes he drew furiously away, occasionally stopping, to make an alteration with the rubber, he kept in his front trouser pocket. Satisfied with his work, he turned the drawing pad towards us and I suddenly realised the whole point of the exercise. Yes it was a great likeness of Dave but in the picture, he was cradling two *matryoshkas* in his arms, bearing the faces of Marina and Sveta, while a caricature of me hovered in the background, with a halo over my head. It was clear that if the threesome implied by the depiction was to become a reality, it was going to cost a lot more than $10! Amazed at the elaborate lengths the girls were prepared to go to, in order to get a "mark" and slightly annoyed at being portrayed, for the first time in my life, as "saintlike", I paid Yuri $10 for the picture and suggested to Dave it was time for bed. With a wry smile, he wished Marina and Sveta a pleasant evening and joined me, as I headed for the lift up to our tenth-floor room. On the way I apologised for initially being taken in by the girls, but Dave just laughed saying, 'Just because we're in Russia Geri, it doesn't mean you know everything.'

Over the next few days, Tolya arranged a series of meetings for us, with various politicians and local businessmen. He had studied economics at Leningrad State University, which had a reputation for educating the country's political elite. In fact, the current president Vladimir Putin, had only graduated from the university, seven years previously. Tolya was a great networker and had an amazing eye for detail. The problem was, he was perceived as being too young and when Dave and I said any investment we made would be through a joint venture, set up with Tolya, they tended to lose interest.

To a certain extent, the business trip turned into something of a holiday. I was glad to be in Russia, without any tourists to worry about and Dave seemed pleased to have a week away from the stresses of running a business, employing over eighty people. He had started the company from his own back bedroom, fifteen years previously and the expansion had been rapid. He complained that now HR matters took up so much time, it was easy to forget what the focus of the business was meant to be. I think in helping me and Tolya, he saw a way of getting back to basics and maybe, just maybe, there might be a pot of gold at the end of the rainbow.

Towards the end of the week, I took Dave to meet my friend Irina, at the Pioneer Palace. It really was a beautiful building and not normally on any tourist itinerary. In the chandeliered ballroom, adorned with baroque frescoes, Irina recounted the history of the palace, including how it had been the childhood home of the last Russian emperor, Nicholas II. Tolya was with us and I sensed immediately, that he felt uneasy in the presence of Irina. Trying to arrange a final meeting, he asked Irina if there was a phone available and she said he could use the one in her office. While he was away, I asked Irina if, in the past, she had ever come across Tolya at the Pioneer Palace but she just smiled and said simply, that she didn't think it would have been his scene. They clearly had diametrically opposed views of the Soviet period. As a communist party member, married to a naval officer, Irina had enjoyed a privileged existence. She had a spacious three-bedroomed apartment in the city centre, close to St Isaac's Cathedral and had been on numerous cultural exchanges to the West, including a couple of visits to Glossop, in the Peak District. Tolya, on the other hand, had returned to Leningrad from Guinea in his early teens, obsessed with the music of Pink Floyd and determined not to conform to any party doctrine. Now, it looked like things were finally moving in his direction but only time would tell.

A couple of months after our return to the UK, I was surprised to get a call from Dave, to say that government grants were now available to help develop trade with Russia and that we should apply. To qualify for a grant, you had to write a report on what opportunities were starting to open-up and I certainly had a few good ideas, although *Bolshoi* ballet T-shirts no longer featured on the list. I was keen on Dave's proposal but knew I wouldn't have the time or expertise to write a report that would be good enough for official scrutiny. This, however, wasn't going to be a problem, as Dave had just taken on a young account manager called Brendan, on a probationary contract and it would be him writing the report. Dave had a free week in November, which was good for me, as this was always a quiet month for touring and so I agreed to arrange flights and accommodation for the three of us. To keep upfront costs down and to avoid paying the dreaded single room supplement, Tolya found us an apartment on the eastern side of the city, close to my old haunt, the Hotel Karelia. The apartment belonged to a friend of his called Ira, who was happy to let us stay the week for $100, while she moved back to her parents' place. With hindsight, we effectively were the first people ever to stay in an *Airbnb*, in Russia. The apartment had one bedroom, which I shared with Dave, while Brendan slept in the lounge on a camp bed. Ever the entrepreneur, Dave had brought a water filtering device that a friend of his had just patented and for the first time, I saw the brown liquid, that normally emerged from the tap, turn crystal clear. I still didn't drink it!

On our first morning, we were picked up by Sergei and Tolya and taken to a succession of pre-arranged meetings across the city. It was always amusing to watch how the two of them inter-acted, constantly bickering about the best route to take. Tolya was an only child, Kira being in her late thirties when she finally conceived and Sergei, when compared to my own father, seemed more like a genial granddad. His driving was definitely "granddadish" in style. Still, we managed to make all our appointments on time and one meeting seemed particularly promising, as the abandoned factory premises would be perfect for setting up a printing press.

Returning to the apartment at the end of a long day, I was surprised to hear the sound of music coming from the kitchen, only for this drop-dead gorgeous blonde, to suddenly appear through the doorway. Tolya had told us that Ira might drop in from time-to-time but hadn't specified when. She was in her mid-thirties, with a shapely body, dressed in a tight-fitting crop top and tracksuit bottoms, the look, rather spoiled by the pair of large pink fluffy slippers on her feet. '*Kak delya?*' (How you doin'?) I asked, but I immediately knew she wasn't interested in me, as she was already staring at Dave. In slightly broken English, she said, 'I've come to make you dinner,' to which Dave replied, in his very limited Russian, '*O-chen pri-yat-no*'. Unfortunately, although Ira clearly had many "attributes", cooking wasn't one of them and after a perfunctory meal of sausage and gherkins, we decided to invite her out for a drink at *Chayka* (The Seagull) the first hard currency bar in Leningrad, named after the play by Anton Chekov and, where you could get some reasonable "pub grub".

Over the next few days, we saw quite a lot of Ira. Every morning she would come and make us breakfast, an oily fried egg, accompanied by some stale, dark, rye bread and in the late afternoon, she would be there when we got back from our meetings, usually on the phone to some friend or other. She seemed to have a lot of friends, one of whom Katiya, started accompanying us on our evenings out. To begin with, I thought Ira might be looking for a "Ticket to the West" but it turned out she was just a "good-time girl", who enjoyed the company of older men. Brendan and I were definitely too young for her.

At the end of the week, Sergei and Tolya came to pick us up, to take us to the airport. We were flying back to Heathrow via Moscow and so needed to get an internal flight from Poulkovo down to Sheremetyevo 1. I had already agreed to give Tolya $1,000, as a fee for all his help. He needed the money to buy a computer and that was the going rate for a top brand. For once, father and son were a bit late arriving and by the time we had said our long goodbyes to Ira, we only had forty-five minutes to make it to the airport. Normally, this wouldn't be a problem but with Sergei at the wheel, I started to get a bit concerned, especially when he decided to take a different route to normal, so as to avoid some road works, he had been told about. As soon as we hit the traffic jam I knew we were in trouble. Unlike Moscow, traffic congestion was a rare occurrence in Leningrad and Sergei seemed completely baffled as to what was going on. Tolya started shouting at him that we were going to miss the flight and it was all his fault for taking the wrong route. Eventually, the traffic started to clear and for the first time in his life, Sergei put his foot down on the pedal. As previously detailed, we did end up making the flight and Brendan did get to watch his beloved Manchester United on the TV that evening, but it was a chaotic end to what had been a successful week. Tolya had pulled out all the stops in getting us to meet the right people, including the city's deputy mayor and he had definitely earned the $1,000, I stuffed into his hands, as I jumped out of the car and ran towards the departure hall.

35

Art for Art's Sake

Over the next few months things went a bit quiet. I returned to tour directing, while Brendan struggled manfully to write the report, in a manner that was acceptable to the panel responsible for administering the government grants. I would always meet up with Tolya, whenever I was back in St Petersburg but I started to sense he was becoming restless, with the lack of progress. While I had my tour directing income, he was having to rely on his parents for financial support and at the age of twenty-seven, he was desperate to start making his own money. One evening, he and his friend Max, came to my hotel room in the Karelia and I was surprised to see an oil canvas tucked under Tolya's arm. It was by a local artist, Georgij Moroz, an acquaintance of Max's. At the time, I knew next to nothing about art but even with my untrained eye, I could see that the painting of lilacs, with a bowl of fruit beside, had value. It transpired that Moroz had already managed to sell a few paintings in the West but it was always a struggle to get the necessary export licences. He was, therefore, prepared to let us have the painting, on a sale or return basis, assuming that I was able to get it out of the country. There would be a 50-50 split on the sale price. This, to me, seemed a good deal. I already had a side line selling Russian dolls and lacquer boxes, through a dealer in Camden Market but I could only get so much stuff in my suitcase and the margins weren't great. Higher value items were what I needed and oil paintings fitted the bill perfectly.

I am not normally a nervous traveller but the first time I went through customs at Pulkovo airport, with an oil canvas rolled up in my suitcase, my heart did start to beat a little quicker. What if I was stopped and the artwork confiscated? Would the customs officers take a bribe or stick to the rules? I also had the pressure of wanting to help Tolya make some much-needed money and the question of whether I would be able to sell the painting, once in London. Luckily, all these fears proved groundless. As per usual, I sailed through customs and a couple of days later, managed to sell the painting to an art dealer, in the West End, for £600. The dealer, who specialised in Russian art, told me that given the lack of supply, prices for Russian artwork, particularly oil canvases, were buoyant and he would happily take more of Moroz's paintings.

It was with an enormous sense of satisfaction, that a week later, I handed over Tolya and Max's cut of £150. Now was the time to scale up the operation. With £300 due to Moroz, we arranged to go and visit him in his studio, situated in a countryside *dacha* (country house) about 20 miles north of the city. On meeting the artist for the first time, it was difficult to believe he was still only in his early fifties. Like many men of his generation, he looked a lot older, the result of too much vodka drinking over the years. As an artist, he was naturally wary of "businessmen" but his face brightened up, when we gave him the envelope containing the money, satisfied that we had held up our end of the deal. He asked us if we would like to join him for a drink to celebrate our new "partnership" and even though it was only 11 a.m., we were unable to refuse.

On the drive out to the studio, in Max's car, I had worked out that I would be able to fit four rolled-up canvases in my suitcase. This would mean each trip would net £600, for Tolya and Max and £600 for me, a great return for no up-front money. Having toasted our new venture at least three times, Russians can never have just one drink, we went into the cavernous barn come

215

studio, where Moroz did all his work. There must have been at least thirty paintings on display and I thought it was going to be a lengthy process, picking out the four best. Spotting a painting at the back, similar to the one I'd sold in London, I said, 'I'll take that one.'

'*Eta sereznya rabota*,' ('that's serious work,') said Moroz, '*Ya ney prodayu*,' ('I'm not selling,'). It quickly became clear that my choice was going to be more limited than I had originally expected, but I wasn't overly concerned, at least the four paintings I ended up with, were on the small side and so, would fit more easily into my case.

It was a confident Geri who walked through the door of the West End gallery a couple of weeks later, to be greeted by a smiling proprietor, anxious to see the latest examples of Moroz's work. As soon as I unveiled the first painting, I knew there was something wrong. 'Very poor,' the dealer said and although the next three got a slightly more positive response, he was only prepared to take two paintings and then only on a sale or return basis. It turned out, that the original painting I had sold, had been done on one of Moroz's good days, i.e., one when he hadn't been drinking and the dealer, who already knew Moroz's work, had snapped up the chance of a genuine bargain. Indeed, I could now make out the painting hanging on the far wall with a £3,000 price tag! I was crestfallen. What had looked like a "cash cow" for Tolya and me, was going to be no such thing. One of the two paintings did eventually sell but with Moroz starting to moan about no paintings and no money, after two months, I had to ask for the other one back and return it to its rightful owner.

There is an old expression in business, "You don't give up because you fail, you fail because you give up." Having experienced the London art market, I knew there was money to be made and I was determined to give it another go. All I needed was an artist able to produce work of a consistent quality. I started to put feelers out through friends and acquaintances and to my surprise, it was Irina who came up trumps. The Pioneer Palace ran numerous after-school activities, one of which was an art class. Each week, a different painter would give a short lecture about their creative process and then run a practical workshop. Out of interest, Irina had sat in on one of these sessions and had been really impressed by the work of a local artist, called Sasha Ivanov, who worked mainly in pastel. I asked her if she could get his contact details and she said that the administration office would definitely have them on file.

A couple of days later, I met up with Sasha in his apartment, on The Boulevard of Enthusiasts, in the western part of the city. I immediately warmed to him as a person. He had an infectious smile and a dry sense of humour. The first thing he asked me was, did I know the reason for the name "Boulevard of Enthusiasts" and when I replied in the negative, he explained that it came from a post-World War II movement, where people gave up their time for free in order to build a better society. Looking out of the window, at the uniform collection of drab apartment blocks, I couldn't help thinking that their idealism might have been a bit misplaced and Sasha clearly agreed with me. He was six years older than me and had been born and raised in Uzbekistan, which helped explain his dark complexion. Originally, he had come to study architecture at The Institute of Engineers of Construction, in Leningrad but five years after graduating, he had decided he no longer wanted to be an architect and had decided to become an artist. In his own words, "'The architect works with his head, but the artist with his heart.'" There was definitely something of the "romantic" about him. However, as he showed me examples of his work, it was easy to see the influence of his architectural studies. Many of the pastels depicted the iconic buildings of St Petersburg, such as St Isaac's Cathedral, the Winter Palace and the Alexander Nevsky Monastery. Maybe, because I come from a family of architects, my father, grandfather and great uncle, all had their own private practices, I really liked Sasha's work and moreover, with my business hat on, it looked very commercial and easy to transport in the bottom of my suitcase. Over a cup of tea, with his wife, Natasha and twin children Alina and Vlad, it was decided I would take two paintings back to London, on a sale or return basis. Unlike with Moroz, I was free to choose which ones I wanted to take and after some deliberation, I settled on a view of the Anichkov bridge, with its four famous horse sculptures and another, looking across the River Neva with the rostral columns in the foreground.

By this time, Luisa and I were renting a flat in north-west London and she told me about a gallery, close to where she worked, on Harley Street, that she thought might be interested. The owner Colin, was a bit of an oddball but he had a good eye and he also knew a picture framer who wouldn't charge me a fortune. It took Colin less than a week to sell both paintings and over the next few months, a steady stream of Sasha's work flowed through the Marylebone gallery. Such was the success, that Colin and I decided to put on an exhibition called, "Window on the West"[70], which was to have thirty of Sasha's pastels on sale. To help promote the exhibition and as a way of transporting the paintings, I thought it would be a good idea to invite Sasha over to London. However, at the time, this was easier said than done. Unbelievably, the only way for me to issue an invitation to Sasha was to get him to come to Moscow and then for me to accompany him to the British Embassy, located on the banks of the River Moskva, close to Arbat Street, where I had to personally vouch for him and give details of my UK bank balance. I had only been to the embassy once before, when a school kid had dislocated a finger and I'd

---

70 To provide a "Window on the West" was the reason Peter the Great built St Petersburg on the shores of the Baltic Sea.

managed to get the British GP seconded there, to strap it up. This time, passing through the large wrought iron gates, I was more nervous, as I was investing a lot of time and some money in Sasha and I couldn't afford for him not to get a visa. In the end, I needn't have worried and a month later, I was waiting at Gatwick Airport for Sasha's flight to land. Unfortunately, I was at the wrong airport.

36

From Russia with Hope!

At the time, all charter flights to Russia went from Gatwick. When working with school groups, I would quite often fly out with *Thomson* and so I naturally assumed that was where Sasha would be landing. You know the expression, "Never assume anything because it makes an ass out of you and me," and as I looked up at the arrivals board, I could see no sign of the *Aeroflot* flight number that Sasha had given me. I went to the help desk, to find out what was going on, only to be told that as of the previous week, *Aeroflot* charter flights were now landing at Stansted. I couldn't believe how stupid I'd been and it was now going to cost me. I rushed out to the parking lot, where my regular minicab driver Sayed was waiting, to give him the unexpected news that we were now going to Stansted. I don't think he could believe his luck, as we were now looking at a 100-mile round trip. Given that I'd already paid for Sasha's flights and visa application, I could only hope that the exhibition proved a success.

I hadn't been to Stansted for nearly ten years. Not since the days of flying out to Bulgaria with Balkan Airlines and as we pulled up outside the arrivals hall, I was amazed at the transformation. Once, little more than a big shack in a field, the recently completed terminal building, designed by Norman Foster, featured a "floating" roof, supported by a space frame of inverted-pyramid roof trusses, creating the impression of a stylised swan in flight. Clearly, not only flights from Russia were re-routing to Stansted. I found Sasha sitting on a bench, close to the terminal entrance and he didn't seem at all bothered that I was over an hour and a half late in picking him up. I was also relieved to see a large, canvas, art-portfolio carrying bag at his feet, which meant he'd had no trouble getting through customs. It took nearly an hour to get back to my London flat, where I handed over the biggest taxi fare of my life to Sayed, just over £100. Luisa was waiting for us and I introduced her to Sasha for the first time. Luckily, on this occasion, I didn't have to do any interpreting, as Sasha had a good command of English, even to the point of being able to flirt with my girlfriend!

The next day, Sasha and I went to the picture framer, located on Dean Street, close to the *BT* Tower. I had already settled on a frame for previous paintings and Sasha agreed to keep the same one for the new works he had brought with him. I'd negotiated a bulk discount of £50 a frame with Gary, the picture framer and he assured me, all the paintings would be ready for the exhibition opening, in a week's time. Handing over £500 with another £500 due on completion, I really hoped he would be true to his word.

Over the next couple of days, I showed Sasha the sights of London. It was the first time he had been out of the Soviet Union and he was like a big kid, eyes wide open in amazement, as he visited all the places he'd only ever read about. I was also keen to have a couple of pastels with a London theme in the exhibition and Sasha said he would have enough time to produce the work, provided I could source the right paper. This wasn't a problem and after some deliberation, we settled on views of Piccadilly Circus and Admiralty Arch.

To publicise the exhibition, I placed an advert in *Time Out* and got a listing in the *Guardian's Guide* section, through a contact I had made on one of my tours. With bottles of *Shampanskoye* on ice and the paintings framed, I was all set for the opening, scheduled for a Saturday lunchtime. I'd chosen a Saturday, so as to allow friends and family time to come down from the north, to witness my debut on the London art scene. Not for the first time, my ego clouded my judgement. Unlike Leeds, where Saturday is always the day with the highest footfall, central London is relatively quiet, with offices closed and people already departed for their "weekend in the country". Any art dealer worth their salt, would tell you that Thursday evening is the best time to launch an exhibition, when critics do the rounds, from opening party to opening party, but this was new territory for Colin, as well as for me and he went along with my Saturday suggestion.

In the end, we did sell a couple of paintings and the *shampanskoye* and caviar went down nicely, but it was a slightly disappointed and hungover Geri, that woke up the next day. Sasha was staying for another week and he was starting to cost me quite a lot. He obviously had very little hard currency and London is an expensive place to live. I had taken him out for a "night on the town", with my best friend Mike, who was, by this time, working as a neurologist at University College Hospital and had managed to go through £200. I needed to find a means for Sasha to pay his way, during the rest of his stay. Realising that one of the two paintings to sell at the exhibition opening, was the view of Piccadilly Circus, I suddenly came up with an idea. I had read in the *Guardian* the previous day, that the United States Ambassador to the UK, was about to return home, having completed his four-year posting. Luisa and I sometimes went on walks through Regent's Park during her lunch hour and I had therefore seen his official residence, Winfield House, a beautiful Neo-Georgian town house, set in 12 acres of private grounds. This seemed an ideal subject for Sasha to draw and maybe, the ambassador would be interested in having a souvenir of his time in London.

The next day was beautifully sunny and so Sasha and I caught the Jubilee Line down to St John's Wood and then made our way through Regent's Park, to a spot close to the fence that enclosed the grounds of Winfield House. In the distance, you could make out the garden front of the house but Sasha wanted to get closer to do his preliminary sketches. Looking back it seems incredible, but at the time the fence was no more than a metre and a half high and made out of black railings. Maybe the Americans hadn't been able to get permission for a security fence, the local authorities wanting to maintain the aesthetic of Regent's Park, whatever the reason, it was definitely not an insurmountable barrier. Half expecting an alarm to go off and for guard dogs to suddenly appear, I helped Sasha climb into the garden and then passed him his sketch pad and pastels through the railings. Telling me to come back in a couple of hours, he headed for a copse of trees about 150 metres inside the perimeter fence and settled down in their shade, to begin his work.

With two hours to kill, I decided to walk over to the London Clinic and see if Luisa wanted to go for an early lunch. When she came down to meet me in the lobby of the clinic, she immediately said, 'Where's Sasha?' and when I explained, she said, 'Are you two crazy? What if he gets arrested and gets charged with being a spy?'

'He's only drawing a painting,' I replied, but I was beginning to see her point. However, it was too late now and I was still desperate to have that picture of the residency.

It was with some trepidation that I returned to Regent's Park and my anxiety levels increased when I realised that Sasha was no longer in the spot where I'd left him. Imagining the beginnings of some diplomatic incident, I skirted the perimeter fence, scanning the grounds for any sign of the Russian artist. Finally, to my immense relief, I spotted him, sketch pad in hand, leaning against a large cherry tree, about a hundred metres inside the garden. I called out and he turned and gestured that he was nearly finished. About five minutes later, he was back on my side of the fence, explaining that he hadn't been disturbed, he had simply moved, to get a different perspective on the house.

It took Sasha a couple of days to complete the picture of Winfield House. I then wrote a letter addressed to the US Ambassador, explaining that the work was on display at the gallery in Marylebone and enclosed a photo. A couple of weeks later, I got a call from Colin to say that the picture had been sold for cash, to a mysterious buyer. I liked to think it was someone acting as a proxy for the ambassador but I never got to find out for sure. In fact, despite the poor beginning, the exhibition proved a success, with two thirds of the paintings sold. One Harley Street surgeon, actually bought five works and didn't even ask for a discount. Over the next few years Sasha's reputation grew, with solo and group exhibitions across Europe and North America. With the advent of the internet, he was able to sell his work directly online and he no longer needed a middle man. I did, however, organise one more exhibition in Leeds, in the late nineties and yes, the opening party was on a Thursday evening.

37

That's a Good Idea!

Sasha was not the only Russian to come and stay with me in the UK. Both Tolya and Max came to visit, which also included some time spent with Dave, up in the north-west. Tolya and Max had set up a business importing clothing from Indonesia and they were keen to source other suppliers. Through my friend Mike, I knew some Indian guys in Leicester, who were clothing manufacturers and on one of my rare visits to my tour operator's head office, I arranged a meeting with them. They were happy to let me have some samples to test the market and so the next time I flew out, I had with me a suitcase stuffed full of cheap shell suits and bomber jackets. Unfortunately, the wholesale prices I had been quoted in Leicester, were not competitive with those obtainable in Jakarta and in the end, the only bomber jacket I saw on the streets of St Petersburg, was worn by Max. This was symptomatic of the many ideas I flirted with at the time. Lots of good intent but little end result.

Some were just plain crazy. I remember having a meeting with a guy in St Petersburg, who was offering me ivory, from the tusks of mammoths discovered in the melting permafrost of northern Siberia. He explained that because the mammoths were extinct, the worldwide ban on the sale of ivory, didn't apply. I, however, was dubious about the ethics of the project. The guy seemed a bit dodgy and I suspected the ivory was probably coming from elephant poaching in India. My suspicions seemed to be confirmed when he gave up on the idea of ivory and instead, asked if I would be interested in buying some liquid uranium!

I was still making some money from selling *matryoshka* dolls and lacquer boxes, through the dealer in Camden market. In addition, my ticket supplier in St Petersburg, Igor, had managed to "find" a source of Russian icons and these provided better profit margins. The problem was, getting them out of the country, as there was an export ban. The solution was to wrap them up in my large, black winter coat, which I placed in the basket of my trolley, as I wheeled my way through customs, a $20 dollar bill in my hand, just in case there were any problems. What I really needed though, was something I could do on a larger scale.

Since the failed coup of 1991, I had noticed that the *matryoshka* dolls depicting the presidents of Russia, had become more popular in the two main tourist markets, Arbat Street in Moscow and outside the Smolny Institute, in St Petersburg. With the inauguration of Bill Clinton as US president, in January 1993, aged just forty-six, suddenly "Clinton Dolls" started to appear, containing other presidents, such as Nixon and JFK. This gave me an idea. What about dolls portraying football teams? I knew Dave's son, Jake, was a massive Manchester United fan, so to test the water, through my supplier in St Petersburg, I commissioned an Eric Cantona doll, containing Peter Schmeichel, Ryan Giggs, Paul Ince and Mark Hughes. Helped by images taken from the 1992 Manchester United album, the artist was able to come up with the world's first footballing *matryoshka* and when I saw the look on Jake's face, as he unwrapped his special present from Russia, I thought I was on to a winner. Clearly, the idea could be used across a multitude of sports. I was particularly excited about the possibility of tapping into the US market, with its five-man basketball teams.

What I now needed to do, was work out how I was going to produce dolls on a commercial scale. I quickly realised that hand-painting the dolls would be too labour intensive and so I got hold of some plain, wooden, five-piece sets and took them up to Dave's factory. He told me there was a new process, whereby you could screen print onto a thin membrane, which in theory could then be stuck onto the wooden surface. Encouraged by the thought of mass production, I returned to St Petersburg the following week, determined to find a reliable source of wooden sets. I also ordered a couple more hand-painted "Cantona Dolls", for promotional purposes.

In the end, it wasn't the technology that scuppered the project but the question of copyright. Having worked in Russia for over four years, where the concept of copyright was non-existent, I had completely forgotten that you might have to get permission to use other peoples' images. If Dave and I were going to produce "Cantona Dolls" on a commercial scale, for sale in the West, then we would have to be licensed by Manchester United. To obtain a licence, was a lengthy and expensive process and couldn't be justified, alongside the cost of the new technology. Of course, nowadays, sports team *matryoshka* dolls are everywhere on the internet but as I look at Eric's face, smiling down at me from the bookcase in my study, at least I can say, I was there before anyone else.

When I first arrived in Russia you could literally say there was absolutely nothing to watch on the TV or anything to listen to on the radio, unless you were a fan of classical music, which I'm definitely not. The only western films you could catch on TV were old, black and white, *Sherlock Holmes* movies starring Basil Rathbone, which were poorly dubbed and often featured a German villain. Meanwhile, at the cinema the only feature film of any note allowed to be shown, was *Cabaret*. This was because of its anti-Nazi sentiment. The Russians had not forgiven the Germans for the invasion of 1941. Through the 1970s, *Cabaret* developed a cult following among the youth of Moscow and

Leningrad, with something of a party atmosphere developing at any given showing, similar to the phenomenon of *The Rocky Horror Picture Show*[71] in the US and UK. It also had an unusual legacy, as it inadvertently supplied the secret word for "gay" into the Russian language. During the Soviet period, homosexuality was illegal, in fact, it wasn't finally decriminalised until 1993. There was, however, a clandestine gay scene, whose members readily identified with the homosexual subtext, that runs throughout the film. At one point, the rich playboy and baron *Maximilian von Heune*, gives the main character, *Brian,* a light-blue cashmere sweater as a present and very quickly the word *"Goluboy"* (light blue) became the euphemism for "gay". Nearly fifty years after the film's release, it is still difficult to be openly gay in Russia and *goluboy* remains the only way to describe oneself as homosexual, apart from the literal translation.

With the disintegration of the Soviet Union, in the early 1990s, the transformation in film, TV and radio was rapid. The biggest change for me, in the early days, was the opening of *Radio Europa Plus*, in Moscow. For the first time, songs I recognised, were on the airwaves and incredibly, it had adverts. I became its number one fan and it got to the point, that I would only take a taxi, if it had a FM radio, capable of picking up the new station. One evening, I was just leaving the Hotel Metropol, in the centre of Moscow, having had a drink with Galya, one of my favourite Intourist guides in the city. She lived fairly close to the Cosmos, so I suggested we get a taxi and I would drop her off, on the way back. Unfortunately, the first taxi I hailed only had an AM radio and so, couldn't get *Europa Plus*. The same applied to the second and third and as it was getting late, I decided that for once, I might have to forgo the pleasures of *Europa Plus*. I was just negotiating the fare, with the latest driver to pull up, trying

---

71 Released 1975.

to get a discount for the fact, he too, didn't have a FM radio, when suddenly another taxi screeched to a halt in front of us, with the driver winding down his window and screaming, 'I've got Europa Plus!' Needless to say, he got the fare and as we drove up Prospekt Mira, he explained that the word had gone out over the internal taxi network, that some crazy westerner was standing outside the Metropol, demanding *Europa Plus* as a condition for travelling. I don't know if it was purely down to me but pretty soon afterwards, every taxi in Moscow was equipped with a FM radio.

If the changes in radio were dramatic, then those in television, were even more so. Channels scrambled to find cheap content, to replace the airtime of government-led programmes. One savvy producer at the Ostankino station, took a punt on, *Los Ricos Tambien Lloran* (*The Rich Also Cry*) a Mexican soap, from the 1970s. Retitled as, *Bogaty Toszhe Plachut*, despite being poorly dubbed, the general public became enraptured with the programme and its popularity blazed across the post-Soviet states. It seemed like every time I was round at Tolya's flat, Kira would have it on in the background and as Sergei looked on exasperated, she would explain in great detail, the latest plot twist. I guess at the time, for most of the Russian masses, escape from the social and political chaos of the emergent Russian Federation was hard to find. For many, *The Rich also Cry*, provided a respite from the daily drudgery. It was estimated that 200 million Russian and ex-Soviets, watched the finale. Compare that to the 52.5 million Americans, who tuned in to watch *Ross* and *Rachel*, finally get it together in 2004[72].

While the content on TV was changing, so too was the available technology. Video recorders were becoming increasingly popular and this presented me, Tolya and Max, with a new business

---

72 Friends US Sitcom.

opportunity. Although the Latin-American soap operas, that were starting to dominate the airwaves, were usually dubbed, most of the Hollywood movies broadcast, simply had a monotone, male voiceover, explaining the action. Given that you could still quite clearly hear the voices of the US actors, this seemed to me a crazy way of doing things. However, Tolya and Max explained to me that the general public, starved for so long of any decent films, were quite happy to put up with it. We, therefore, decided to enter the movie business.

Rather appropriately, the film we chose was, *Green Card*, starring Gerard Depardieu and Andie MacDowell. At the time, our friend Inga, was literally living the film's story[73] and we thought it would appeal to a mass audience. With me supplying a copy of the film, Tolya writing the "script" and Max providing the voiceover, we were able to produce the first Russian version, available for video release. As usual, my role was the easiest one. For Max and particularly, Tolya, it was really hard work. I couldn't help marvel at Tolya's determination to get things done, often cajoling Max to do just one more take, to get the delivery absolutely "nailed on". Unencumbered by copyright issues, we expanded our video portfolio, including a couple of "artistic" French films, sent to me by my old friend Renaud, which unsurprisingly, didn't need any voiceover!

---

73 Trying to get permanent residency in the USA.

38
Growing Up (A Bit)!

By the spring of 1993, I was already in my thirtieth year and with the big "3 0" now on the horizon, I started to take stock of where I was. Yes, I was still making decent money through tour directing but there was no way I was going to carry on doing that for ever. Things had gone quiet on the joint venture idea, as, "out of the blue", Tolya had taken a job with the bank, *Credit Lyonnais*, who had recently opened an office in St Petersburg and unsurprisingly, was concentrating most of his efforts, on making a good impression on his new employers. In addition, I was due to marry Luisa, later in the year.

I had proposed, following a drunken night out with Mike, at the London Hippodrome, located just off Leicester Square, in the heart of the capital. On returning to the flat in the early hours of the morning, I had managed to throw up all over the living room carpet and then fall asleep on the settee, only to be woken by a fuming Luisa, throwing a bucket of cold water over my head. Things weren't looking great. I had a terrible hangover and I was due to fly out to Russia the following day. Not wishing to have a whole day of getting the cold shoulder from Luisa, I decided to ask her to marry me, thinking that if she said yes, given the circumstances, then she must truly love me. Amazingly, she agreed straightaway, although the lack of a ring seemed a slight concern. I explained you didn't have to get engaged in order to get married and that we could go and look for wedding rings, once I was back from Russia. Then, ever the salesman, in order to clinch the deal, I said she could have a Moroz oil painting, that I had kept as an investment and which she had admired for a long time. That painting still hangs above the mantlepiece, in my living room and whenever I look at it, I can't help thinking what a "lucky bugger" I was, to get Luisa to marry me.

Following our September wedding and honeymoon travelling around Turkey, I returned to my tour directing duties but my heart was no longer in it. Moreover, price inflation was rampant. One day, I bought a banana from a street vendor on Nevsky Prospect, only to realise I'd paid more for it than I would have done at my local Waitrose, on the Finchley Road. I was committed to touring until the new year, by which time, I resolved to find something else to do and preferably, London based. I decided to get in touch with my old friend, Tom and for once, my timing was perfect. Maria had accepted a new job with *CNN* in London and although he was coping at the moment, he knew he was going to need help come the springtime, when he would be having to deal with increased numbers of Russian visitors.

Throughout my tour directing career, I had always tried to maximise my own personal time away from the group. For example, when I was in Paris and my clients were visiting the Eiffel Tower, I would quickly run across the Champs de Mars, to see friends who had a beautiful apartment over-looking Les Invalides. With the decision taken to stop tour directing and no longer bothered about customer service questionnaire scores, for the final few months, I spent as little time as possible in my groups' company.

I arranged for my mother to come out to St Petersburg to see me and got her a room in the Hotel Astoria, located directly opposite St Isaac's cathedral. Like the Grand Hotel Europe, it too, had been recently renovated and the new staff were very different from their Soviet predecessors. One in particular, Sasha the bar manager, was especially personable and over an after-dinner drink, he was keen to tell me about a side line he was running, which involved promoting helicopter tours of the city. He asked me if my mother and I would like to have a free trial and then I could sell it as another "Geri optional". I thanked him for the offer but explained that my tour directing days were coming to an end. In any case, I was slightly dubious about the health and safety aspect of the project. The helicopter in question, was an old red army one, which had recently been decommissioned and I wasn't sure what the levels of maintenance would have been like over the years. Sure enough, a couple of months later the helicopter crashed, with the pilot and two western tourists, all losing their lives. Not for the first time, I thought, 'There but for the grace of God go I.'

Sadly, it was during my mother's visit, that the dangers of the "New Russia" revealed themselves in their most graphic form. We had been invited to dinner by Tolya's mother, Kira but when Sergei opened the door to us, I knew immediately there was something wrong. First, there was no food on the table, which was very unusual and then I caught a glimpse of Kira, sitting at the kitchen table, in floods of tears. Sergei explained to us in French, that Tolya had been attacked by four thugs and had taken a severe beating. Leaving my mother with Sergei in the sitting room, I went into Tolya's bedroom to see the extent of his injuries. Propped up in bed, he gave me a faint smile as I entered the room but he was in a very bad way. All his face was covered in swellings and he could barely open his left eye. Through gritted teeth, he explained that he had just parked his car outside the flat, when he had been set upon by four masked men, wielding iron bars. Clearly, they had been waiting for him, this was no random attack. It turned out, he had been approached a couple of days before, by a man wanting to get inside information on the Credit Lyonnais operation, in St Petersburg. Tolya had instantly told him to get lost and now he was paying the price. I was anxious not to alarm my mother but Tolya insisted on seeing her and there then followed a rather surreal conversation in French, whereby he tried to downplay the severity of what had just occurred. Now, Tolya was a really tough guy, he and Max both practised mixed-martial arts, but in fighting back, he had provoked his attackers into using even greater force, which I later found out, had resulted in severe internal bleeding. The next day, he was rushed to hospital, where for three days, it was in the balance whether he would live or die. Thankfully, in the end, he pulled through but the whole episode only strengthened my resolve to re-locate permanently to London.

Things were getting increasingly violent in Moscow as well. With me now married, Juliyanna had found herself a Russian boyfriend and was living with him in a flat, just off Leningradski Prospect, on the way out to the airport. When I met the guy for the first time, I took an instant dislike to him and I don't think he liked me very much either. He reeked of mafia. The flat was large by Russian standards and he said he had paid cash for it. In addition, all the latest technology was present, including satellite TV and CD player. The décor could best be described as "nouveau riche" and I noticed Juliyanna was wearing a new pair of Adidas designer trainers. When I asked him what he did, with a smug smile, he just said, 'Bizness,' and left it at that. I couldn't help feeling disappointed, that Juliyanna had ended up with a guy like this but as she correctly pointed out, when Vitali had gone off to "work", at least he was taking care of her, something which I had singularly failed to do, since our very first meeting at the airport duty free.

However, Juliyanna's life as a "kept woman", was destined to be short lived. A couple of months later, having dropped my group off at Sheremetyevo, I called in at the flat, only to have a distraught Juliyanna tell me that Vitali had been killed in a car crash, the previous weekend. The official explanation was that it was a normal traffic accident but there had been no witnesses and the road conditions were good at the time. Clearly, Juliyanna thought that Vitali had been murdered and I couldn't help thinking she was probably right. I asked her what she was going to do now and she said she was going to move back to her parents, as a business associate of Vitali's had just been round, to tell her he would be moving into the flat and she had twenty-four hours, to get all her stuff out.

The next time I met Juliyanna, it was to say goodbye. Shaken by Vitali's death, she had decided to leave the country and through an old school friend, who had emigrated to Australia, in the mid-eighties, she had managed to get an entry visa that would allow her to stay in Sydney for six months. It was rather ironic that we were both leaving the country at the same time. Appropriately, we met for the final time at the Spanish Bar. Over a few *San Miguels*, we talked about all the changes we had witnessed during the past five years, some of them good, some of them bad. As the taxi pulled away from outside the Hotel Moskva, I shouted, '*Uspekh,*' ('Success,') and she turned in the back seat and gave me one of her knowing smiles. I never saw her again or got to find out what happened to her in Australia. I did send a letter to the address she gave me for her friend in Sydney but I got no reply. Unlike Tolya, I think she had always seen her future overseas and now she was just getting on with it. Occasionally, when watching TV with Luisa, back in London, I would hastily have to change channel, if Mary Nightingale (Juliyanna's lookalike) was presenting the evening news but otherwise, she faded to the back of mind. After all, I now had more pressing affairs to deal with.

39

The Ruskies are Coming

It was a sign of how much things had changed, that by the spring of 1994, it was now Russians who were paying my wages. At the time, a lot of new Russian money was finding its way to London and areas like south Kensington, were becoming increasingly "Russified". My role was to look after visiting VIPs and show them the sights. Although the visits were quite frequent, the numbers were small, only a couple of people at a time. This was definitely a different kind of tour directing. In fact, it was a bit unclear what the company I was working for, actually did. Tom said it was a holding company for Russian investments in the UK, but that could mean absolutely anything.

The first couple I looked after were a bit strange. They were young newly-weds, probably in their late teens and the wife was already ten weeks pregnant. I had been told that the girl's father was some political bigwig in Moscow, a close ally of Yeltsin's and I suspected that he might have been keen for her to come to England to have the baby and then return to Russia, at which point, it would be unclear if the baby had been born out of wedlock. As previously mentioned, some Russians can be extremely puritanical and he probably didn't want to risk something that might cost him popular support. They were staying in an apartment owned by the holding company, close to Gloucester Road tube station and it was my job to get them settled in and show them around the city. The apartment itself was beautiful, taking up the whole of the first floor of a Georgian town house. Luisa and I had recently bought our first flat in north-west London and so, I had a good idea of property prices. I reckoned this one must be worth at least ten times the value of our place, i.e., well over £600,000. Clearly, my new employers had money to burn.

For the first two weeks, I had very little to do. The girl, whose name was Anya, was suffering with morning sickness and spent most of her time in bed. The husband, Dmitri, meanwhile, seemed to be enjoying the delights of satellite TV, I think he had found some "artistic" channels to watch and my main role, was to keep them topped up with supplies from the local supermarket. With Anya feeling a bit better, I managed to persuade them to do a bit of sightseeing but I soon realised they weren't "culture vultures". They were more like bored schoolchildren, on an organised excursion. There was only one thing they really wanted to do and that was to, 'Go to *Alton Towers*.' I thought that when I explained it would be a seven-hour round trip by car, then they would lose interest but they were adamant. Reckoning it would be a good way of justifying my existence, no one was going to keep on paying me for the odd visit to the shops, I hired a car with the company credit card and one sunny March morning, we set off on the 200-mile drive, to *Alton Towers*. I had got Luisa to take the day off work and I hoped some female company might bring Anya out of her shell. Fat chance! I soon gave up pointing out places of interest, instead chatting to Luisa about the recently completed five nations rugby championship, in which my team, Wales, had been narrowly victorious.

Neither I nor Luisa had ever been to *Alton Towers* and the final stretch of the journey, after leaving the motorway (M1) seemed to go on for ever. When we finally arrived, I thought Anya and Dmitri might cheer up but as we wandered through the grounds, it soon became evident that they didn't want to go on any of the rides, they simply wanted to see the place. Personally, I've never been a big fan of theme parks and Luisa felt the same. In the end, we had what, undoubtably, must be the most expensive stroll through the Staffordshire countryside ever recorded. With the *Alton Towers* visit over, there seemed very little for me to do, even Dmitri had, by now, managed to find his way to the shops and so it was time for me to move on.

A couple of weeks later, I was asked to go out to Heathrow, to meet a mother and daughter, who were flying in from Moscow and from the moment I met them, I knew this was going to be more fun. The mother, Natasha, immediately reminded me of Yelyena, the Intourist guide who had been with me on the "Luisa Tour". She was small and round but had beautiful eyes and an infectious laugh. Her daughter, Valentina, was taller and darker skinned and spoke a smattering of English. We took a taxi into town and I asked the driver to do a mini tour of the main sights, on our way to the Dorchester Hotel, where they were staying for ten nights. Unlike Anya and Dmitri, they seemed genuinely interested in my tour guide spiel and when we pulled up outside the hotel, on Park Lane, I was able to tell them with some pride, that they would be staying in one of the world's most prestigious and expensive hotels.

After checking them in, I arranged to meet up the following morning, as I had been told to take them to a solicitors' office, close to Oxford Street, where some papers were waiting to be signed by Natasha. This seemed a bit strange, as I had understood, it was Natasha's husband, a government minister back in Moscow, who was the real VIP and "the girls" had just come for a holiday. It was, therefore, with some curiosity, that I entered the oak-panelled, thick-carpeted office of the senior partner, the following morning, accompanied by Natasha and Valentina. The guy must have been in his mid-fifties and was all smiles and pleasantries, almost to the point of being obsequious. It transpired that Natasha's signature was required to release funds from the English bank account, that had been set up in her name. It was clear from Natasha's expression, that she didn't really understand what was going on, but when the guy said, 'it was just to get "a bit of pocket money,"' she signed on the dotted line.

A bit of "pocket money" turned out to be £10,000 in crisp £50 notes, with more to come, if we needed it. Given that all hotel bills were being picked up by the holding company, I really thought we might struggle to get through £10,000, let alone any more, in the nine days remaining but ever the optimist, I was prepared to give it a try!!

Natasha insisted on me taking charge of the money, saying that it was a man's job and five minutes later, I was walking down a sunlit Oxford Street, praying that nobody realised what was inside the bulging envelope sticking out of my jacket pocket. I took "the girls" to *Selfridges*, thinking this would be an easy way of making inroads into the £10k but they declined to buy anything, perhaps overawed by the amount of products available, or maybe, more likely because they weren't used to having a man present, on their shopping expeditions. Deciding to change tack, I took them for lunch at Langan's Brasserie, in Mayfair. It was somewhere I'd always wanted to take Luisa but hadn't had the resources. Part owned by the actor, *Michael Caine*, it had a great reputation for its cuisine and atmosphere, along with the possibility of a bit of celebrity watching. With Natasha adamant that I was to order for them, I perused the menu handed to me by the rather snooty waiter and suddenly realised spending £10k, in just over a week, might not be that difficult after all. When I asked for the bill, the waiter said, 'I assume you'll be paying by cash, sir?' Clearly, Natasha and Valentina weren't his first Russian customers. In fact, at the time, stories were starting to circulate that even central London properties, were being sold to Russian businessmen, carrying briefcases stuffed full of used banknotes.

Over the next few days, we continued to make serious inroads into the girls "pocket money". Both Natasha and Valentina loved to eat and drink and they also developed a liking for West End musicals, the favourite one being, *Starlight Express*. We took taxis everywhere, including a day trip out to Oxford, to have lunch at the Randolph Hotel. Luisa started to get a bit fed up that I was out every evening but I just said it was work and that I had no choice. In truth, I was really enjoying myself. It felt like I was back in the old Soviet Union, when I could go anywhere and do anything, with money no object. On the taxi ride out to Heathrow, for the return flight to Moscow, I handed the envelope containing what was left of the original £10k, to Natasha. She took a quick peek inside and then returned it to me saying, *'Bolshoye spasibo,'* ('Thanks a lot,') and for a moment, I regretted having been so profligate but then, as I said in my wedding speech, 'I've spent 90 per cent of my money on women and champagne and the other 10 per cent, I've wasted!' In any case, it was still easily the biggest tip of my life.

Of course, by this time, I wasn't naïve about what was going on. A pattern was beginning to emerge, whereby an unholy alliance was being made between business and politics. State assets, such as oil and gas, were being privatised on a massive scale and the new owners, always had close ties to the political elite, ensuring the price they paid was ridiculously low. For example, I heard that the Luzhniki Stadium, built for the Moscow Olympics, of 1980 and occupying a prime site, on the banks of the Moskva river, had been sold for next to nothing, the price being determined, solely on the cost in roubles, of the bricks used in its construction. Looking back, I do feel a bit guilty, that I was prepared to turn a blind eye to some of the injustices but I was still obsessed with Russia and working with Tom, seemed the only way to keep the dream alive of creating my own joint venture. Little did I know that, in less than six months, I would be back home in Leeds, working for my father, the dream over.

In early July, I got a call from Tom to say Natasha's husband, Nikolai, was coming to the UK for a heart bypass operation and he had asked for me to act as translator, during his convalescence at the Wellington, a large private hospital, in St John's Wood. The hospital was relatively close to my flat in Cricklewood, just five stops down the Jubilee Line and so, it was easy to be around for help with ordering meals and interpreting the updates, given by his surgeon. The operation had proven a success and day-by-day Nikolai was getting stronger, I even joked about taking him nightclubbing at the Hippodrome. However, one afternoon, I walked into his large private suite, only to find someone I didn't recognise, lounging in a bedside chair, looking like he owned the place. He was speaking in Russian and I could see from the look on Nikolai's face, that he was uncomfortable with what was being said. Hearing me enter, the guy slowly rose to his feet and came towards me. He was well over 6-feet tall and thick set, with hands like shovels but the thing that most struck me, was that when he spoke, it felt as if he was looking straight through me, his eyes betrayed no emotion, they were literally dead. He introduced himself in English, as Ruslan and gave me a company business card, which described him, simply as an "Associate". It didn't take a genius to work out what kind of an associate he was and I immediately began to feel my throat go dry. Speaking in Russian, so that Nikolai could understand, I asked him what he was doing here and he simply replied in English, 'We're taking care of Nikolai now, you're no longer needed.' The words, "'taking care of...,'" sent a shiver down the back of my spine and I turned to Nikolai and asked, in Russian, if this was the case. Rather deliberately, he nodded his head, a slightly despairing look on his face. I felt in an invidious position. Clearly, Nikolai was being intimidated but what could I do about it? Playing for time, I said I would have to check with my office, that I was no longer required and he just smiled and said, 'Go ahead... by the way, we know where you live!' Relieved to be out of the room, I took the lift downstairs to the hospital reception and used one of the pay phones, to put a call through to Tom. When I explained what had happened, he didn't seem the least bit surprised. The way he described it, was that back in Moscow, there was a "turf war" going on between our company and a larger, rival "company", for political influence and currently, we were losing. Now, normally, I hate being on the losing side but for once I didn't care. I had no desire to receive a home visit, from Ruslan and his friends. Needing a drink to relax, I took the tube into town, remembering that Italy was due to play Bulgaria, in the semi-final of the football World Cup, later that evening. Luisa had already gone down to Eastbourne, to watch the match with her father, so I headed for Bar Italia in Soho, where I knew there would be a good atmosphere and if I got there early enough, I might even get a seat. With a couple of hours to kill before the match, I downed a succession of *Peronis* and thought about what I was going to do.

Luisa had already mentioned about wanting to start a family at some point and the thought of raising kids, in a small flat, in London, wasn't overly appealing. Property prices in London were starting to rocket up, ironically, partly due to the influx of Russian money and now would be a good time to move, before the ripple effect reached the provinces. But most importantly, I was scared about what might happen, if I didn't end my Russian obsession. I had never been threatened before and I had to admit, I didn't like it. By the time the match kicked off, I'd resolved to make a clean break and when Mike joined me to watch the second half, I told him of my decision. To my surprise, he said he was relieved that I had finally seen sense. He had been worried for a while, that I was wasting my talents on some Russian pipe dream and now was the time to start a proper career, before it was too late. I agreed, but what was I to do? Luckily, I didn't have to wait too long for the answer. Oh, and by the way, Italy won, 2–1, with Roberto Baggio, getting both the goals.

40

Tempted Back

When I left Leeds, aged eighteen, I never could have imagined that fifteen years later, I would be back, living in the city, with a wife and three children. Following my decision to change direction, things had moved very quickly. Possibly, sharing Mike's concern for my career prospects, my father had asked me if I wanted to come and work for him, taking on the role of business manager, for his expanding architectural practice. With Luisa's support, I had agreed, reasoning it would be better working for "The Tafia", rather than "The Mafia"! We had relocated to Leeds and in less than three years, with Luisa's help, I was the father of three bouncing, baby boys (Vito, the eldest and identical twins, Guido and Cristian). Benefitting from the boom in London property prices, we had swapped our two bedroom, Cricklewood flat, for a large Victorian terrace, on the outskirts of the city. With a young family to take care of and a busy working life, the practice was taking advantage of the recent introduction of GP Fundholding[74] and had a number of commissions for new medical centres, thoughts of Russia were very much, at the back of my mind. I was, therefore, surprised to get a letter from Tolya, asking me to come to St Petersburg, as he had a business idea to discuss and he needed my input. He was offering to cover all my expenses, including flights, so clearly things were looking up for him. I was intrigued to see how things had changed during my time away but I was concerned about leaving Luisa home alone, with three young babies and I couldn't help thinking about Al Pacino's line in,

---

74 Conservative policy launched in 1991 to give GPs more control over their budgets which had financial benefits for their pensions.

The Godfather Part III, "'Just when I thought I was out, they pull me back in.'" However, Luisa was, as always, supportive, saying her mother would come up to help while I was away and in truth, I could do with a break from changing nappies and making up bottles of milk.

On arrival at Pulkovo Airport, I was pleased to see that the new airport terminal had been completed. No need for riding on any carousels this time! Tolya was there to pick me up and I immediately noticed that he was now driving a shiny, *Toyota Celica* and no longer reliant on his father's old *GAZ M20 Pobeda*. On the drive into the city, Tolya updated me on the events of the past few years. The big news was, that Max had emigrated to the US and was now working as a taxi driver in New York, while he had left Credit Lyonnais and was now with a newly-founded, Russian investment bank. He had also recently bought his own apartment, close to where his parents lived and that was where I was going to be staying. Having dropped my stuff off at the apartment, Tolya said he had something to show me and I guessed this might have something to do with his business idea. We caught the *Metro* into town, alighting at Pushkinskaya and then walked a couple of blocks, until we were outside a building with a large fluorescent sign saying, *Bilyard*. 'You were right Geri,' Tolya said and I instantly knew what he meant. Since childhood days, I have always loved playing pool and it had been one of my pet projects, to introduce the game to the Russians. However, Tolya had always dissuaded me from pursuing the idea, saying it was likely to attract mafia interest. Now, someone had built a pool hall in St Petersburg and for the first time ever, in Russia, I was going to get to play the game I loved. As we entered the building, Tolya explained that as I had predicted, pool was becoming increasingly popular and this was just one of a few venues that had sprung up around the city. There had also been a revival of interest in Russian billiards and I spotted a number of the modified snooker tables, with narrower pockets, on which the game was played. Strangely, I had played the game once before and in the most surreal of venues.

In the summer of 1992, Mahesh's mother had come over from India, to see her new grandson for the first time and through a mayoral contact, he had managed to let a *dacha*, on the outskirts of the city. However, this was no ordinary *dacha*. It had previously been used for entertaining, by the Communist Party elite and was more akin to an English country, manor house. Secluded in a thickly wooded forest, it was like entering a different world. At the time, Dave and I were on a "working holiday", Dave accompanied by his wife Sue and me, by Luisa. Janet had invited us over for lunch, which proved to be the one and only time, I ate curry in Russia. With the women fussing over the baby and who was going to do the washing up, Dave and I went off to explore the rest of the residence and were amazed to come across a wood-panelled billiard room, with a full set of balls and cues. Needless to say, we had to have a game, little knowing how long it was going to take us. This is because the pockets are only 3mm wider, than the diameter of the balls. To pot a ball, is a major achievement and when I compared the game with American Pool, it seemed to reflect the nature of Russian society, where everything is a struggle, as opposed to the instant gratification, common to US culture. Unsurprisingly, snooker, the archetypal English game, falls somewhere between the two extremes.

Recalling my previous experience at the *dacha*, I naturally chose to play a game of American pool and over a few frames and a couple of cans of beer, Tolya began to explain why he needed my help. In his new role at the bank, it was his job to place investors' money in ventures that would return a high dividend, in a short period of time. He told me that the sector currently delivering the highest returns, was the hospitality one and so he had decided to create St Petersburg's first, authentic, English pub. He had already earmarked premises on Nevsky Prospect and now, what he needed, was a design concept, a marketing strategy and most importantly, a supply of English cask beer. My initial reaction was that the first two requirements wouldn't be a problem. One of the architectural technicians in the practice was a wiz, on our recently acquired AutoCad system and could probably knock something up in less than a week, while I could deal with the marketing side of things. In fact, I already had a name in mind for the pub, "The Sherlock Holmes". It seemed to tick all the boxes, familiar to an older Soviet generation, through the films of Basil Rathbone, while being quintessentially English. Also, the expression, "Elementary my dear Watson," was known by Russians of all ages and could be played on, for advertising slogans. The problem was going to be the cask beer, necessary to give the pub it's USP[75], so as to distinguish it from the other bars, which were starting to appear in the city centre. When Tolya had stayed with me in London, I had taken him on a pub crawl, down the Kilburn High Road, including a stop at the infamous, Molly Maguires[76] and he had loved the way the barmaids hand-pulled pints of beer. It was this that he wanted to replicate in Russia, where the only beer drunk, was out of imported bottles and cans. I thought it was rather ironic that he was moving into an area associated with organised crime but then again, maybe his investors were the type of people who could offer protection, as well as money!

While we continued to play pool, I thought about people back home, who knew about the brewing industry and suddenly, I remembered an acquaintance from my ski racing days, who had been the financial director of *Sam Smiths*, one of the leading UK brewers. As far as I knew, he still lived in a village 10 miles north of Leeds and I resolved to look him up, on my return.

---

75 Unique Selling Point.
76 Rumoured to be a hang out of the Irish Republican Army (IRA).

With Tolya at the bank during the daytime, I had plenty of time to catch up with old friends and acquaintances. Now that I was no longer cash rich in Russia, I tended to avoid getting taxis, instead choosing to take the *Metro* or to walk. To be honest, the city didn't seem to have changed that much in appearance. Yes, there were a few more western brands about, particularly on Nevsky Prospect and in Gostiny Dvor (the St Petersburg equivalent of GUM) but in general, it was the same old drab shop fronts and *Ladas* still predominant on the roads. One thing I did notice, however, as I traversed the city, was that there were far more beggars on the streets, clearly, the effects of the new market economy, were not benefiting everyone.

One evening I was invited to dinner by my artist friend, Sasha and his wife, Natasha. Given that I now had newly born twins, we had lots to celebrate and the vodka flowed quite freely. Sasha's own children, Alina and Vlad, were also twins, although obviously not identical and were, by now, in their final year of high school. I was interested to find out what they were planning to do. Vlad, was a bit unclear, mentioning something about graphic design but Alina was dead set on becoming a lawyer, saying that the only future for Russia, was if the rule of law could be respected and not used as an instrument of state power. Wow, the idealism of youth. At the time, I really hoped the younger generation could atone for the sins of the fathers but as I write, Alina has been living in Barcelona for the past ten years, with Vlad moving to Finland, shortly afterwards.

A little bit the worse for wear after the evening's celebrations and with it already well past midnight, I decided to revert to type and to flag down a car, for the journey back to the flat. It didn't take long for an old, black *Lada* to pull up and I was pleased to find that I was still able to negotiate a reasonable "fare". There was, however, a slight problem, as I couldn't remember the exact address of the flat and so, when the driver asked me at which point he should turn off Moskovsky Prospect, I hesitated and then chose the incorrect option. Realising we were heading in the wrong direction and in any case, needing to get a bit of fresh air, I asked the driver to stop, got out of the car and started to head, in what I thought was the right direction. By this time, it was pitch black and Russian street lighting could at best, be described as dim. The other problem was that in this area, all the buildings were exactly the same, five storied apartment blocks, called *khrushchyovkas*, developed in the early 1960s and named after the then Soviet leader, Nikita Khrushchev (note to Elton John, Nikita[77] is a boy's name, although he probably knew that already.) After about fifteen minutes, I was relieved to spot a small park I thought I recognised and taking this as my reference point, I was soon standing outside the padded door of Tolya's fifth-floor flat. Putting the only key I had, in the lock, I was concerned to find it didn't quite fit. Numerous, slightly drunken attempts to force the lock proved fruitless and, in the end, I decided that there was nothing for it but to bang on the door, in order to wake Tolya. Imagine my surprise, when in response to my repeated banging, an old woman's voice called out in a frightened manner, '*kto eto?*' ('who is it?') Suddenly, I realised I was in completely the wrong apartment block and not wishing to cause a scene, hastily ran down the staircase and slightly out of breath, regained the street. By now, totally disorientated, I started to wander around, desperate to find some point of recognition. In the end, by pure chance, I came across a group of teenagers on their way back from a late-night party and they were able to point me in the direction of the Park Pobyeda *Metro* station, from where, I was sure I could find my way home. Finally, back in the flat, nearly an hour after first being dropped off, I was relieved to find that Tolya was fast asleep in his room and so, I was spared the

---

77 Elton John song from 1985, Nikita is portrayed as a female army officer in the video.

embarrassment of having to explain why I was so late. A couple of days later, meeting up with Sasha, to discuss the possibility of an exhibition of his work in Leeds, he asked me if I'd had any problem getting back to the flat, as he and Natasha had been a bit worried that I might have had a bit too much vodka. When I told him the story, he simply smiled and said, 'You're a real Russian man now.' Apparently, it happened all the time.

On the flight back to the UK, I tried to digest what I'd experienced over the previous seven days. Russia was definitely changing but was it for the better? Max was not the only one to have left. Inga's mother had also gone to the US, to join her daughter and other people I met, still talked about emigrating. The one person, however, who was definitely staying, was Tolya. He was absolutely determined to make the new Russia work for him. As it turned out, it would be another twenty years before I could sit and have a drink in Tolya's pub and it wasn't called *The Sherlock Holmes*. On my return home, I found out from my *Sam Smiths* contact, that cask beer couldn't be transported over long distances and the idea was put on hold. The exhibition of Sasha's work did go ahead, with the few unsold paintings going to friends and family in Leeds. And that, to all intents and purposes, was it. Russia slowly faded into the background, as the demands of raising a young family, took over my life. All that remained as a reminder was the Moroz painting, hanging on the dining room wall and the black overcoat I used to wear on winter evenings out.

41

A New Millennium

In the year 2000, after thirty-seven years working as an architect, my father decided to follow my mother into retirement. They had recently bought a house, in a quiet corner of south-west France, an area they had been visiting since their student days, at Liverpool University and he was keen to spend more time, on his favourite naturist beach. His decision had also been influenced by the fact that the young female architect, he had been grooming to be his successor, so as to continue the practice with me, had tragically been killed in a cycling accident and it therefore made sense to wind up the business. I went to work in sales for a Leeds-based tour operator, specialising in holidays to France, followed by a period teaching in the Travel and Tourism department, of the local FE[78] college. By this time, Luisa was working as a film reader, for the *National Breast Screening Service* and so it made sense for us to share child-minding responsibilities, with both of us working part-time. This arrangement made even more sense, when in 2006, following a routine mammogram, Luisa self-diagnosed herself with early stage breast cancer and embarked on a course of treatment, that would last for three years. Unbelievably, having "beaten" breast cancer, she then discovered in 2010 that she had Hodgkin's lymphoma. The two diseases were totally unrelated, she was just very unlucky. I can't help thinking that working in radiography since the age of eighteen, might have been a contributory factor but we will never know for sure. By 2014, after large amounts of chemotherapy and ultimately an

---

78 FE – Further Education.

autologous stem cell transplant[79], she was finally in remission and in the year of our fiftieth birthdays, we decided that she should take early retirement, on the grounds of ill health and move to Eastbourne, to be closer to her parents. Our eldest son, Vito, was due to start an Economics degree at Durham University, while the twins would accompany Luisa to East Sussex, where there was an excellent Sixth Form College, in the county town of Lewes. I, meanwhile, would stay in Leeds, where I was enjoying a successful career in sales, for *BP[80] Fuel cards.*

The move to Eastbourne proved a huge success. We bought a flat at the foot of the Sussex Downs and managed to acquire a beach hut, on the sea front, close to the famous bandstand. After so much time spent in hospital, it was great for Luisa to be able to enjoy the bracing sea air and the spectacular views of the *Seven Sisters*[81] and beyond. In addition, both Guido and Cristian, excelled in their new Sixth Form, gaining, perhaps unsurprisingly, identical marks in their 'A' Levels of A*, A, A. (Strangely, this was exactly the grades that Vito had achieved). Obviously, the boys got their brains from their mother but their wanderlust came from me.

In the summer of 2016, Guido was due to spend two months doing voluntary work for an educational charity in Uganda, prior to taking up his place at Edinburgh University. Meanwhile, Cristian was planning to visit his grandparents in France. This, however, seemed a bit unfair, as the cost of the Uganda trip, far outweighed that of the air fare to La Rochelle. Luisa and I, therefore, asked Cristian if there was anywhere he would like to go. Imagine my surprise when he instantly replied, 'Russia.' Working in Leeds, I

---

79 Healthy blood stem cells from your own body are used to replace your diseased or damaged bone marrow.

80 BP p.l.c. (British Petroleum) is a British multinational oil and gas company headquartered in London, England. It is one of the oil and gas "supermajors" and one of the world's largest companies measured by revenues and profits.

81 A series of chalk cliffs close to Eastbourne.

had had very little involvement in the twins' 'A' Level studies and so I had not realised that the "Russian Revolution", now formed a part of the History syllabus. Apparently, Cristian had really enjoyed learning about the rise of the Bolsheviks and was now keen to see where the "action" had taken place. I must admit, at first, I was a bit reticent. I had totally lost contact with all my Russian friends and the last thing I desired, as a former tour director, was to go on an organised trip. Still, Cristian was adamant that this is what he wanted to do and so, I agreed to look into it.

Working in sales, I always preferred to take time off during school holidays, as the decision makers in the organisations I targeted, tended to be of an age when childcare became an issue. I had recently booked ten days for a summer break, down in Eastbourne, so I already knew the time frame for the trip. For many years, I had been advising people thinking of going to Russia, to spend more time in St Petersburg than Moscow and in addition, air fares were always cheaper to the second city. I therefore decided to book return *BA* flights, from Heathrow to St Petersburg and to arrange accommodation for the first three nights there, followed by two nights in Moscow and a final two nights, in St Petersburg. I knew that there was now a high-speed rail link between the two cities (just four hours) and so, two nights in Moscow would be ample. Cristian was anxious to stay at the Cosmos, keen to go for the communist retro feel that I was sure would still exist. It was also comparatively cheap, when compared with the plethora of international hotels that now existed. Similarly, a hotel I'd never heard of called the Anabel, just off Nevsky Prospect, seemed good value and booking each over the internet, proved a painless operation. With flights and accommodation secured, there only remained one small problem, visas. Somethings never change! As we were travelling independently, we had to fill out an online application, via the Russian Consulate website. The amount of detail required was mind-boggling, with proof of flights and accommodation a pre-requisite, as well as financial status and travelling history. I wasn't sure what they would make of my answer to the question, "How many times have you been to Russia?" just hoping that a figure of approximately 100, would not trigger any alarm bells. Having already paid for the flights and hotels, I was in danger of losing close to £1,000, if the visa request was turned down. It was therefore, with some relief, that I got an email a week later, saying that our application had been successful and that we were both to come to London, to pick them up in person. Obviously, it would have been too simple to send them in the post! We were given a set time to be at the Consulate in Kensington Palace Gardens and remembering the legendary stories of how long the queue could be, I resolved to get there before opening time, to ensure we didn't miss our slot.

I drove down to Eastbourne the day before our appointment and given the unreliability of *Southern Trains*, decided the safest way to ensure not being late the following day, was to drive up to London and park the car at the Royal Marsden Hospital, where we had an annual pass. Unfortunately, two years previously, Luisa's lymphoma had returned and she was now being treated at the UK's premier cancer hospital, while waiting to find a donor for a stem cell transplant. The drive to London passed without incident and having got the overground train from Sutton, into the centre of town, by 8.30 a.m., we were in the ticket hall at Victoria Underground station, about to get the Circle Line for the few stops, round to the Consulate. Luisa had given me a couple of Oyster cards, which had some credit left on them and so, I gave one to Cristian and kept the other for myself. Anxious to get to the Consulate as early as possible, I headed briskly for the ticket barrier with Cristian following behind. Once through the barrier, I could hear the sound of a train approaching and sure enough, once on the platform there it was, doors open, waiting to depart. Sensing Cristian on my shoulder, I sprinted the last few metres and just made it in time as the doors closed behind "us". Relieved to know we were now sure to be at the Consulate well before opening time, I turned to Cristian and said, 'That was close!' only to be stunned to find that it wasn't Cristian at all, just some random bloke. I looked back at the platform as the train pulled away but there was no sign of him. I couldn't believe it. For years I'd led groups of up to fifty American high-school students on trips across the *Underground* and I'd never lost anyone, now, I'd somehow managed to lose my eighteen-year-old son. Trying to think logically, I decided to get off at the next stop and wait for him but after the next two trains revealed no Cristian, I started to worry that something serious must have happened. Unable to get a mobile signal, I went up to street level and tried calling his mobile but it went straight to voicemail. What to do? There was only one thing for it, call Guido, if anything had happened to his identical twin, he was sure to know. As always, Guido answered straight away but he didn't have any news and so I told him I was going to head back to Victoria and if he heard from Cristian, to tell him to wait for me there. After a five-minute wait, I caught the next eastbound circle line train, back to Victoria and made my way to the ticket hall. Just then my mobile rang, with an incoming call from Guido. Much to my relief, he told me that Cristian had called to say there had been a problem at the ticket barrier but he was now going to get the tube round to Bayswater station, where he would wait for me. This was starting to get a bit crazy, as our trains must have literally crossed, with me heading east and Cristian heading west. By now it was past 9 a.m. and on the ride over to Bayswater, I kept on looking at my watch, hoping that the lost thirty minutes wasn't going to cost us our trip to Russia. I was also intrigued to find out what had been the problem at the ticket barrier. As we pulled into the station, I spotted a rather worried looking Cristian, standing at one of the platform exits, scanning the length of the train for a sign of the father, who had seemingly abandoned him. 'What happened to you?' I called out, as I approached, to which he replied, 'You gave me an *Oyster* card with hardly any credit on it.' Apparently, when the card was refused, he'd called out for me to stop but as is my wont, I'd just careered on ahead, with the sole aim of not missing the train. The problem had been exacerbated by the fact that I had his wallet in my rucksack and so he couldn't buy another ticket. Finally, he had been able to persuade a sympathetic Underground employee, to let him through, by which time, I was long gone.

My Welsh grandmother used to say, "'All's well, that ends well...,'" and in this instance, she couldn't have been more correct. Despite arriving way later than I'd intended, the queue for the visa section was virtually non-existent and we were even slightly early for our allotted appointment. I hadn't been in the company of Russians for nearly twenty years and I was comforted to find that some things hadn't changed, particularly the level of customer service. You really felt they were doing you a favour by letting you visit their country and the exasperated sigh of the immigration official, as I failed for the third time, to get my fingerprint to register on the scanning device, reminded me I was in the process of returning to a very different world.

With our visas finally secured, I could relax and turn my attention to tracking down as many of my old friends as possible. Unfortunately, I had long since lost my old contacts book but with the aid of the internet, I managed to get back in touch with Tolya, who seemed to have become CEO of a bank in St Petersburg and with Sasha, who still had his own website selling his artwork. With the joy of technology, I was able to have a long *Skype* conversation with Tolya, during which, I could see his father Sergei, hovering in the background, Kira had sadly died, four years earlier. At first, it looked like the timing of the trip was all wrong, as Tolya and his family (he now had a wife and two daughters) were due to be in Florida for the whole of July, staying in their holiday home. However, Tolya said he would delay his own departure by a week, so that we could meet up. Clearly, he was doing ok, as during the *Skype* conversation, he showed me round his countryside *dacha*, which looked more like a Beverly Hills mansion, than a rural cottage.

42

Friends Reunited

On a perfect July morning, our *BA* flight from Heathrow to St Petersburg, eased itself off the ground and started to slowly bank round, in order to start the journey east. I was pleased to be on my way but slightly annoyed, that for the first time in many years, I had not managed to be the last person onto the plane. This was not only a badge of honour for me but a practical step, in order to get the pick of any free seats going. However, for once, I had come up against someone more determined than me and with Cristian starting to get a bit embarrassed, I had finally relented and allowed the bespectacled guy, reading *The Financial Times*, to have his way. To no great surprise, the same thing happened on the return journey a week later, he was clearly, a regular commuter. For the previous couple of days, Luisa had been checking out the weather app on her phone and it looked like the good weather in England, was going to be replicated in Russia. We were therefore travelling light and I was looking forward to showing Cristian the gleaming spires of the Peter and Paul Fortress, in the early evening sunshine.

Unfortunately, about two hours into the flight, we started to experience some turbulence and thirty minutes later, as we started our descent into St Petersburg, we entered a thick cloud base, accompanied by the occasional flash of lightening. We touched down, in what could best be described as a monsoon and I was already starting to regret not having brought an umbrella. At least these days, the aircraft pulled up at its own stand, so no need for getting soaked walking across the tarmac to the transfer bus. The line for passport control was as long as ever, with each inbound passenger having to spend at least ninety seconds being scrutinised by the uniformed official. Given the rigour of the visa application process we'd been through, it still amazed me that they could take so long to check your details. Then again, it's probably more about showing you from the very outset, who is boss. Despite my jaunty '*Kak delya?*' ('How you doin'?') I didn't manage to get a smile out of the rather attractive, female border guard, who inspected my passport, so no change there, twenty-seven years after my first arrival in the country. Our shared case was one of the last to come on to the carousel and so, by the time we had made our way through customs, the queue for the taxi rank, to my mind, was prohibitively long. In any case, I could already spot a couple of guys, who were obviously offering "private hire", which was the way I always used to travel when I was in the city. This would be the quicker and cheaper option. Approaching the older of the two men I asked, '*gostinica Anabel skolko?*' ('How much to the Hotel Anabel?') To which I think he replied, '*vosemsot*' ('eight hundred'). This seemed a pretty good price, about £7.50 and I felt an inward sense of pride, as I demonstrated to one of my own sons, that the "old man" could still cut a deal in Russia.

The vehicle, a brand-new *Mercedes*, was located close to the terminal, in one of the many multi-storey car parks, which had sprung up since my last visit. The driver, not the guy I'd done the deal with, was all smiles and soon, we were on our way. It was still raining heavily but I knew the route like the back of my hand and soon we were on Moskovsky Prospect, heading into town. As is my custom, even in the UK, I was keen to talk to the taxi driver, to get his take on the current situation in the country and I was pleased to discover that my Russian held up pretty well, despite the odd grammatical slip. I was a bit surprised, when after about ten minutes, we took a turn off Moskovsky Prospect, but the driver explained there were road works about one kilometre ahead and it would be best to take a detour. It was at this point that I started to get a bit disorientated. It was still raining heavily and pretty soon, we were in an area of the city I didn't recognise and where a lot of new build was going on. At one point, I became convinced we were going round in circles but finally, we found ourselves on Nevsky Prospect, with the driver pulling up outside the courtyard entrance to our hotel. I took out a 1,000 rouble note to pay the fare, deciding that, as the driver had been so friendly, I'd include a two hundred rouble tip. Suddenly though, the driver wasn't smiling, '*Nyet,*' he said and pointed at something I hadn't noticed before. Below the dashboard, opposite the front passenger seat, was a taxi meter and it was showing the number eight thousand! Cristian and I had been sitting in the back and even if I had been concentrating, it would have been difficult to spot. Suddenly, I realised I'd been had. Eight thousand roubles were the equivalent of seventy-five pounds and now the reason for the detour became crystal clear. It wasn't because of roadworks; it was to clock up the meter. There was no arguing with the guy and if I did decide to get the police involved, I wouldn't have a leg to stand on. Begrudgingly, I handed over the money, reconciling myself with the fact that I was effectively paying for all the times I had "screwed" Russian taxi drivers, in the past. On the return journey to the airport, a week later, we booked an official taxi, through the hotel for the standard rate of £10. By this stage, I had realised that in the "New Russia", most of the time, it made sense to play the game. My traditional way of operating had become obsolete.

Checking into the hotel, I was surprised to find that the receptionist's English was better than my Russian. It reminded me how much things had changed over the past few years. For example, even Luisa's numerous Italian cousins, now wanted to speak English with us, whereas, when I had first met them, over twenty-five years ago, everything was in Italian. The hotel had described itself as "*bijou*" on the internet, which is why I had chosen it, as a contrast to the decidedly, "non-*bijou*", Hotel Cosmos. The room was nice with an en-suite bathroom, which would come to serve more as a drying room, over the next few days, as the rain continued to fall.

I had arranged for Tolya to come round to the hotel at 7 p.m. and with Cristian keen to get in touch with his girlfriend, Amy, I settled down on the bed and started to watch what Russian TV now had to offer. The answer, not much. A succession of variety shows, soap operas and state-controlled news, which made me long for an episode of *Pointless*[82], to accompany my pre-dinner G&T. Just like in the old days, Tolya was bang on time. While twenty years ago, he had been starting to lose his hair, now he was completely bald, a spitting image of his father, Sergei. Although his hair had disappeared, he was clearly looking after himself, as his physique was exactly as I remembered, tall and lean. When I mentioned this, he said he had his own private gym at home and that he worked out every day. Clearly, he was doing well for himself, which probably explained why he wasn't overly impressed with our accommodation, saying this part of Nevsky Prospect, had now become the city's red-light district and why weren't we staying at the Grand Hotel Europe, where I used to hang out? I said something about experiencing the real Russia but the truth was, at £200 a night, the Grand Hotel was a bit out of my price bracket. At least I now understood that "*bijou*" as a description, could have a number of meanings and in fact, the first Russian I taught Cristian was, *nyet spasibo* (no thank you) as a response, to the kind offers we received from the girls, who hung around the courtyard, outside our hotel.

After a long day's travelling, both Cristian and I were pretty hungry, so Tolya took us to a beer tap room, where as well as a large selection of craft beers, they also served burgers and

---

82 British teatime quiz show.

chips. For the first time in my life, I was able to sample a genuine Russian cask ale and Tolya proudly told me that microbreweries were popping up, all over the country. This reminded me about the failure of our "*Sherlock Holmes*" project and I asked Tolya if anything had ever come of the idea and he simply replied, 'just wait and see.' The food, when it came, was of a good standard and the bar owner, an amiable guy. Tolya was obviously something of a "regular" and I got the impression that our host was keen to retain his business. After a couple of pints, both Cristian and I were a bit light-headed and I said something about going to see Tolya's apartment, where we would also be able to book our train ticket down to Moscow. I had been reluctant to do this in the UK, instinctively wary of handing over my credit card details to a Russian website. Tolya, however, with his wife and two daughters far away in Florida, was definitely up for a night out and so the evening carried on. After visiting a couple of other bars, we ended up in a place that could best be described, as an Irish pub. As soon as we walked in, I knew that this was Tolya's "local", as he knew all the waiters and bar staff by name and the female manager, was straight over to take us to his "usual" table. To our surprise, Tolya said now was the time to eat, as Cristian and I had naturally assumed, that the burger and chips at the tap room, had served as our evening meal. I was even more surprised, when along with the menus, the manager brought some financial papers for Tolya to peruse. Slowly, it dawned on me that Tolya owned the place. It turned out he wasn't just the CEO of a Russian investment bank, it was his bank and by now, he had diversified into related areas. For example, he had introduced chip and pin machines to St Petersburg and was also running a fleet of security vans, collecting takings from businesses across the whole of the city, to deposit in his bank. I was really pleased and somewhat proud that he had come so far, in the twenty-five years since I had first met him, but was a little concerned about the circles he was moving in, money and security usually only meant one thing, mafia! I politely voiced my concerns and Tolya patiently explained to us that, as long as he limited his business activities to St Petersburg, he could slip under the radar, whereas, if he ventured into Moscow, he would be, in his own words, "'looking for trouble!'" He did accept, that with the lack of an independent judiciary, everything could be taken away from him in the blink of an eye, but so far, so good.

Given the fact that we had already eaten, it's probably not fair to judge the quality of the huge amounts of food Tolya foisted on us, best just to describe it as traditional "pub grub". By now, it was approaching midnight and even with the three hour time difference, Cristian and I were starting to flag. Finally, Tolya said it was time for him to show us his apartment and with no need to pay the bill, we headed off into the semi-gloom, that is characteristic of the later period of St Petersburg's "white nights". The rain had eased off slightly and it was only a short walk to the recently refurbished apartment block, where Tolya now lived. Having visited family in Italy, I am used to apartments on a large scale but this one took the biscuit. An industrial sized kitchen, with numerous, sparsely-furnished rooms leading off it, including the aforementioned gym and a home cinema. What struck me most, was the lack of personal memorabilia one would normally expect to find in a family home. The only photo, was a huge blown-up one of Tolya, with his wife, who was clearly much younger and his two teenage daughters. Everything had a slightly temporary feel, as if the family were reluctant to put down any roots.

Before sorting out the train tickets, Tolya was keen to show us his two, large *Range Rovers,* parked in the basement garage. As I sat in one of the mechanical beasts, with Tolya explaining all the latest technical gadgetry, I couldn't help thinking back to Sergei's rickety old *GAZ M20 Pobeda* and the time I nearly missed my flight. I asked Tolya if his father was still driving and he said yes, but he now had a new *Skoda Fabia* hatchback to potter around in, the *Pobeda* having long since departed for the scrapheap. I gathered that he now divided his time between the original family apartment, off Moskovsky Prospect and Tolya's countryside *dacha*. Tolya said that during the summertime, Sergei preferred to spend more time out of the city and so he was currently staying at the *dacha* and we would visit him at the end of the week. Back upstairs, Tolya got out his laptop and put in a google search for Russian Railways. I was surprised he didn't already have a login, but then again, for obvious reasons, he never went to Moscow. Whether it was Tolya's inexperience or a problem with the website, we simply couldn't book a ticket and after twenty minutes of failed attempts, Tolya decided it would be best to go round to the station and purchase them on the spot. Given that it was already half past midnight and we were a fifteen-minute walk away from Moskovsky Vokzal, I didn't think this was a great idea, however, by this time, pretty drunk Tolya, was insistent and so we set off at a brisk stroll down Nevsky Prospect. Sure enough, when we got to the station, the queue for the one ticket desk that was still open, made it look like people had come for an audition of *Russia's Got Talent*. Despite the late hour, the place was heaving, with many people bedding down for the night, in expectation of an early morning train. Even Tolya had to admit, this wasn't going to work and so there was nothing for it, other than to return to the apartment and try the internet again. By this time, I was determined to get the issue sorted, as the whole success of the trip depended on securing the four hour journey down to Moscow and I didn't want to spend the limited time we had in St Petersburg, messing around trying to get tickets. Whether it was because the website was now working properly or possibly because by this time, Tolya had sobered up a bit, our second attempt was more successful and it was with some relief that the message, "Payment Accepted", finally appeared, although only after Tolya's third attempt to put in his credit card details. I wasn't totally clear what type of seats Tolya had booked but the timings were good and the price not exorbitant. Having given Tolya the cash for the tickets, Cristian and I headed back to the Hotel Anabel and wished our new lady friends, in the courtyard, *'spokoynoy nochi,'* ('goodnight.') Clearly, it was a 24-hour operation.

The next morning, to my dismay, the rain had increased in intensity and the weather app on Cristian's phone wasn't promising any improvement soon. We had breakfast, fried eggs with some rye bread, in the small hotel dining room and I was pleased to find, that not all the hotel staff spoke English. The small, rather plump lady who served us, looked like she'd been in a time warp since Stalinist times and she was more than happy to indulge my banter, about how great it was to be back after twenty years. With Cristian eager to see where the Russian revolution had been born, we set off along Nevsky Prospect, the rain pouring down, in the direction of the Winter Palace. On the way, we stopped off in a couple of department stores, to try and buy an umbrella each, but the store assistants were as unhelpful as I remembered and none were to be found. We were just going to have to get wet.

Arriving in Palace Square, already drenched, our spirits were lifted by the sight of the beautiful, Rastrelli designed Winter Palace. Cristian was fascinated to be in the place he had read all about in his history books, while I was more interested in how long the queue for the Hermitage Museum was. Unsurprisingly, given the weather, it was on an epic scale, not helped by the fact that it was the cruise ship season, with large groups of foreign tourists descending on the city for the day. No longer able to blag my way in with a five dollar bill I said to Cristian, that we would come back the following day, when I hoped the queue would be shorter but he didn't seem bothered about missing out on the collection of three million pieces and so I decided to take it off the itinerary.

Instead, I took him over the River Neva, via the Kirovsky bridge, heading in the direction of the Peter and Paul Fortress. This was where Peter the Great originally founded St Petersburg and normally, it afforded great vistas of the city, from the small sandy beach found at its foot. However, today was definitely not one for sightseeing (see the photo I took of Cristian on his disposable camera) and we decided to head back to the hotel. As we were leaving the small island, on which the fortress stands, I spotted the place, where in winter, an enterprising local bather, would "set up shop" and offer to dive into the freezing waters, through a hole in the ice, in return for a dollar. At the time, I remember thinking, *'there's got to be easier ways to make a living.'*

It took half an hour to get back to the hotel, by which time, taking a shower could be seen as a way of drying off! Cristian and I had only brought two pairs of long trousers each, having opted to bring more shorts, for the expected good weather. With the temperature hovering in the low teens, we now had a problem, as we couldn't afford to get a second pair of trousers soaked. We therefore decided to take the afternoon off, while our morning attire dried in the bathroom. Luckily, Cristian had already bought his *iPad* a subscription to *Netflix* and we finally came to the compromise solution, of watching Tom Hanks in *Saving Private Ryan*. As most people know, this is a rather violent film, so it was a bit disconcerting to have heart emojis keep appearing at the bottom of the screen, as Cristian's girlfriend, Amy, responded to his texts. By the end of the film, we were feeling quite hungry and the Anabel definitely wasn't the type of hotel doing room service. We therefore decided to brave the 400 metres, that separated us from the nearest *Burger King*, on Nevsky Prospect, covering the rain-sodden distance, in a time that must have been close to an Olympic record. This was my first time back in a fast-food restaurant since my tour directing days. At that time, I had the tradition of going for lunch on the final day of a tour, at the only

McDonalds in the country, on Pushkinskaya Square in Moscow. Often, groups would have some free time before we set off for the airport, so I would set a rendez-vous for the Intourist Hotel at the bottom of Gorky Street and then take a leisurely stroll up to *McDonalds*, where I would gorge myself on two *Big Macs* with fries, a large milk and a piping-hot apple pastry. Particularly if I had been on the Golden Ring tour, where the food was notoriously bad, I would feel almost as if I was in heaven. In those days, the concept of the "meal deal" hadn't yet filtered through but as Cristian and I queued up to place our order, I noticed a sign saying, *pitanie sdelki* (food deals) and I realised they'd caught up.

With the rain continuing to lash down in biblical proportions, we spent the evening in our room. Luckily, *Euro 2016* was taking place in France at the time and Russian TV was showing all the games live. Amazingly, my team Wales, had qualified for the quarter-finals, ironically having beaten Russia 3–0, in a group qualifying game. In a sense of utter wonder, Cristian and I watched as Wales beat Belgium, the number two ranked team in the world, 3–1 and progressed through to the semi-final, where they would play Portugal. I thought this might be a sign that our luck was changing but the next day it was still raining.

After breakfast, I asked at reception about where to buy an umbrella, when to my surprise the receptionist pulled out a large golfing umbrella from under the desk. Apparently, a guest had checked out early and forgotten to take it. Now that I could guarantee not having to sit around in wet clothes, I flipped into tour director mode, determined to show Cristian all that the city had to offer.

We caught the *Metro* up to St Isaac's Cathedral and then took in the Admiralty Building, along with the Bronze Horseman, the impressive monument to Peter the Great, followed by a visit to the *Marinsky Theatre*, scene of so many wonderful nights in the past. Unfortunately, there was no ballet planned for the evening performance, but for once, that didn't really matter, as I'd already arranged to meet for dinner, with my artist friend, Sasha. It's a short walk from the *Marinsky* to the Hotel Astoria, where my mother had stayed all those years ago. In the elegant lobby, we had morning tea with chocolate cake, looking slightly out of place, when compared with the other immaculately-clad hotel guests. For lunch, I decided to take the *Metro* down to the Hotel Moscow, at the other end of Nevsky Prospect, one of my old haunts and where Luisa and I had spent our first evening together. The hotel was pretty much as I remembered it and the rather thin borscht I was served in the canteen, took me back to my time working with school groups.

After lunch, we crossed the major road junction outside the hotel, to get to the Alexander Nevsky Monastery. As usual, I couldn't be bothered taking the designated subway and just told Cristian to follow me, as I sprinted across the road, as passing cars hooted their disapproval. In the grounds of the monastery there were a number of school groups and I was struck by how uniformly thin the children were, despite the arrival of fast food in Russia. At least some things hadn't changed. Deciding not to pay the entrance fee to the monastery itself, we retraced our steps to the hotel, where we took the *Metro* from the adjacent station, back to the Anabel.

Given that a visit to the Hermitage was going to be out of the question, I decided the best way to show Cristian some artwork, would be to take him to the Russian Museum, situated in the centre of town and with the added advantage of being right by the Grand Hotel Europe, where we could have pre-dinner drinks. Conscious of how I'd felt in the Astoria earlier that morning and now with a full set of dry clothes to choose from, I changed into my best outfit, including my signature lilac-coloured linen jacket. Often overlooked by tour groups, the museum houses an impressive collection of Russian art, dating from the tenth century up to the present day. As I had expected, the queue was virtually non-existent and we spent a leisurely hour going through the high-ceilinged rooms, of what had once been the Mikhailovsky Palace, the neoclassical residence of the Grand Duke, Michael Pavlovich. While in the museum, I became aware that the rain outside might be easing and as we made our way over to the Grand Hotel Europe, I caught my first glimpse of sunshine in the past 48 hours.

Sitting at the long, art-deco bar and chatting to the pleasant female bartender, I was taken back to a time when this had been my second home. Taking Cristian on a mini-tour after our first drink, we passed the general manager's office, where I used to meet up with Mahesh and I was pleased to see that the magnificent atrium had lost none of its wow factor. After a couple more drinks, I started to get a bit sentimental and I think Cristian felt slightly embarrassed, as I waxed lyrical to Tanya, the bartender, about my halcyon days in the city.

I had arranged to meet Sasha at our hotel, as he was now living out of town and would be driving in. He had suggested eating at a restaurant close to the hotel but was a bit concerned about where he was going to leave his car, as I had told him the Anabel had no car park. There had always been a lack of parking in the city centre and the police had traditionally used this fact as a way of supplementing their income, by fining drivers for the most minor infringement. When he arrived, a little late, Sasha explained that he had finally found a spot to park and that it should be ok for a couple of hours, but I could tell he was a bit apprehensive and appreciated the fact that he was prepared to risk a fine or bribe, in order to meet up. Then again, during the lawless time of the early nineties, I had once kept a loaded revolver of his in my hotel room, while we sorted out a visa for him, at the British Embassy, in Moscow. It was great to catch up with Sasha after so many years. He could still talk for Russia and had retained his impish sense of humour. Sadly though, both the twins were now living abroad, Alina in Barcelona and Vlad in Helsinki and so, Sasha rarely got to see his new grandchildren. It seemed like a certain generation had given up on Russia ever changing while Putin was in power and with his presidency now due to last until 2036[83], the status quo is set to continue. The restaurant where we ate was one of a new breed, reviving traditional Russian classics and for the first time ever, the beef stroganoff I ordered, actually tasted of meat. Having said our goodbyes to Sasha, we made our way back to the Anabel for an early night, as we had the Moscow train to catch the next morning.

---

83 New law April 2021.

43
Big Changes

I'd only taken the day train between Russia's two major cities once before, a nine-hour ordeal, when leading the *Women's Institute* tour, back in 1992. I was, therefore, looking forward to catching the *Sapsan* (literally Peregrine Falcon) the first high-speed electric train in the country, which had been operating since 2009. With a top speed of 175 mph, the journey time had been cut down to four hours, meaning, that we would be in Moscow in time for lunch. As we pulled effortlessly out of Moskovsky Vokzal and accelerated up to optimum speed, I was reminded of the first time I had caught the TGV[84] from Geneva to Paris, many moons ago and feeling like I was on an aeroplane, powering down the runway, heading for take-off. Cristian and I had forward-facing seats, at a table for four people and the guy opposite us, immediately struck up a conversation in English, enquiring as to what we were doing in Russia. When I explained that it was a mixture of seeing old friends and showing Cristian the sights, he was keen to know what differences I had noticed since my last visit, nearly twenty years ago. Thinking about it, I said that' 'physically, the centre of St Petersburg had changed relatively little but obviously, there was a lot more money about.'

'Just wait until you get to Moscow,' he said, 'You ain't seen nothing yet!'

It transpired, he was a property developer and was going to Moscow to finalise a deal, for the construction of a new shopping mall, in the eastern part of the city. Obviously, he was well-

---

84 Abbreviation for a high-speed passenger train (in France) *train à grande vitesse*.

connected and enjoying the fruits of capitalism. He even invited us to go out for a day, on the Gulf of Finland, on his own personal yacht. As we chatted away, I sensed that a few of our fellow passengers were listening in on our conversation, with the odd knowing smile being exchanged. It was, therefore, something of a surprise, when the female train attendant, who, for some reason, was sitting in a seat, two rows behind us, suddenly told us, in no uncertain terms, to quieten down. From the glazed look in her eyes, she was probably nursing a hangover and we were interrupting her attempt to get some much needed shut eye. Although, the trains had changed, it was almost comforting to realise, that the staff had stayed the same. Our new friend, Alexei, gave her a withering look and told her to mind her own business, while other passengers in the compartment, said it was nice to hear "proper" English being spoken and not the Americanised version, that had come to prominence. Sheepishly, she curled up in her seat, resigned to having been so comprehensively outvoted.

As we entered the outskirts of Moscow, I started to understand what Alexei had meant by 'You ain't seen nothing yet!' It is commonly accepted that the best way to judge the state of a city's economy, is to count the number of cranes you can spot across its skyline, in which case, Moscow was booming. Everywhere you looked construction work was taking place and as we approached the centre, I saw the first examples of the New York style skyscrapers that now towered above the city. Having said our goodbyes to Alexei and with his business card in my wallet, for future yachting opportunities, we alighted the train and headed for the Komsomolskaya *Metro* station, where we took the brown circle line, one stop, to Prospect Mira, changing on to the orange line, for the three stops north to VDNKh. The *Metro* was pretty much as I remembered it, that is, always busy but with hardly any wait for a train. It also brought into focus, what a melting pot of nationalities comprised the old Soviet Union. Unlike St

Petersburg, many of our fellow passengers were clearly of central Asian descent and spotting a person of colour, was no longer a rarity.

Approaching the Hotel Cosmos, I was slightly perplexed to see a large statue had appeared on the forecourt, in front of the building. At first, I couldn't make out who it was but as we drew nearer I recognised the unmistakeable features of the man, who, in a nod to his prominent nose, the French call *Cyrano*, namely Charles de Gaulle. Cristian asked me what he was doing there and at the time I had no answer. I have subsequently discovered, that on 9th May, 2005, in order to mark the 60th anniversary of Russian Victory Day[85], the statue was unveiled in the presence of the then French president, Jacques Chirac. However, historically speaking, the links between De Gaulle and Russia are tenuous at best and the statue simply looks bizarre. I suppose in some respects, it symbolises the crazy place that the Cosmos remains to this day, a giant monolith, out-of-step with the modern world.

In the old days, I always used to take a room on the twentieth floor, with views out over the Park of Economic Achievement and with the Ostankino TV Tower, in the distance. At the current time, however, my bargaining tools were much reduced and I had to content myself with a room on the fifth floor, affording a rather diminished vista. Entry to the room, was now via a key card, meaning that the days of the *dezhurnaya* had definitely come to an end. No more service washes for the cost of a packet of *Marlboro Red*. At least the large bathroom remained and I remembered how I used to spend many a leisurely morning, soaking in the piping hot water in the deep tub, while my Intourist guide led the city tour.

---

85 End of World War II.

As we had a limited amount of time in Moscow, we headed straight off to the centre of town. I wanted to find out how the ticket system for the Kremlin grounds was now working, as entry was still only allowed at 10 a.m. and I didn't want to miss out the following morning. Unlike St Petersburg, the weather was sunny and warm and I was keen to show Cristian where I used to sunbathe, in the Alexander Gardens, at the foot of the Kremlin walls. The ticket office was now a much grander affair, with digitised notice boards but in essence, nothing had changed. Tickets would be available from 9 a.m. each day and only valid for entry the same day. This would mean an early start, as I wanted to be first in the queue, when the office opened the following morning. With the ticket question settled, I led Cristian through the Alexander Gardens, up towards Red Square. In so doing, we automatically passed the Tomb of the Unknown Soldier, with its eternal flame burning brightly. I was slightly surprised to see that a fairly large crowd had assembled and I wondered what they were waiting for. As the Kremlin clock struck 5 p.m., everything became clear, as this is now where the changing of the guard took place, Vladimir Putin, having decided to distance himself from Lenin, by moving the showpiece from outside the mausoleum on Red Square. To me it seemed a shame as everything felt on a smaller scale, nestled in a corner of the Alexander Gardens. Still what Putin wants, Putin gets.

After taking in the grandeur of Red Square, we headed off for something to eat at the original *McDonalds*, located at Pushkin Square at the top of Tverskaya (formerly Gorky) Street. In so doing, we passed the Moskva Hotel, where I used to meet Juliyanna, in the basement Spanish Bar and the site of the old Intourist Hotel, now rebuilt as the Ritz Carlton. One block up Tverskaya, I noticed that the Central Post Office had remained in situ and still had groups of African students hanging around outside. Back in the 1980s, this had been one of the few places in Russia where

273

you would see a black face, as the only way for students from countries such as Zimbabwe to contact home, was to come and join the massive queues that formed outside its doors. Speaking of queues, I was pleased to see that unlike at its opening, when people were prepared to stand for hours outside in the freezing temperatures, we were now able to walk straight into *McDonalds* and order the ubiquitous *Big Mac* and fries.

Our appetite sated; we headed across the square to take some photos of the statue of Alexander Pushkin. Since the fall of the Soviet Union, this had become the spot where demonstrators of various political persuasions, would come to meet but today, with the sun beating down, it was only populated by young families eating ice cream and old men playing chess. With the time now approaching 6 p.m., I was anxious to get down to the *Bolshoi* to see about arranging tickets. From the internet, I had gleaned that, although there was no performance today, an "evening of ballet" was scheduled for the following day and I assumed that there would be some touts about, outside the theatre. There was just one guy there and he didn't have any tickets, but he said if we came back at 3 p.m. tomorrow, he would be able to sort us out. He seemed genuine enough and more importantly, he didn't want any money up front.

To end our afternoon tour, I took Cristian over to the Monument of Karl Marx, which stands opposite *Teatralny Ploshchad* (Theatre Square) and then up to Lubianka, the home of the KGB. After so many years of not taking photos, it was strange for me to be snapping away on my mobile phone but Cristian was revelling in seeing all the places he'd read about and of course, now you don't have to pay to get photos developed. We took the *Metro* back to the Cosmos, from the Kuznetsky Most station and headed for the mezzanine-floor bar, that still dominated the hotel lobby. No longer called the *Heineken* bar, it had been rebranded as the

"Sports bar" and according to a sign, had a pool table. Looking forward to an evening of beer and pool, we entered the bar, only to discover that the table didn't exist. As the barman patiently explained, given that the majority of the hotel's clients were now tourist groups from South Korea, a country not known for its love of pool, the table had long since gone but nobody had bothered to remove the sign. As I scanned the deserted bar, I couldn't help thinking some serious marketing was needed but then again, this was the Cosmos. We ordered our drinks and took a seat, while a young waiter loaded a tray with a bowl of peanuts and brought the drinks over. He clearly was pleased to have something to do and as soon as we had downed our first pint, he was straight over asking if we wanted a refill. In the background, Russian TV news was running an item on Theresa May, who had recently been elected British Prime Minister, describing her as the new "Iron Lady". Isn't it funny how they always get it wrong!

As Seoul is six hours ahead of Moscow, I saw little chance of the bar filling up, all the Koreans must already be tucked up in bed and so after a second pint, we headed for our room. As we walked through the deserted foyer towards the lifts, it was clear to see that the Cosmos was no longer the "biggest brothel in the world", the girls had moved on to greener pastures. Where the *dezhurnaya* had once sat at their desks, now stood Asian vending machines, selling "Buddha knows what".

While Cristian struggled manfully, to find a spot to get the advertised Wi-Fi to work, in order to message Amy, finally settling on a spot at the end of his bed, where he assumed something like the lotus position, I pulled up one of the armchairs, poured myself a G&T, from one of the cans I had brought with me, from the UK and looked out over the Moscow skyline, dominated by the Ostankino TV tower, in the distance. For the first time in Russia, I was able to enjoy a chilled G&T, having put some cans in

275

the minibar when we first arrived. Still not trusting the water to have ice in my drinks, I thought what a great invention the can of G&T was and of course, I would no longer be in danger of missing a train, due to a lack of tonic water!

The next morning at breakfast, we came face-to-face with the hotel's new clientele, hordes and hordes of Korean tourists, who seemed keen to make the most of the continental buffet that was on offer. At least, for once in my life, I felt relatively tall, as I stood in the queue for scrambled egg and *blini* (pancakes). The waiters who I used to change money with, had long since gone, to be replaced by tiny women, probably Vietnamese in origin, who scurried around the cavernous dinning-hall, collecting up the used cutlery and crockery. Breakfast in the old days, with hungover waiters and kitchen staff, could prove to be a drawn-out affair but the buffet system was relatively efficient, which was good, as I was keen to be first in line for Kremlin tickets.

We took the *Metro* into town, arriving in the Alexander Gardens as planned, at 8.30 a.m.. I was pleased to see that there were very few people lined up outside the ticket office, so it looked like we were going to be ok. The office opened at nine on the dot and we were one of the first to secure their entrance for the day. We made our way round to the Kutafiya Tower, which is the main entrance to the Kremlin and joined the orderly queue that was starting to form, for the 10 a.m. opening. Whilst waiting in line, we got into conversation with a couple of young female backpackers, from Germany, who said they were in transit to Berlin, having flown in from the Far East that morning. I was a bit mystified as to how they had got their tickets and they explained they had simply bought them on the internet, a couple of hours earlier. I guessed they had paid a premium for this but in fact, the price was the same as the ticket in my hand, the equivalent of £12. Not for the first time, I felt like a bit of a dinosaur, struggling to embrace new technology, Russia had moved on, but I seemingly hadn't.

Like me, Cristian isn't particularly interested in visiting old monuments and after an hour and a half, we decided that we had exhausted all that the Kremlin has to offer. I was keen to see how GUM had changed and Cristian had discovered in his, *Lonely Planet* guide book, that there was a new retro diner called *Stolovaya* (dining room) 57, on the second floor, where we would be able to get lunch. No longer a single department store, the beautiful nineteenth-century building, with its spectacular glass roof, was now given over to a series of boutiques, selling designer clothes, at exorbitant prices. Slightly nervous that lunch was going to prove expensive, we joined the queue for *Stolovaya*, only to be pleasantly surprised by the quality of the food and the good value on offer. Maybe, the prices were kept low by the fact everything was self-service and you were instructed to clear your own plates away. The only people working in the place, were those preparing and serving the food, the Soviet days of monumental over-staffing were no more.

After lunch we headed for the Arbat, where I had explained to Cristian there was a great street market, where we could do some souvenir shopping, for family and friends back home. In the early 1980's, the Arbat had become the first pedestrianised zone of the Soviet Union and at the time of my tour directing days, if you wanted to see the biggest selection of *matryoshkas* in the country, then it was the place to go. In fact, on the tour with Luisa, I had spent a good couple of hours going up and down the street, while she decided which eleven-piece doll to buy. Typically, once she had finally chosen one and I had negotiated the price and handed the money over, then she decided she wanted a different one, but much to Luisa's disquiet, there was no way of getting her money back. As I explained at the time, 'You're not in *Marks and Spencers* now.'

It is only a short walk from GUM to the eastern end of Arbat Street and with the weather set to be fine, I expected the place to be heaving. Unfortunately, I was to be severely disappointed. The street market no longer existed. All that remained as a reminder of its former existence, were a few shops, selling expensive dolls, amber jewellery and lacquer boxes. I struck up a conversation with one of the shop assistants and he explained the market traders had been forced out, as the area became gentrified. It transpired that the Arbat was now one of the most sought after places to live in the city, with property prices going through the roof. Deciding that souvenir shopping would have to wait until we returned to St Petersburg, we headed off for the *Bolshoi* and our 3 p.m. meeting with the ticket tout.

44

A Night at the Ballet

Having famously been let down on the day Misha was kidnapped, all those years ago, I was slightly apprehensive as we approached Theatre Square. However, I needn't have worried, as the tout was already waiting for us by the fountain, directly in front of the *Bolshoi* and the tickets he was offering, were for the central, upper circle. Checking that there was no mention of restricted view, I negotiated a price, the equivalent of £30 a head and handed the money over. When I had looked on the internet back in England, agents were offering the same tickets for £100 each and I felt a sudden sense of pride, that doing things the old way, could still sometimes work. It definitely helped ease the pain of the St Petersburg taxi ride and the guy even showed us the exact point of entry for our tickets, on the left-hand side of the building, as no longer, was all entry via the main front doors.

With four hours to the start of the performance, we made our way back to the Cosmos, in order to get scrubbed up and to put some decent clothes on. I also quite fancied trying out the hotel swimming pool. I'd always known of its existence because of an infamous story, dating back to a time just after the hotel's opening in 1979. Apparently, a group of Italian tourists had arrived late one evening, only to be told that there had been a double booking and no rooms would be available until the following morning. The only option, was to provide them with camp beds in the empty swimming pool, which had been drained for maintenance purposes. Decidedly unhappy but with no other choice, the group had literally set up camp in the pool and bedded down for the night, only to be woken the following morning to the sound of water gushing in, with their belongings floating around them. Unfortunately, the engineer responsible for refilling the pool, had not been informed of the group's arrival and had gone straight to the pump room to turn on the water. I can only imagine what the scene must have looked like, with a bunch of screaming, soaking-wet Italians, trying to get themselves and their belongings out of the pool and I'm pretty sure that any loss or damage, wouldn't have been covered by their travel insurance.

Smiling at the memory, Cristian and I went in search of the pool, which the hotel receptionist told me was now incorporated in a new fitness centre, in the hotel basement. Entering the cavernous bowels of the Cosmos for the first time, I was struck by the brutal nature of the architecture, which recalled the tyranny of the Soviet period. The desk at the entrance to the fitness centre was staffed by two attractive young women, in designer track suits, who told us that as we were hotel guests, we could use the pool for free but we would need to wear swim caps, which could be hired for £10. Needless to say, we chose not to take them up on their generous offer and looking around the deserted pool and adjacent gym, I could see we weren't the only ones to give the place a miss.

I'd decided to have a drink before the evening's ballet, in one of my old haunts, the Hotel Metropol, located a stone's throw away from the *Bolshoi*. Like the Grand Hotel Europe, it had been completely renovated in the early 1990s, regaining its art nouveau splendour. One of the deputy managers had been a Scots guy called Andy, who I got on well with and so, I had always been assured of a warm welcome. Twenty-five years later on, Andy was long since gone but as we sat at the bar chatting to the friendly barman, it felt like I'd never been away. I remember Cristian being a bit worried that the tickets I had bought would prove to be fake, so I explained to the barman how I'd got them and he just gave me a knowing smile, indicating that I'd done the right thing.

The evening's ballet was a slightly unusual one, in that it was split into three pieces, with music by Faure, Stravinsky and Tchaikovsky, respectively. Cristian's girlfriend, Amy, was an accomplished dancer and he had been to watch her perform on a number of occasions but nothing could have prepared him for the technical brilliance of the leading male dancer, with his earth-defying leaps and endless pirouettes. Sitting next to us, was a young American woman, who it turned out was an exchange student at Moscow University. I was keen to find out what student life was now like in the capital, but she was decidedly frosty and unwilling to get into a conversation. She struck me as one of those types whose daddy picks up the bills, for wherever in the world she fancies going and of course, she spoke no Russian. In the two intervals, we each had a large glass of white wine, in the sumptuous Upper Circle bar, with its polished, marble floor and by the time the evening's performance came to a spectacular finale, I was feeling pretty animated, as the two of us cried, 'Bravo! Bravo!' while the leading soloists took their curtain calls. Needing to get a bit of fresh air before taking the *Metro* back to the hotel, we wandered over to Red Square, where for a few minutes, I wallowed in nostalgia, remembering all the times I had watched the changing of the guard, in the middle of the night. Of course, Putin had now put a stop to that and I guessed it was now, literally, "time to move on".

The next day, was our final one in Moscow but the train back to St Petersburg, wasn't until 5 p.m., so we still had some time left to explore the city. With a check-out time of noon and a fine weather forecast, I decided to take Cristian down to Gorky Park. Traditionally, the place where Muscovites come to relax, my main memory of the place was being dragged round numerous modern art installations, by an enthusiastic Juliyanna. There were still

281

art exhibits to be found but other than that, the park had been completely transformed. Along the banks of the River Moskva, designer bars had sprung up and Cristian's *Lonely Planet* guide informed us that there was a vibrant music scene in the evenings. It was only mid-morning and most of the bars were yet to open but we found one with a riverside terrace and ordered a couple of iced, lemon teas. If we'd had more time, I would have definitely come back for a meal and an evening's socialising, especially as the weather was now starting to really warm up.

We got back to the Cosmos just in time for the midday checkout and went down to the porters' lodge, where we left our suitcase, while we went for a stroll around the nearby VDNKh (Park of Economic Achievement). It being the school holidays, the huge site was teeming with thousands of young families, enjoying the afternoon sunshine. There were numerous food outlets and for our lunch, we settled on what looked like the Russian version of *KFC*. I had always joked that VDNKh should be called the "Park of Economic Under-Achievement" but to be fair, the one area in which the Soviets had excelled during the Cold War, was in the space race and this was still in evidence throughout. The massive Vostok rocket, the first crewed spacecraft in human history, dominated the far end of the park and I remembered visiting the old space museum, where a stuffed version of Laika, the first animal to orbit the earth, was on display. Known as the "space dog", Laika was a stray mongrel from the streets of Moscow, selected to be the occupant of the rocket, Sputnik 2, launched into outer space on 3rd November, 1957. At the time, the technology to de-orbit had not been developed, so Laika would inevitably die. It seemed typical of the Soviet era mentality, to pretend that Laika had survived but I didn't have the heart, to tell the many school groups I took to the museum, the true story.

Tolya's *dacha* proved to be the fifth one in the row and was easily the biggest. It had an extensive garden, with a large brick barbecue as its focal point. On the drive was his father's Skoda Fabia and as we pulled up, Sergei appeared from the house. He was pretty much as I remembered him. Although now nearly ninety, he still had the same boyish smile and as I introduced him to Cristian in French, I hoped I would end up ageing as well. I chose to speak French, as Cristian had just finished his 'A' Level and was basically fluent, however, it soon became clear that Sergei was struggling to keep up and so I reverted to Russian. As Tolya and Sergei prepared the BBQ, it was funny to watch them in action, all the time bickering about how best to cook the meat and what sauces to use. It reminded me of how they used to be before Tolya got his own car and had to rely on Sergei for transport.

After a delicious lunch of *shasklik* (skewered kebab) and stuffed tomatoes, Sergei offered to do the tidying up, while Tolya gave us a tour of the private estate. In all, there must have been about forty properties, each one with its own unique design and it transpired that Tolya himself, had been one of the main investors in the project. At the heart of the gated community, was a fitness centre containing gym, sauna and swimming pool, along with a games room for table tennis and most importantly pool. Now I've played pool all over the world but this table must rank as the best I've ever encountered. The only problem was that there was no rest, or as some people call it, "The G Stick". In the past, much to peoples' amusement, I've fabricated rests out of parasols and ski sticks to compensate for my height disadvantage but for once, I was forced to play "restless", however, true to form, I still managed to win.

We returned to the house for drinks on the terrace with Sergei and I noticed that Tolya was now limiting himself to orange juice, rather than vodka. He explained that given his desire to "stay under the radar", he couldn't risk being stopped by the police for being over the limit. What a change from the old days, when drink driving seemed to be a national pastime! Soon it was time to say goodbye to Sergei, as he was staying on at the *dacha*, while Tolya was away on holiday, with his family, in Florida. During the course of the afternoon, I'd sensed that he wasn't entirely happy with all this new found wealth and maybe he thought it would all end badly. As I gave him a final hug I said, *'uvidimsya,'* ('see you again,') but the look in his eye told me he doubted it.

The return trip to St Petersburg was more direct and took just under an hour. This worked out well as the Wales game against Portugal, in the *European Championship* semi-final, was due to kick off at 9 p.m. local time and I didn't want to miss a minute of the most important game in Welsh football history. Tolya was flying out to Orlando, early the next morning and naturally, wasn't bothered about the result. Rather appropriately, we said our goodbyes on Nevsky Prospect, promising to keep in touch. His eldest daughter was fifteen and he was planning like many other wealthy Russians, for her to finish her education in an English boarding school. With our flat on the south coast, I suggested Eastbourne College or Roedean as possibilities and if he wanted to check them out, we'd be more than happy to have them as guests. He said that would be nice, but I'm not entirely sure he meant it. As the white Range Rover pulled away, I couldn't help thinking that we now lived in two totally different worlds and maybe, it was better that from now, "never the twain shall meet".

Goals from Nani and of course Ronaldo, ensured that the Welsh dream came to an end that evening. With Cristian keen to get hold of some Russian memorabilia for himself and his brothers, I'd set aside the following morning for some shopping and a boat trip around the city. Our flight wasn't until 3 p.m. but this would still mean an early start, so after the final whistle, we decided to hit the sack, hoping that the weather would remain good for our final day.

We woke to another bright, sunny morning and the first forty-eight hours of continual rain seemed to be something of a distant memory. After breakfast we headed out on to Nevsky Prospect to hit the shops, in search of presents for Luisa, Vito and Guido. I was tasked with finding something for Luisa, while Cristian was to take care of his brothers. I must admit, I really struggled to come up with anything. Luisa already had enough stuff from Russia to sink a ship and in the end, I settled on a couple of fine, bone-china mugs, with images of the Winter Palace. *'At least they'll get used,'* I thought. Cristian rather predictably, for someone who had just turned eighteen, went down the alcohol route, buying a selection of Vladimir Putin shot glasses, along with a bottle of Peter the Great Vodka, to put in them. Our shopping complete, we returned to the Anabel and finished packing our case, which we left with the receptionist, having booked a taxi for 1 p.m. to take us out to the airport. This time it was going to be an official taxi and the receptionist assured me it would cost 1,000 roubles (£10). Once again, I felt a pang of regret for having been duped on the initial transfer but at least by now I was learning from my mistakes.

It might seem strange that I had never been on a boat trip around the canals of St Petersburg but a lot of the time I had been there was in winter, when everything, including the River Neva had been frozen over. The boat left from its berth on the Griboyedov Canal, just off Nevsky Prospect and soon we were passing one of my old haunts the "Chaika" bar and approaching the Church of the Saviour on Spilled Blood, which had been erected on the site where anarchists had assassinated Emperor Alexander II, in March, 1881. Further along the Griboyedov, we passed the spot where me and a couple of members of my tour party had "bumped" a car out of the way, which had been double-parked and was blocking the road, as my coach driver looked on with incredulity. He had been prepared to sit there and wait, until whatever time the miscreant driver decided to return. That, however, was not my way of doing things.

After about twenty minutes, we found ourselves out on the Neva itself, with spectacular views of the Winter Palace, Peter and Paul Fortress and the Rostral Columns available. Cristian was happily snapping away, making up for our previous time in the city, when everything had been obscured by the torrential rain. He took one particularly good selfie of me and him, with the Rostral Columns in the background. I remembered how, when time permitted, I would do an extra evening's tour of the city, on the way to catch the overnight train to Moscow, which always included a stop off at the columns, for my group to take pictures of the Winter Palace, from across the river. Usually, I would be accompanied by my favourite driver Misha, who worked for me on a quasi, full-time basis and I recalled how, in the early days, when I was still learning the ropes, I used to simply say, *'pozhar,'* ('fire,') when I wanted to go to the columns, referencing the braziers that used to burn brightly on top of them, during ceremonial occasions.

The boat trip over, we returned to the hotel and picked up our suitcase. The receptionist gave us the registration number of the taxi that was coming to pick us up, to ensure we didn't get fleeced again. I thought this was a bit over the top but sure enough, as we were waiting out on Nevsky Prospect, a car pulled up with the driver claiming he was here to take us to the airport. He got out of the car and made to put our suitcase in the boot, however, the registration didn't match the one I'd been given, so I simply said, *'ischeznite,'* ('get lost,'). Rather sheepishly, he got back in the car and pulled away, no doubt off in search of someone a bit more gullible than me. A couple of minutes later, the genuine taxi appeared and in little over a quarter of an hour, with no unnecessary detours, we were passing the Pulkovskaya Hotel, where Sarah, the *Thomson* rep used to be based and nearing the airport itself.

We were dropped outside the departures hall and I paid the friendly driver the 1,000 rouble fare, along with a 200 rouble tip. *'Myagkiye posadki,'* ('Soft landings,') he said and we headed off to join the queue for the *BA* check-in. It felt slightly strange to be exiting the country, for once, with nothing to hide but my art trading days were long since over.

Entering the departure lounge, I was struck by the scale of the place. Clearly, St Petersburg was booming. Whereas in the 1990s, there had only been one, small, hard-currency bar, now there was a plethora of bars and restaurants, along with a number of designer boutiques. Having not eaten since breakfast, we were pretty hungry and wanting a change from the predominantly fast food diet we had experienced over the past seven days, we decided to try out the *Jamie's Italian* franchise, located on the mezzanine floor. Normally, as a family, we don't eat in Italian restaurants, away from the home country but for once, I was prepared to make an exception, craving some freshly made lasagne. However, as we took our seats and started to peruse the menu, I realised that my need for pasta was going to have to wait. None of the main courses was under £50 and the cost of a beer made my eyes water. Hastily, we beat a retreat and instead settled for a final *Whopper* and fries in the *Burger King* downstairs.

Waiting at the departure gate for our flight to be called, I thought about how every time I'd left Russia in the past, I had been expecting to come back but this time it was different, I knew I wouldn't be returning. Maybe I was secretly a bit jealous of the success Tolya was enjoying. When we had started out together, over twenty-five years before, all the cards had seemingly been in my favour and yet, it was now he who was the multi-millionaire, while I was just comfortably off. Perhaps I hadn't really wanted it enough and had been too easily distracted by the women and *shampanskoye*. Then again, without Russia, I wouldn't have met my beautiful wife Luisa and go on to become the father of three rugby-playing sons, who I am immensely proud of. As the *BA Boeing 737* eased off the runway and started to climb into the sunlit sky, banking to the left as it gained height, I took one last look at the city that at one time I'd imagined would become my home. Feeling slightly emotional, I mouthed the traditional Russian farewell of, '*Do svidaniya*,' but then, remembering that this literally meant 'until the next meeting,' I decided to lapse into French and simply said, quietly under my breath, '*Adieu.*'

Epilogue

There is an old saying that Russian stories don't have happy endings. Luisa died at 8 a.m. on Sunday 12th March, 2017, she was only fifty-two. Judy and I had been at her bedside constantly, for the past two months, as her health had steadily deteriorated. The stem cell transplant she had received from a donor in New York, the previous autumn, had initially been deemed a success but over the Christmas period, she had caught an infection from which she never really recovered. At the funeral a couple of weeks later, we played the Sinead O'Connor song, *Nothing Compares 2 U*, which pretty much summed up the way everyone felt about Luisa. It was also from the album, *I Do Not Want What I Haven't Got*, which had been my favourite cassette to listen to, during our first trip together, on the *Trans-Siberian*. She had always said that I should write a book about my time in the Soviet Union and, in the mid-noughties, I had made an attempt, starting with the working title, "Russian Mineral Waters I Have Known". However, for whatever reason, my heart wasn't in it, the few pages of prose I managed to produce, ending up in the waste-paper basket.

Shortly after Luisa's death, my father also passed away and so, I gave up work and returned to the family home, to help look after my eighty-two-year-old mother. Requiring another income stream, I converted the office space my father had used for his architectural business, into a self-contained studio, to be run as an *Airbnb*. Needless to say, there was no problem finding artwork to hang on the walls of the new accommodation and it was nice to be able to display properly, for the first time, some of Sasha's unsold pastels. With the *Airbnb* proving a success and pretty much running itself, I was in danger of becoming like *Pechorin* in, *A Hero of Our Time*, a *Lishnyi Celovek* (Superfluous Man) and so, I decided in order to get some focus in my life, that I would finally put down on paper, all the stories I had been "boring" people with over the last thirty years. In addition, the arrival of the pandemic, definitely helped kick start the creative process, giving me some form of structure, in a crazy world.

When close to completing the book, I thought it only right, that I should get in touch with some of the main protagonists, to ensure they were happy for me to use their names. Not everyone consented and for this reason, some names have been changed to protect the innocent. There was, however, one person I couldn't track down... Tolya! His mobile number was dead and his email address came back as unrecognised. I had originally got back in touch via *LinkedIn* but now his profile page had disappeared. Resorting to *google*, I typed in his full name and was shocked to find that in 2019, he had been arrested and charged with embezzling hundreds of millions of roubles, from his financial organisation. His days of "flying under the radar" were over. No doubt, the charges were trumped up but with no independent judiciary, he wouldn't have stood a chance.

The inevitability of Tolya's demise, in many ways, crystalised the way I thought about the new Russia. "*Plus ca change, plus c'est la meme chose*"[87]. There is something in the Russian character that seems to get a masochistic pleasure out of suffering and it is, perhaps, this more than anything else, that allows dictators like Putin to endure. Churchill once defined Russia as a, "'riddle, wrapped in a mystery, inside an enigma,'" but for me, the flowery language obscures the meaning. The best I can come up with is, 'If in Europe you feel Asian and if in Asia you feel European, then you are Russian.'

---

87 Literally "The more things change, the more they stay the same".

A couple of weeks ago, I was flicking through the tv channels, when I came across a documentary by the comedian Frankie Boyle, from three years ago, about his visit to Russia, prior to the *2018 Football World Cup*. It had been his first time in the country and during most of the programme, he seemed like a fish out of water, particularly given that, as a recovering alcoholic, he didn't drink, something his Russian hosts simply couldn't understand. At the end of the hour-long episode, the director had obviously asked him to sum up his feelings about the country. For a moment he had paused and then simply said, "'Fuck this place,'" and he's probably right.

Milton Keynes UK
Ingram Content Group UK Ltd.
UKHW030650240724
446081UK00004B/240